Rulers of Liter

MW01717012

Rulers of Literary Playgrounds: Politics of Intergenerational Play in Children's Literature offers multifaceted reflection on interdependences between children and adults as they engage in play in literary texts and in real life. This volume brings together international children's literature scholars who each look at children's texts as key vehicles of intergenerational play reflecting ideologies of childhood and as objects with which children and adults interact physically, emotionally, and cognitively. Each chapter applies a distinct theoretical approach to selected children's texts, including individual and social play, constructive play, and play deprivation. This collection of essays constitutes a timely voice in the current discussion about the importance of children's play and adults' contribution to it vis-à-vis the increasing limitations of opportunities for children's playful time in contemporary societies.

Justyna Deszcz-Tryhubczak is Associate Professor of Literature at the University of Wrocław. She has published among others on utopianism in children's literature and participatory approaches in children's literature studies. She is Director of the Center for Young People's Literature and Culture at the Institute of English Studies (University of Wrocław).

Irena Barbara Kalla is Associate Professor at the University of Wrocław, Dutch Studies. She has published on Dutch and Flemish literature, including *Huisbeelden in de moderne Nederlandstalige poëzie* (2012) and *Minoes, Minnie, Minu en andere katse streken* (with J. Van Coillie, 2017). She is Coordinator of the Centre for Research on Children's and Young Adult Literature at the University of Wrocław.

Children's Literature and Culture
Jack Zipes
Founding Series Editor

Kenneth Kidd and Elizabeth Marshall
Current Series Editors

'The Right Thing to Read'
A History of Australian Girl-Readers, 1910–1960
Bronwyn Lowe

Battling Girlhood
Sympathy, Social Justice and the Tomboy Figure in American Literature
Kristen B. Proehl

Cyborg Saints
Religion and Posthumanism in Middle Grade and Young Adult Fiction
Carissa Turner Smith

Out of Reach
The Ideal Girl in American Girls' Serial Literature
Kate G. Harper

The Arctic in Literature for Children and Young Adults
Edited by Heidi Hansson, Maria Lindgren Leavenworth and Anka Ryall

Terror and Counter-Terror in Contemporary British Children's Literature
Blanka Grzegorczyk

ChicaNerds in Chicana Young Adult Literature
Brown and Nerdy
Cristina Herrera

Rulers of Literary Playgrounds
Politics of Intergenerational Play in Children's Literature
Edited by Justyna Deszcz-Tryhubczak and Irena Barbara Kalla

For more information about this series, please visit: www.routledge.com

Rulers of Literary Playgrounds

Politics of Intergenerational Play in Children's Literature

Edited by Justyna Deszcz-Tryhubczak and Irena Barbara Kalla

Routledge
Taylor & Francis Group
NEW YORK AND LONDON

First published 2021
by Routledge
605 Third Avenue, New York, NY 10017

and by Routledge
2 Park Square, Milton Park, Abingdon, Oxon, OX14 4RN

First issued in paperback 2022

Routledge is an imprint of the Taylor & Francis Group, an informa business

Library of Congress Cataloging-in-Publication Data
A catalog record for this book has been requested

ISBN: 978-0-367-50147-1 (pbk)
ISBN: 978-0-367-50143-3 (hbk)
ISBN: 978-1-003-04898-5 (ebk)

DOI: 10.4324/9781003048985

Typeset in Sabon
by Apex CoVantage, LLC

Contents

Figures and Tables

Figures

Tables

Acknowledgments

The initial idea for this book was developed after the 2016 Child and the Book conference, whose focus was children's literature and play. The conference was held at the Faculty of Letters, University of Wrocław. We are grateful to Professor Marcin Cieński, the dean of the Faculty of Letters, as well as to the Institute of English Studies and the Department of Dutch Studies at the University of Wrocław for their financial support of our publication.

Special thanks should be given to our colleagues from the Centre for Research on Children's and Young Adult Literature for their unrelenting motivational support from the very outset of our project. In addition, we are deeply indebted to Dr. Patrycja Poniatowska for her meticulous editorial work.

We want to thank the editors at Routledge for their assistance in the preparation and production of this book. Our gratitude also goes to all copyright holders for their permission to include visual materials in the volume.

Finally, we would also like to thank our contributors for their trust, enthusiasm, responsiveness, and timeliness while this volume was taking shape.

Justyna Deszcz-Tryhubczak and Irena Barbara Kalla

The Playground of Children's Literature

Justyna Deszcz-Tryhubczak with Irena Barbara Kalla

The title of this collection is a direct allusion to *Rulers of the Playground* (2017), a picturebook by Joseph Kuefler, which has inspired us to reflect on linkages between children's literature and play, and in particular on their significance for fictional and real child–adult relations. The young characters depicted by Kuefler compete for the domination of the playground space. When their peers have finally had enough of being ordered around, they move away to a patch of trees. The two competitors reach a compromise and the others come back. However, one girl is readying herself to take control of the playground right after an earlier disagreement has died down. Kuefler's evident fascination with children's play as rough and conflictual questions Brian Sutton-Smith's conclusion that adults often do not find attractive the fact that the playground is "a political world in which children establish their own power hierarchies and loyalties" (ix). This dark and disturbing side of play, including competition so vividly represented by Kuefler, is believed to be crucial both for children's well-being and for their identity. As indicated in the *Children's Playground Games and Songs in the New Media Age* project funded by the Arts and Humanities Research Council Beyond Text program (2009–2011) in the UK, children's culture has always involved such disturbing elements as "depictions of death and mutilation, of the death or absence of parents, of abduction, malign magic and bogeymen" (15), all of which not only are "thrillingly pleasurable" but also enable children to realize that they are "people with their own interests in phantasmagoric pleasures as well as more 'socio-dramatic' play" (15). For Susan Linn, such play develops children's sense of control of their helplessness and fear when facing the world (142).

Kuefler's book also celebrates children's agentic imagination and their defiance of norms and expectations in relation to play spaces designed for them by adults. The child characters' re-appropriation of the playground space and equipment as parts of their kingdom reflects real children's repurposing of the play space in often non-compliant or unpredictable ways. Playgrounds usually signal and yet do not fully determine play activities (Sicart 52). However, children's creative freedom of play coexists with their interactions with adults involving not only supervisory intervention but also intergenerational exchange and collaboration. In Kuefler's book, no grownups interrupt the interactions among child characters, which may reflect a popular sense "that adult and children's worlds are and should be separate" (Blackford 241), that play is "natural and naturally incorrupt" (Cook 123), and that children's play is something children do with peers or alone. However, in real life, adult influence on play manifests itself in how material and aesthetic elements of playgrounds invite, resist, or discourage some forms of play behavior for political, legal, moral, or cultural reasons. As Miguel Sicart explains, "[t]he way spaces are articulated for play is dependent on more than design or playful considerations. Strong norms, rules, and laws govern the use of public and private spaces, and play design must be done in accordance with them" (53). Parents may also manipulate children and use play to keep their offspring busy to get them out of their way (Smith 196). In broader terms, adults enter into children's play in a number of ways: they encourage or discourage some forms of play, they discuss play, or they structure it to make it educational (181). It is thus impossible to detach children's play from adult life.

This interdependence between adults' and children's worlds in the context of play is not exclusively directed at children but may also be initiated by them, as illustrated by the following phenomenon: on the one hand, children playing at playgrounds are usually monitored by adults sitting on the benches nearby; on the other hand, as children climb the structures available at playgrounds to a level sometimes even three times their standing height, they are able to view the surroundings and those who might be observing them. In a Foucauldian analysis of the performance of mothering at suburban playgrounds, Holly Blackford argues that this two-way "panopticism" not only regulates children's lives and spaces but also reinforces the power of the social gaze as a catalyst of self-control for both children and adults (228). As Blackford explains, while the supervision of children's play by adults is commonly seen as a way to keep it safe, "panopticism also seeks to produce a certain kind of subjectivity in children, an internalization of discipline through self-monitoring" (228). Simultaneously, it results in a certain subjectivity in mothers and adults in general as well as in the formation of "a community that gazes at the children only to ultimately gaze at one another, seeing reflected in the children the parenting abilities of one another" (228). As Blackford concludes, although playgrounds were originally meant as spaces detached from the world of adults, they are in fact "metaphors for cultural meanings and spaces" that both reflect and transform ideologies of adulthood and childhood (237).

Blackford's study of the playground self-governmentality confirms and extends in an interesting way the interpretive reproduction theory proposed by William A. Corsaro, according to which children both participate in and belong to "two cultures – their own and adults,'" which "are intricately interwoven" (4). This means, as Jaipaul L. Roopnarine and Aimbika Krishnakumar remark, that children actively use adult cultural and social "messages" to develop representations of themselves and their social and mental worlds, which includes adjusting to adults' expectations and goals concerning play. Simultaneously, adults follow cultural scripts or their own beliefs concerning the beneficial influence of play on children's development (276), often projecting their current fears and concerns onto how they monitor children's activities. Finally, parents are often manipulated by media and toy producers relying on "the prevalent 'play ethos,'" that is, a categorical and unqualified assertion that play is essential to human development and that it is the most significant form of the child's learning (Smith 182, 196).

As mentioned earlier, Kuefler's picturebook does not depict play as supervised by adults. However, the playground equipment used by the child characters enables them to observe the surroundings from above and, potentially, return the gaze of the "hidden" adults (to paraphrase Perry Nodelman) monitoring their play off the page. The picturebook itself participates in the previously mentioned panoptical exchange as it is both a result of an adult's observation of children at play and a window through which child and adult readers may reflect on the playground dynamics in real life. Simultaneously, the book may become a plaything both encouraging and regulating play, including child–adult interactions in the reading act itself and beyond it. Intrigued by the panoptical status of Kuefler's picturebook and by what it reveals about the complex creative, appropriative, normative, and restrictive capacities of play, in *Rulers of Literary Playgrounds: Politics of Intergenerational Play in Children's Literature*, we propose to explore children's literature as a playground subject to the intergenerational dynamics of playful spaces discussed previously. We argue that children's books concerned with play as a theme or as an extratextual function afforded by the text are sources of cultural meanings regulating play and, more broadly, childhood and adulthood, in similar ways as it happens with the space of the playground. As such, they are also vehicles of intergenerational communication about co-construction of play. Therefore, the collection addresses the following questions: how does children's literature impose norms on child and adult readers or subvert them in relation to play? How do children and adults appropriate or follow these norms in their joint playful engagements with these texts? Such a focus departs substantially from the one offered in the most recent study of connections between play and literature, *Children's Play in Literature Investigating the Strengths and the Subversions of the Playing Child* (2019), edited by Joyce E. Kelley. This collected volume aims at exploring "how various authors of literature and film for both children and adults incorporate not merely child life and child characters but children's play as a key part of their works" (18). While our book also examines the play motif in children's literature, it nevertheless goes beyond representation: just as Blackford's analysis of the playground panopticism and the mutual surveillance and control among children and adults extends a hierarchical model of child–adult relations by pointing to the combination of dependence and autonomy regardless of age, our intention is to provide insights into the potential of children's literature to inspire and turn into intergenerational play involving authors and readers.

To address child–adult relationalities in the context of children's literature and play, *Rulers of Literary Playgrounds* draws on Robin Bernstein's *Racial Innocence Performing American Childhood from Slavery to Civil Rights* (2011), where she contends that toys and books are "scriptive things" representing "distinct genealogies of performance" and inviting different behaviors in children and adults (200). Bernstein defines a script "as dynamic substance that deeply influences but does not entirely determine live performances, which vary according to agential individuals' visions, impulses, resistances, revisions, and management of unexpected disruptions" (71). As she further remarks, although it is difficult to determine individual behaviors and actions, it is nevertheless possible to discover "the act of scripting" or the "issuing of a culturally specific invitation," that is, what things, including children's texts, encourage their users to do (11). In addition, contrary to Jacqueline Rose's conclusion that children's culture is imposed on children (the oppressed group) by adults (the empowered group), Bernstein also argues that children are "experts in the scripts of children's culture" who do not passively receive it but "expertly field the co-scripts of narratives and material culture and then collectively forge a third prompt: play itself" (28).[1] Finally, children's books and toys participate in culture in general "so as to script performances whose meanings cannot be easily contained or controlled" (29). Hence, children's behaviors resulting from their engagements with children's literature are usually culturally situated and involve a complex combination of resistance to, appropriation of, and compliance with received prompts and scenarios.

Simultaneously, our approach concurs with Karen Sánchez-Eppler's perception of children's play as both shaped by and transforming "adult expectations and the pressures of the real" (42). While Sánchez-Eppler focuses on child-made things as material traces of children's play, we propose to explore how the cross-generational co-scripting of play inspired by children's texts is a vital element of child-adult relations as it is shared by readers and authors. We are especially interested in what kinds of performance related to play are scripted in children's texts and what forms of child–adult communication these scripts prompt or discourage.[2]

Taking such an open approach to children's books and play, we both acknowledge their positive preparatory and adaptive role in child development and examine them as a complex, nuanced, and dynamic network of intersecting influences that shape child–adult connections either by contributing to the development of children's and adults' agency, creativity, and empathy or by restricting these capabilities. With this twofold interest as its central concern, *Rulers of Literary Playgrounds* follows W. George Scarlett et al.'s plea to find a middle way between the conviction that, if play is so essential to children's development, they cannot decide about it on their own and the idealization of play, which may prevent adults from noticing and stopping dangerous and harmful behaviors (5–6). We are also cautious about a frequent tendency to (re)essentialize play as synonymous with some true child and childhood, in particular "the rather pleasing notion of an incessantly innovative, creative child whose liberation can be realized in and through play" (Cook 123, 125). We thus choose to explore child–adult fictional and real relations – both partner-like and hierarchical – that emerge in relation to play and children's literature.

Rulers of Literary Playgrounds develops this reflection from a twofold perspective: (1) play is a multifaceted literary motif reflecting tensions between normative and subversive childhood and adulthoods; (2) play resulting from reading is also a manifestation of how children's books influence children's and adults' lifeworlds. The central focus of the first section of the volume, "Social and Political Contexts of Play," is fictional children's play as mirroring specific agendas addressing broader sociopolitical trends and cultural phenomena aimed at regulating children's and, by implication, adults' lives. Birgitte Beck Pristed opens this discussion by examining Soviet propaganda booklets and paper recycling posters published between 1956 and 1991 to show that while the early Soviet propaganda stressed pioneers' patriotic duty to collect wastepaper for economic reasons, late Soviet campaigns presented paper as a valuable natural resource used to create children's literature and schoolbooks. Beck also argues that the campaign posters depict child labor as both pleasurable and productive play. Family recreation is also the subject of Jan Van Coillie's chapter, which elucidates ideological tensions around models of children's play as reflected in the nineteenth-century Flemish children's literature and educational publications. Van Coillie shows that the conflict between conservative and liberal approaches to children's play, especially the propagation of family games as a way of protecting children from the risks involved in street play, is a manifestation of more general socioeconomic changes affecting society, including the emergence of socialism. Sarah Hoem Iversen's contribution examines the role of entries on play in nineteenth-century children's dictionaries in gendered socialization of children.

Hoem Iversen argues that despite the moral didacticism permeating the dictionaries, some lexicographers in fact used this genre to question restrictive gender models imposed on girls. Yoo Kyung Sung discusses more egalitarian intergenerational aspects of play in picturebooks about transnational Mexican families as they emerge as a result of negotiations between contemporary childhood cultures and heritage-oriented cultural agendas. Finally, the contributions by Sally Sims Stokes and Blanka Grzegorczyk address the significance of intergenerational play in times of military conflicts, violence, and terror. Sims Stokes reads the image of intergenerational play in Streatfield and Hutton's *Harlequinade* (1943) as a means of communication across generations and a source of consolation for both children and adults living under threat of war. Grzegorczyk looks at representations of play in contemporary children's novels dealing with terrorism, arguing that they offer a powerful critique of the global reign of terror.

Section Two, "Constructs of Children's Agency in Representations of Childhood and Play," discusses diverse normative conceptions of children's play and their actual and potential influence on texts for young readers. Elliott Schreiber argues that Ludwig Tieck and Hans Christian Andersen revised the Grimms' model of the evolution of the fairy tale as a genre rooted in ancient sources by connecting fairy tales to children's capacity for imaginative play. Schreiber also contends that both models remain relevant to the contemporary psychology of intergenerational storytelling and play. Ilaria Filograsso provides an analysis of another model of intergenerational play in children's literature: her chapter explores Gianni Rodari's ideas concerning language play as a bridge between child and adult readers. Filograsso contends that, for Rodari, children's authors should foster their readers' understanding of narrative mechanism as a way to encourage them to actively participate in the story. Elizabeth L. Nelson's contribution argues for the partly fictional nature of play anthologies: although they refer to children's actual experiences, they are unavoidably interpretations of the observed phenomena affected not only by anthologists' methodological approaches but also, as Nelson shows, by their own experiences of children's play. Hence children's play anthologies are not only sources of information about children's culture but also reflections of how adults perceive childhood and play, which in turn results in a close affinity between these texts and children's literature. Looking at more contemporary contexts of play, Taraneh Matloob Haghanikar and Linda M. Pavonetti comment on play deficit by presenting the results of their study of images of play in Caldecott Medal and Honor books: the awarded books contain increasingly fewer representations of outdoor and communal play, while substantial growth has occurred in the production of multimodal texts that encourage children to engage in new kinds of creative play activities.

Section Three, "Materialities of Play," centers on children's books as objects of play directly catalyzing or influencing extratextual child–adult interactions. Jennifer Farrar focuses on the influence of parents' encounters with metafictive picturebooks on their perceptions of reading and literacy. She also argues for the potential of metafiction to foster critical literacy in both older and younger readers. The development of young reader's literacy is also the subject of Zofia Zasacka's contribution, which proposes that intergenerational play around texts should be a vital element of activities aimed at promoting reading for pleasure and engaged reading. Literacy is presented in a broader socioeconomic context in Elżbieta Jamróz-Stolarska's chapter, where she looks at the Polish children's literature market to examine the limited production of digital books aimed at fostering children's interactions with literature through play enabled by novel technological features, potentially attractive both to younger and older readers. Finally, Jean Webb's chapter constitutes an apt coda for the collection: Webb, a children's literature scholar, presents an autoethnographic account of her own playful intergenerational experiences with children's texts. She emphasizes the significance of such interactions both for children reading books here and now and for the adults they are going to become as reaffirming continuities between childhood and adulthood.

Rulers of Literary Playgrounds: Politics of Intergenerational Play in Children's Literature unravels the diversity of interconnections between children's play and children's literature. It shows in particular their complex entanglements with one another as they contribute to and structure fictional and real child–adult relations and interdependencies. The culturally and historically situated perspectives shaping all the chapters invite readers to engage in play-related explorations in the field of children's literature studies beyond European and American contexts. Furthermore, discussions of children's play in literary culture could be substantially enriched with the inclusion of child-authored texts, increasingly recognized as vital contributions to children's literature and as expressions of children's cultural agency.[3] Finally, we hope that, regardless of its academic focus, this volume provides a valuable resource not only for other scholars but also for parents and professionals interested in using children's literature to communicate effectively with children and adults in play situations and on other occasions.

Notes

1. Rose's position has recently been questioned in numerous publications. See Gubar, "On Not Defining Children's Literature," "Risky Business"; Joosen; Cowdy and Halsall.
2. A recent instance of the kind of study proposed by Bernstein is Jacqueline Reid-Walsh's *Interactive Books: Playful Media Before Pop-Ups* (2017), which

argues that movable books are examples of interactive media that have been available to child readers since the seventeenth century. By examining examples of movable books, Reid-Walsh explores children's engagement with interactive media in the context of historical participatory culture.

3. See Conrad; Cumming; Wesseling.

Works Cited

Bernstein, Robin. *Racial Innocence: Performing American Childhood from Slavery to Civil Rights*. New York UP, 2011.

Blackford, Holly. "Playground Panopticism: Ring-Around-the-Children, a Pocketful of Women." *Childhood*, vol. 11, no. 2, 2004, pp. 227–49.

Burn, Andrew, et al. "Children's Playground Games and Songs in the New Media Age 2009–2011." Project Report, http://projects.beyondtext.ac.uk/playground games/uploads/end_of_project_report.pdf. Accessed 20 Dec. 2018.

Cook, Daniel Thomas. "Panaceas of Play: Stepping Past the Creative Child." *Reimagining Childhood Studies*, edited by Spyros Spyrou, et al. Bloomsbury, 2019, pp. 124–36.

Corsaro, William A. "Interpretive Reproduction in Children's Play." *American Journal of Play*, vol. 4, no. 4, 2012, pp. 488–504.

Cowdy, Cheryl, and Alison Halsall. "Editorial: 'Possible' and 'Impossible' Children." *International Research in Children's Literature*, vol. 11, no. 2, 2018, pp. v–x.

Conrad, Rachel. "'My Sole Desire Is to Move Someone Through Poetry, and Allow for My Voice to Be Heard': Young Poets and Children's Rights." *The Lion and the Unicorn*, vol. 40, no. 2, 2016, pp. 196–214.

Cumming, Peter. "Introduction to 'Another Children's Literature: Writing by Children and Youth' Taking Writing by Children and Youth Seriously." *Bookbird: A Journal of International Children's Literature*, vol. 55, no. 2, 2017, pp. 4–9.

Gubar, Marah. "On Not Defining Children's Literature." *Publications of the Modern Language Association*, vol. 126, no. 1, 2011, pp. 209–16.

———. "Risky Business: Talking About Children in Children's Literature Criticism." *Children's Literature Association Quarterly*, vol. 38, no. 4, 2013, pp. 450–57.

Joosen, Vanessa. *Adulthood in Children's Literature*. Bloomsbury, 2018.

Kelley, Joyce E. "Introduction: Caution – Children at Play: Investigations of Children's Play in Theory and Literature." *Children's Play in Literature: Investigating the Strengths and the Subversions of the Playing Child*, edited by Joyce E. Kelley. Routledge, 2019, pp. 1–23.

Linn, Susan. *The Case for Make-Believe: Saving Play in a Commercialized World*. New Press, 2008.

Roopnarine, Jaipaul L., and Aimbika Krishnakumar. "Parent – Child and Child – Child Play in Diverse Cultural Contexts." *Play from Birth to Twelve: Contexts, Perspective and Meanings*, edited by Doris Promin Fromberg and Doris Bergen, 2nd ed. Routledge, 2006, pp. 275–88.

Sánchez-Eppler, Karen. "Geographies of Play: Scales of Imagination in the Study of Child-Made Things." *Reimagining Childhood Studies*, edited by Spyros Spyrou, et al. Bloomsbury, 2019, pp. 41–56.

Scarlett, W. George, et al. *Children's Play*. Sage Publications, 2005.
Sicart, Miguel. *Play Matters*. The MIT Press, 2014.
Smith, Peter K. *Children's Play*. Wiley-Blackwell, 2010.
Sutton-Smith, Brian. "Foreword." *Children's Imaginative Play: A Visit to Wonderland*, edited by Shlomo Ariel, Praeger, 2002, pp. ix–xii.
Wesseling, Lies. "Researching Child Authors: Which Questions (not to) Ask." *Humanities*, vol. 8, no. 2, 2019, p. 87, https://doi.org/10.3390/h8020087.

Part 1

Social and Political Contexts of Play

1 The ABC of Late Soviet Wastepaper for Pioneers and Their Parents

Birgitte Beck Pristed

The act of playing with literature transgresses purely linguistic notions of literary communication as abstract decoding of verbal and/or visual signs. Instead, playing with literature inevitably points to the materiality of its medium – that is, to books as toy objects – and extends activities evolving around these textual items far beyond merely reading, speaking, and listening. Media historians, focusing on the nineteenth- and twentieth-century development of modern mass media such as newspapers, radio, TV, and computers, have often tended to overlook the traditional book as a medium. However, the digital advent of children-friendly apps for computer tablets, which has certainly challenged the status of paper as the given and transparent medium of children's literature, has provoked a new interest among a number of scholars in the contrastive material aspects of old-fashioned printing paper, its intrinsic qualities, sociocultural status, and political functions within textual communication.[1] Such ideological functions of paper are especially evident and important in the context of Soviet children's culture, literature, and play.

In the Soviet era, paper played a pivotal role as a medium of the Socialist enlightenment project, with its development of mass education and agitation systems, mass printing, and modern bureaucracy. At the same time, paper represented a so-called deficit material, and the state publishing and printing industry suffered under permanent problems with paper deliveries. The lack of paper not only affected the material quality of Soviet children's books, children's access to and handling of reading and writing materials, and their creative use of paper as a toy, but it also sparked the institutionalized practice of children collecting recycling paper. This chapter discusses the changing political and didactical rationale of late Soviet paper recycling campaigns addressed to pioneers and schoolchildren by examining the visual and verbal rhetoric of propaganda books and paper recycling posters from 1956 to 1991.[2] How do the poster and propaganda material visualize and imagine the medium of paper in relation to late Soviet concepts of childhood, adult–child relations, play and work, books and literature?

Early Soviet propaganda campaigns stressed pioneers' patriotic duty to collect wastepaper to overcome economic and industrial scarcities for the sake of the country. However, in the late Soviet period, a more developed concept of paper recycling added new environmental-symbolic and cultural meanings to paper as both a valuable natural resource and a source of a future, allegedly blossoming abundance of children's literature and schoolbooks. Thus, the main propaganda rationale for children's collection of wastepaper changed from an early focus on production to a later focus on Socialist consumption. The wastepaper campaigns aimed at turning the adult, economy-orientated goal of waste recycling into a playful and seemingly pleasurable competition in young pioneers' everyday life. However, the article argues that by encouraging and stimulating pioneers to participate in the extraliterary activities of paper circulation, the wastepaper campaigns staged Soviet children not merely as passive consumers but instead as active co-creators of literary paper products and cultural renewal. Furthermore, Soviet children assumed a leading, organizational role by guiding their parents to collect household waste, thus reversing the traditional model of the adult–child relation.

Paper and Pioneers from the Early to Late Soviet Period

At a first glance, recycling and revolution seem to be mutually exclusive concepts. The spirit of revolution wants to throw the old overboard and start anew from scratch. In contrast, the concept of recycling implies that old stuff is valuable and may be useful and reused. This inherent contradiction is evident in the development of Soviet recycling concepts over time. The early Soviet period was characterized by de facto extreme paper scarcity. After the Revolution and Civil War, paper production had dropped to a catastrophic 10 per cent of the prerevolutionary period, and though Soviet paper production expanded during the years of forced industrialization under the First Five Year Plan (1928–32), a parallel stop to paper import from politically foreign Capitalist enemies turned the paper crisis into a chronic condition (Chuiko 30–31).

The pioneer organization, founded in 1922, mobilized schoolchildren between the age of 10 and 15 to participate in wastepaper collection campaigns as children's own economic contribution to the fulfilment of the adults' Five Year Plans. Participation in wastepaper collection was part of the pioneers' political education and a patriotic duty. Thus, children should learn to become active, responsible future workers by helping to provide the industry with valuable material resources from an early age. Although the iterative practice of collecting wastepaper remained a more or less stable aspect of children's everyday life throughout the Soviet era, the rhetoric and rationale for doing so significantly changed from the early to the late Soviet period. This may be illustrated by a comparison of two propaganda graphics from recycling campaigns, aimed at mobilizing pioneers and schoolchildren in 1929 and 1984, respectively.

Under the headline "We'll give the country paper. We'll clean out wastepaper from institutions, depots, and houses," the January 5, 1929 edition of the newspaper *Pioneer Pravda* presents a cartoon of an angry-looking young pioneer, Kolia, whose remarkably long, rebellious Pinocchio nose sweeps like a sword through a huge pile of chaotically unordered paper. Self-assertive Kolia aggressively puts his foot down on the paper stack while pointing to his forehead and rolling eyes in contempt of the adult bureaucrat below him, who is being crushed and pulped himself under his mountain of superfluous paper files.[3]

This piece of propaganda originates from Stalin's attack on "bureaucratism" and the Stalinist so-called *makulatura* campaign December 1928–February 1929,[4] which exploited the labor of eight million schoolchildren to remove "wastepaper" from institutions, archives, and enterprises for the need of the paper industry. Out of the 80,000 tons of collected wastepaper, a conservatively estimated 14,069 tons were irreplaceable archival material, primarily belonging to the historical and cultural heritage of Tsarist Russia. Notably, it was not archivists but employees from the state recycling agencies who selected materials for recycling. Eventually, many of the "old specialists" of the state archives became victims of Stalin's purges (Khorkhordina 181–82, 203–4).

The *Pioneer Pravda* article's catchy and playful rhyme "without all these clerical letters / our work moves on much, much better"[5] invites children to take part in a symbolic act of purging by pulping history and deleting memory in a terrifying form of intergenerational play, which was mocking rather than pleasure-driven. The campaign took place in a political atmosphere where public press was soon to celebrate children for denouncing their parents, and propaganda imagined the child as the unspoiled Soviet citizen of the future (Kelly 79–80). Hence, by instrumentalizing the destructive force inherent in some processes of children's play, the cartoon and article present early Soviet paper recycling as a radical modernization practice with the economic goal of increasing and speeding up the industrial production of the paper plants. The cultural/political argument for recycling appears to be that, by cleaning out the waste of an unnecessary elder generation, the young generation combat the paper crisis. The text argues that this is important, because without paper there cannot be any books, journals, or "culture," but the cartoon clearly focuses on the destruction of old culture.

On the face of it, artist Aleksandr Chantsev (1949–2002) seems to repeat this argument in his 1985 poster "School children, collect wastepaper! It is a resource for new books and notebooks."[6] However, here all similarities stop. Chantsev's bright yellow poster presents a schoolgirl and a boy who have not much in common with their predecessor Kolia from

Пролетарии всех стран, соединяйтесь!

К борьбе за рабочее дело БУДЬ ГОТОВ!

ПИОНЕРСКАЯ ПРАВДА

Орган Ц. К. и М. К. ВЛКСМ.

Цена отдельного № 2 коп.

Газета юных пионеров и школьников—выходит три раза в неделю. 5 января 1929 г.

Дадим стране бумагу

ОЧИСТИМ УЧРЕЖДЕНИЯ, СКЛАДЫ И ДОМА ОТ БУМАЖНОГО ХЛАМА

СБОР БУМАГИ

Как проведем каникулы

ДВА ДНЯ В ДЕРЕВНЕ

В ОКРЕСТНЫЕ СЕЛА

КУДА СДАВАТЬ БУМАГУ

Культотряд „Бауманец"

Figure 1.1 Frontpage of the January 5, 1929 edition of the newspaper *Pioneer Pravda*

Source: Russian State Children's Library.

1929 apart from the red scarf. The rosy-cheeked smiling children appear friendlier, harmless, and better behaved than Kolia. Symmetrically, they carry a neat bundle of newspapers and a string bag, respectively, full of paper waste, which they drop down into a container, formed as a

Figure 1.2 Aleksandr Chantsev's 1985 poster "School children, collect wastepaper! It is a resource for new books and notebooks!"

Source: Russian State Library, Poster Collection.

huge arrow. The downward arrow also represents the page opening of a large book, on which the children stand, indicating the direction to an abundance of text and exercise books, whose topics cover an entire ABC or Cyrillic *Azbuka*, from *A*stronomy and space exploration, to *B*otany and *G*eometry. Between these leaves of paper, green leaves of blossoming plants are growing, suggesting a harmonious symbiosis between the flowers of culture and nature. In contrast to Kolia, these schoolchildren are not cleaning out old waste in a violent act of modernization; rather their careful collecting of past materials nurtures and protects both nature and culture. Revolution is now history. Hence, the emphasis in the 1985 poster on the large arrow indicates a more developed concept of recycling, which may even be understood as a postmodern practice of an eclectic re-use of the scraps of the past to create cultural products.[7] Obviously, this poster visualizes a different concept of the child, of the relation between old and new, and of how to handle and play with paper. What happened between the two graphics from 1929 and 1985?

After another devastating blow to Soviet paper industry during World War II, the Communist Party gave high priority to the expansion and modernization of paper production in the 1960s and 1970s and initiated the building of several new mass-scale plants (Chuiko 52). In parallel to rising paper production rates, the publishing industry's print-runs of books, newspapers, and journals also seemed to be ever-growing. Late Soviet growing urbanization, an increasing level of education, better living conditions, and more leisure time were all factors that contributed to an increasing book and paper demand in the population. However, since readers did not want to buy million-high print-runs of Party-conform and Marxist-Leninist agitation literature, much of this literature was simply pulped again, while schoolbooks and children's literature were often difficult to obtain (Dinerštein 167). In fact, annual Soviet paper consumption per inhabitant remained less than 10 per cent of the corresponding American figures (Häkli 350–53). Despite such paper deficit, "gasification" of urban households led to a hitherto unseen accumulation of old newspapers, previously used to light fire in the stoves. This development called for more efficient ways of collecting wastepaper. Until the early 1970s, only approximately 20 per cent of all wastepaper was collected from Soviet households, and in Moscow, which had the best but far from sufficiently developed net of recycling centers, the figure was still only around 30 per cent (Shamko 1–2; Smolianitskii and Moiseev 23).

A Task for Children or Adults?

In the main literary newspaper *Literaturnaia gazeta*, the progressive intelligentsia of the 1960s began voicing environmental concerns about the forest and water resources threatened by the expansion of Soviet paper plants and criticized the extensive production and wasteful transportation practices of the paper and printing industry. In this context, the biologist and author of popular Soviet books about the life of bees,[8] Iosef Khalifman (1902–88), complained that Soviet citizens had too long considered themselves too rich in forest resources and thus neglected the collection of wastepaper. Instead, they left this important task to schoolchildren and pioneers and organized it amateurishly as children's play (Khalifman

10). In her study of metal scrap collection in the more resource-scarce Socialist and post-Socialist Hungary, Zsuzsa Gille observes in the late 1970s similar protests against leaving the waste collection of valuable industrial secondary resources in the hands of children and pioneers (110–11). She interprets this as part of a changing attitude toward waste from early Socialism's use of waste collection as a *political* instrument to control, discipline, mobilize, and educate young Socialist citizens to late Socialism's *economic* monetarization, rationalization, modernization, and professionalization of waste collection and reutilization – in short, a task for adults!

Despite such a critical debate and the 1970s introduction of incentives for the adult population to participate more directly in wastepaper collection campaigns,[9] the Soviet household wastepaper collection system continued to depend fully on children as its most stable workforce. The pioneer organization was a well-functioning tool for mass mobilization of this workforce, and through the children, campaigns could also reach out to the parents at home.

The headline of the anonymous poster "Participate actively in the All-Russian Competition for the Collection of Wastepaper and Household Secondary Resources" is followed by a remarkable imperative in red and black capital letters of Constructivist style: "Pioneers and schoolchildren! Organize the collection of daily residues in your own apartment." In the foreground, a stylized boy is looking straight at the viewer, carrying a big bundle of wastepaper. In the background, we see the child again, now leading his parents as a small procession of demonstrators toward the recycling center, carrying their collected scrap together with agitation banners displaying recycling slogans. The poster shows both father and son marching forward, strictly disciplined in gray uniforms. The militaristic-looking school uniform originates from the patriotic postwar period of high-Stalinism but remained in use until 1962.

The poster centers on the child as the connection point between the wastepaper-hungry industry (presented as the silhouette of a factory with smokestacks in the background) and the family household. Compared to the cartoon of the early Soviet wastepaper campaign, which had an institutional setting of the bureaucrats' office, wastepaper collection has now moved to domestic sphere of the family apartment. This testifies to the increased availability of consumed wastepaper in the households. Indeed, another agitation booklet from a later collection campaign emphasizes the role of school pedagogues and teachers to instruct children about both the competition terms and the ideological and economic aspects of collecting recycling materials (Malikov 10). However, this poster makes it evident that, once instructed, the schoolchildren were supposed to go home and instruct their parents to collect scrap. Thus, the child assumes the organizational role of the household and thus reverses the traditional adult–child relation. For contemporary parents, it may seem a rather

Figure 1.3 Anonymous 1962 poster, presumably by G. German and I. Shoifer: "Pioneers and Schoolchildren! Participate actively in the All-Russian Competition for the Collection of Wastepaper and Household Secondary Resources"

Source: Russian State Library, Poster Collection.

utopian scenario that children would come home and tell the adults to clean up their apartment. The 1962 poster still points to some continuities from the early Soviet period in the perception of children's role in intergenerational wastepaper collecting. On the one hand, the propaganda message of the poster testifies both to a constructivist belief in the child as an active revolutionary agent, capable of leading the older generation into the bright and ordered future of Communism. On the other hand, it suggests a certain "infantilization" of adult Soviet citizens who are receiving instructions to behave as dutiful and obedient children of the state (Dobrenko 167). In reality, however, parents often simply had to help their children with the quite demanding and difficult task of fulfilling the obligatory wastepaper collection quota.

Working or Playing?

The 1962 poster depicts the boy carrying a considerable load of wastepaper. It is a characteristic feature of the posters in the Russian State Library collection, especially of the poster from the 1950s and 1960s, that they display children, boys as well as girls, carrying quite heavy burdens of paper in their arms, on their backs or shoulders, or between each other in string bags, boxes, or carrying frames. Hence, posters and propaganda photographs do not hide the fact that it is hard, physical work to collect wastepaper. Instead, the posters celebrate the children as strong, athletic, smiling, and hardworking: The heavier the weight, the more successful a campaign. However, by the 1970s and especially the 1980s, some of the posters get brighter colors and a slightly "lighter" touch by depicting the children on the top op paper stacks, playing trumpet or holding for example books, flags, balloons, or paper kites with campaign slogans in their hands instead of wastepaper. This presents the collection campaigns in a more festive manner, suggesting that they give room for more pleasurable forms of play and leisure, not just hard work.

One may compare the Socialist iconography of the wastepaper-collecting pioneer with the contrasting Capitalist icon of the paperboy. On the one hand, this typically first (low) paid job of the child embodied the very dream of individual, free entrepreneurship, following the cliché "from paperboy to company director." On the other hand, to a number of socially engaged documentary photographers such as Lewis Hine, the American paperboy represented the social injustice and exploitation of child labor in industrial society (Kubie 884–85). Soviet visual propaganda primarily depicted pioneers as collectors of old newspapers rather than distributors of fresh news. Unlike their Western fellow child workers, pioneers did not receive any individual payment for their job since personal profit making was certainly not an educational goal of the campaigns. In the 1960s, it was each schoolchild and pioneer's obligation to collect a minimum of 10 kilograms of wastepaper annually as a contribution to the national economy. In return, the Soviet Supply Committee's (Gossnab) recycling agencies provided a small monetary compensation to the savings of the local pioneer networks, which they spent collectively on social activities and cultural events such as excursions. To encourage children to over-fulfill their quota, Gossnab organized in cooperation with the Ministry of Enlightenment annual competitions within each schoolyear. During such campaigns children competed with each other at group, institutional, and national levels, in collecting the most wastepaper. Through such competitive "games" with rhymes, rules, and rewards, state authorities turned unpaid child labor into a "productive" play. Hence, in contrast to classic notions of play as a pleasurable, spontaneous, and voluntary activity without extrinsic goals (Else 7, 147), late Soviet recycling campaigns represented an opposite pattern of an organized, disciplined, and goal-driven activity for children. Nevertheless, propaganda visualized wastepaper collection as a seemingly child-organized, freely chosen activity to a point where paper recycling appeared a goal in itself.

For Industry or Nature?

One of the largest late Soviet paper recycling campaigns was "A Million for the Fatherland!" (Million – Rodine!), which ran from 1974 to 1980. The goal of the All-Union campaign was that pioneers and schoolchildren should collect one million tons of wastepaper during this period. Similar to the rhetoric of contemporary digital crowdfunding campaigns, a 1979 agitation booklet for the campaign opens with the announcement that actively participating children have already collected 900,000 tons, but, to reach the final goal, they have to unite all their efforts. Thus "million" refers not only to the quantity of wastepaper but also to the millions of schoolchildren engaged in the mass-scale campaign.

The booklet opens with a Brezhnev quote stating that to economize with material resources is rule number one in the life and work of Soviet people. Hence, saving resources and recycling primarily involved economic, rather than environmental, concerns. However, in parallel to the 1970s growing public interest and political concern with environmental questions in the West, the USSR developed official environmental politics, which were maybe less directed at solving the specific and alarming environmental problems of planned economy but rather more ideologically centered on rediscovering "pollution" as a weakness of the over-production and consumption of growth-based late-Capitalist society. Though the Brezhnev government never established a Ministry of Environmental Affairs, the General Secretary had announced at the 24th Party-Congress in 1971 that "while taking measures to speed up scientific and technological progress, it is imperative to do everything in order that this progress should be combined with a proprietary attitude towards natural resources" (Josephson et al. 189–90).

The tree as a new type of visual motif and environmental argument enters the posters of the 1970s and 1980s, while the dominant color of the posters literally shifts from red to green. This picture is confirmed by a 1982 recycling poster motif by Boris Reshetnikov (b. 1921), also depicting a pair of school children carrying a string bag with paper waste between them. A triangular color photo of a birch forest is inserted behind the children pointing down at their full string bag. The text below says that 60 kilograms of collected wastepaper protect one 50–60 year-old tree from being felled, thereby alluding to the lifespan of man. The imperative economic needs of the state and country and material needs of the Soviet pulp and paper industry are completely absent in the text and image on both Reshetnikov's and Chantsev's 1980s recycling posters. Instead, schoolchildren appear to collect wastepaper for the sake of nature and culture, respectively, rather than for the sake of industry. This does not make their act less patriotic; after all, the birch tree is a national Russian symbol. While the early posters of the 1950s depicted the forest primarily as a "production site" displaying industrial uses of nature such as floating timber, the later posters insert motifs such as butterflies and flowers among the trees, suggesting a more romantic perception of the forest and a recreational use of nature. Furthermore, the posters present literature, books, and reading as one such direct product of the forest, as if literature itself was a natural "material resource."

This visual metaphor is evident on the booklet cover of *A Million for the Fatherland*. Here fading, falling autumn leaves blend with a young pioneer's fresh flower-decorated schoolbooks, suggesting that old leaves become new and that pioneers support the very seasonal cycle. In the background, the former obligatory motif of smokestacks has been replaced by white pigeons and drifting fleecy clouds.

Books or Board?

Throughout the late Soviet period, a repeated slogan of the campaign posters is that one metric ton of recycling paper equals 25,000 notebooks for the school (see for example Figure 1.3, bottom of poster). *A Million for the Fatherland* expands this type of calculation by stating that the campaign has so far saved 15 million trees, corresponding to more than 50 per cent of the material resources needed for the union-wide annual publication of schoolbooks and children's literature (Malikov 1). Furthermore, the propaganda piece claims a direct proportional correlation between the quantity of collected wastepaper and the number of available publications: "The more wastepaper you will collect, the more children's books, schoolbooks, journals, and newspapers will be published"

Figure 1.4 Front and back cover of the Soviet state publisher of youth literature Molodaia gvardia's 1979 publication *A Million for the Fatherland* (Million – Rodine!) propagandizing the 1974–80 school and pioneer campaign for collecting one million tons of wastepaper

Source: Russian State Library.

(Malikov 4). Pioneers support not only the industry and national economy but also nature *and* culture! Hence, the recycling campaigns present children as cultural agents whose transformative power co-produces new children's books and schoolbooks. The campaign sustains this work ethos by encouraging and reporting from school excursions to paper plants and by explaining the history of paper to children, thus engaging the children in the material means and labor processes of book production (Malikov 10–15).

The campaign refers to the Brezhnev government's decision to introduce a system of state-funded, free textbooks for schoolchildren and suggests that in return children bring back wastepaper to the state and thus allegedly become suppliers of their own educational means. Interestingly, the campaign also states that the economic value of one metric ton of high quality printing paper is two to three times higher than the price of one metric ton of refined steel (Malikov 2), thereby challenging the status of a hard metal that has been considerably more propagandized through the history of the Soviet Union than soft paper. Hence, iron and steel symbolized the forced industrialization under Stalin, who also took his name from this metal, and it was literarily evoked in Nikolai Ostrovsky's mass-published Socialist realist novel classic *How the Steel Was Tempered* (org. 1932, several revised editions).[10] This new late Soviet emphasis on printing paper as number one in the hierarchy of materials testifies to a paradigmatic shift from a proletarian industrial society to a society of so-called developed Socialism that offered higher education to a broader part of the population. However, in reality, Soviet paper plants did not possess sufficiently developed recycling technologies to process fine printing paper out of wastepaper. Hence, the children's collected wastepaper was more likely to end up as rough board, packing material, and pulp for the chemical and construction industry rather than as new books.

Conclusion

The yellowed, ephemeral paper posters, now stored in the Russian State Library's collection, present an ABC of Soviet paper politics, visualizing paper as a scarce, valuable material, an economic and natural resource, and finally as a medium of cultural renewal, enlightenment and literary education. In the hands of children, paper transforms pioneers into active revolutionary agents who lead their parents from a wasteful present into an ordered future of Communism. Pioneers instruct adult citizens to behave as dutiful and obedient children of the state and thus challenge the traditional role division between parents and children. In reality, however, parents often simply had to help their children handle the quite heavy burden of wastepaper since wastepaper collection also implied hard physical work. The recycling campaigns stage such child labor as competitive "games" or "productive" play, through which wastepaper collection becomes a seemingly child-organized, freely chosen activity to a point where paper recycling appears a goal in itself. By gradually introducing environmental motifs, the posters present books and literature as direct "natural products" of the forest and emphasize the role of children as mediators between nature, state industry, cultural institutions, and home. Hence, the posters encourage pioneers to engage in role-play as co-producers of new children's books and schoolbooks, while at the same time providing and supplying the industry with board and building materials.

Notes

1. Recent media and cultural historical approaches to paper include Gitelman's 2014 monograph *Paper Knowledge*; Häkli, especially 350–453; Derrida 33–57. For a survey of material approaches to communication technologies, see also Parikka, chapter 4, "Media Theory and New Materialism," 63–89.
2. I have selected the posters from the Russian State Library's poster collection with the catalogue code У-211 "Отходы производства и их использование; сбор утил. инф." (Industrial residues and their use, recycling information), which contains several hundred posters, hereof approximately 50 posters from paper recycling campaigns. The earliest posters date from 1956, when the library established "recycling information" as a separate collection category, which testifies to the growing institutionalization and significance of recycling campaigns in the late Soviet period.
3. I have examined this and other examples of the representation of paper in early Soviet children's books further in my contribution "The Fragile Power of Paper and Projections." *The Pedagogy of Images: Depicting Communism for Children*, edited by Serguei Oushakine and Marina Balina. University of Toronto Press, forthcoming.
4. See the decree of the People's Commissariat of the Workers' and Peasants' Inspectorate, 20 Dec. 1928, "О порядке изъятия из учреждений и предприятий архивной и иной бумажной макулатуры для нужд бумажной промышленности" (On the removal procedure of archival and other wastepaper from institutions and enterprises for the need of the paper industry).
5. «Без канцелярской тучной кучи //мы работу двинем лучше!»
6. «Школьники, собирайте макулатуру! Это сырье для новых книг и тетрадей» А. Чанцев. Издательство «Плакат». Москва. 1984 г. Изд. № 1525277. З. 5003. Т. 2 млн. А-12164–84 г. Ц. 2 к. Тип. изд-ва «Зоря».
7. For a theoretical perspective on modernity as a rational cleaning practice versus postmodernity as a recycling practice within Western thinking and art history, see Fayet. For a comparative example of Russian postmodernist artistic use of garbage materials, a playful dialogue on waste between the Moscow conceptualist artist Ilya Kabakov and art historian and philosopher Boris Groys, see Grois and Kabakov 319–30. For a further discussion on the notions of Russian postmodernism, see Lipovetsky – especially 42–50 – and Epstein 188–210. According to Mark Lipovetsky, early Russian postmodernism differed from Western postmodernism because of its attempt to revive the modernist tradition after the hegemony of socialist realism within Soviet art and literature. In contrast, Mikhail Epstein regards socialist realism itself to be a forerunner of Russian postmodernism because of its eclectic mixture

of all previous classical styles and deliberate – though not self-ironic – use of literary clichés.

8. *Пчёлы. Книга о биологии пчелиной семьи и победах науки о пчёлах* М.: Государственное издательство культурно-просветительной литературы, 1952, several later editions, all in high print-runs.
9. For example, during the so-called *makulatura* experiment of 1974–91, adult readers could exchange collected waste paper for vouchers for popular book titles; see Levinson, 63–88, and Pristed.
10. See Gille for a detailed account on "Metallic Socialism" 41–78.

Works Cited

Chuiko, Vladimir Alekseevich, editor. *Istoriia tselliulozno-bumazhnoi promyshlennosti Rossii*. RAO Bum-Prom, 2009.

Derrida, Jacques. "Le papier ou moi, vous savez . . . (Nouvelles spéculations sur un luxe des pauvres)." *Les Cahiers de médiologie*, vol. 4, 1997, pp. 33–57.

Dinerštein, Efim. "Kniga v sovetskom obščestve." *Kniga – issledovanija i materialy*, vol. 74, 1997, pp. 166–78.

Dobrenko, Evgenii. "Vse luchshe – detiam (totalitarnaia kul'tura i mir detstva)." *Wiener Slawistischer Almanach*, vol. 29, 1992, pp. 159–74.

Else, Perry. *The Value of Play*. Continuum Books, 2009.

Epstein, Mikhail. "The Origins and Meaning of Russian Postmodernism." *After the Future: The Paradoxes of Postmodernism and Contemporary Russian Culture*. The U of Massachusetts P, 1995, pp. 188–210.

Fayet, Roger. *Reinigungen: Vom Abfall der Moderne zum Kompost der Nachmoderne*. Passagen-Verlag, 2003.

Gille, Zsuzsa. *From the Cult of Waste to the Trash Heap of History: The Politics of Waste in Socialist and Postsocialist Hungary*. Indiana UP, 2007.

Gitelman, Lisa. *Paper Knowledge: Toward a Media History of Documents*. Duke UP, 2014.

Grois, Boris, and Il'ia Kabakov. "Dialog o musore." *Novoe literaturnoe obozrenie*, vol. 20, 1996, pp. 319–30.

Häkli, Esko, editor. *Ingen dag utan papper: Om papper och dess roll som kulturbärare*. Söderströms, Atlantis, 2008.

Josephson, Paul, et al. *An Environmental History of Russia*. Cambridge UP, 2013.

Kelly, Catriona. *Children's World: Growing Up in Russia, 1890–1991*. Yale UP, 2007.

Khalifman, Iosif. "Budem uvazhat' bumagu! Pust' pogasnet koster." *Literaturnaia gazeta*, 29 Nov. 1967, p. 10.

Khorkhordina, T. I. "'Makulaturnaia' kampaniia." *Istoriia i arkhivy*. Ros. gos. gumanit. un-t, 1994.

Kubie, Oenone. "Reading Lewis Hine's Photography of Child Street Labour, 1906–1918." *Journal of American Studies*, vol. 50, no. 4, 2016, pp. 873–97.

Levinson, Aleksei. "Makulatura i knigi: analiz sprosa i predlozheniia v odnoi iz sfer sovremennoi knigotorgovli." *Chtenie: Problemy i razrabotki*, edited by Valeriia Stel'makh, Gos. biblioteka SSSR m. Lenina – Nauchno-issledovatel'skii otdel bibliotekovedeniia, 1985, pp. 63–88.

Lipovetsky, Mark. "Russian Literary Postmodernism in the 1990s." *The Slavonic and East European Review*, vol. 79, no. 1, 2001, pp. 31–50.

Malikov, N., editor. *Million – Rodine (Fotoocherk o sorevnovanii po sboru makulatury mezhdu pionerami i shkol'nikami)*. Mol. Gvardiia, 1979.
Parikka, Jussi. *What Is Media Archaeology?* Polity Press, 2012.
Pristed, Birgitte Beck. "Reading and Recycling: The Soviet Paper Debate and Makulatura Books, 1974–91." *The Russian Review*, vol. 78, no. 1, 2019, pp. 122–40.
Shamko, V. E. "O sostoianii pererabotki makulatury v SSSR i za rubezhom." *Tezisy dokladov: Vsesoiuznoi konferentsii 'Puti ratsional'nogo ispol, zovaniia makulatury v proizvodstve bumagi, kartona i drugikh vidov produktsii.'* Belbumprom, 1981, pp. 1–10.
Smolianitskii, Boris, and Boris Moiseev. *Sbor i pererabotka makulatury*. Lesnaia promyslennost, 1971.

2 How Delightful Is a Child at Play? Play in Children's Literature in Flanders during the Nineteenth Century

A Systemic Approach

Jan Van Coillie

We take it for granted today that children play, but playing has not always been considered an obvious part of a child's life. The attitude toward children and play in Western society changed radically during the nineteenth century (Chudacoff 46; Cross 269–70). Children's books provide fruitful material for the study of this changing attitude. Hence, in this chapter I investigate various representations of play in children's books in Flanders in the nineteenth century and their changes over time. Given this focal thematic concern, the central question of this study is not what games are described in children's books but how play is represented, approached, and valued in these books.

In order to answer this question, I have carried out a combined content and critical discourse analysis on a sample of stories and collections of poems selected from among more than 300 books. The results of this study will be interpreted in light of the dominant images of childhood and the relationship between adults and children. The main focus will be on the tensions between what I call the *regressive* child image – according to which a child should remain a child as long as possible – and the *progressive* child image, which demands that the child should become a responsible adult as soon as possible. The former is rooted in the Romantic tradition; the latter is rooted in the tradition of the Enlightenment.

Representation and Ideology

Representations of children's play are inextricably linked to representations or so-called images of childhood, that is, ideas about what children are, what they can handle, and what is appropriate, good, or useful for them. Personal images of childhood always arise in interaction with collective images of childhood in a given period (Oittinen 4; Joosen & Vloeberghs 28–30). In her article on the images of childhood in Western modernity, Katrien Vloeberghs characterizes the dominant collective image during the second half of the nineteenth century as "bourgeois" (18). According to Vloeberghs, this image integrates elements of the prior

Enlightenment and Romantic images of childhood, adding a repressive dimension, which limits the child's freedom and autonomy and increases its dependence on adults.

Representations or "images" are never value-free: they are always ideologically charged, with ideology understood in its broadest sense as "a system of beliefs which a society shares and uses to make sense of the world" (McCallum and Stephens 360). In fact, ideologies form the basis of images. Teun van Dijk calls them "the basis of the social representations shared by members of a group" (8). According to John Stephens, "fiction must be regarded as a special site for ideological effect, with a potentially powerful capacity for shaping audience attitudes" (3). Therefore, analyzing representations in texts implies revealing their underlying explicit and implicit ideologies. To that end, researchers can focus on the values and norms that are being associated with the object of research. In writing for children, these norms and values are often communicated quite overtly, "its intention being to foster in the child reader a positive apperception of some sociocultural values which, it is assumed, are shared by author and audience" (Stephens 3).

Because my purpose in this chapter is to provide an overall account of the variations and evolution of the representations of play in a large corpus, I have selected a limited number of focal points in order to analyze the explicit and implicit attitudes of the authors toward play. First of all, I focus on the evaluative words, which, according to Fairclough, can be interpreted "in terms of what authors commit themselves to with respect to what is desirable or undesirable, good or bad" (164). I also pay special attention to metaphor, which Jack Weber views as a form of implicit evaluation (180). As another focal point, I examine generic sentences, defined by Roger Fowler as "generalized propositions claiming universal truth and usually cast in a syntax reminiscent of proverbs of scientific laws" (132). Following Stephens, I also explore narrative viewpoints and focalization. According to Charles Sarland, they "imply certain ideological assumptions and formulations, and construct implied readers who must be expected to share them" (42). Finally, because ideologies are inevitably formulated in and by language, I also seek to establish how far (the lack of) playfulness pervades the literary style.

Interpretation and Systems Theories

The secondary research question of this study is: "How and why does the representation of play vary and evolve?" In order to interpret these variations and changes, I draw on the systems theories of Itamar Even Zohar (290) and Niklas Luhmann (20) and approach children's literature as a system that is inextricably intertwined with other systems to form a sociocultural polysystem. Therein, I concentrate on the pedagogical system, which has usually been associated with children's literature. Indeed, children's books have typically been viewed as an educational tool (Zohar Shavit 33; Nikolajeva ix–x; Ewers 77). The images of play in children's literature are subsequently discussed in conjunction with ideas about play, playfulness, and imagination in educational periodicals and handbooks.[1]

Finally, the findings are interpreted in the context of broader transformations in society. Changing images of childhood can be indications of socio-economic and/or political tensions. According to Vloeberghs, "what a child represents, plays out or stages, expresses a view on the way a specific culture or society understands or judges itself" (11). Play in particular can be seen as "a human activity liable to carry heavy ideological markings" (Stephens 186). As Johan Huizinga claims, freedom is a fundamental characteristic of play, which makes it, according to Stephens, "subject to adult attempts to impart order, structure and meaning to it" (186). It is precisely because children are the adults of tomorrow that adult authors project both their hopes and their fears in children's books. They are colored by the ideology of the group to which they belong as well. In this study, I address the Catholic and liberal ideologies, which divided the Flemish bourgeois culture during the nineteenth century. After Belgium regained its independence in 1830, the Catholic Church dominated political and cultural life for a couple of decades. This monopoly was broken after 1850, when the liberals came to power. The liberal agenda claimed exclusive authority for public education, which caused what has come to be known as the "school battle" to erupt, increasingly dividing the country into two camps, which in turn affected culture and literature. It also resulted in a strict split into separate Catholic and liberal publishing houses. The impact of these politically and religiously inspired ideologies has received little attention in the study of children's literature so far.

1830–1870: Sweat and Soap Bubbles

Before 1850, children's literature in Flanders mainly consisted of devotional books promoting Catholic values by means of moralistic stories and poems. The titles of the stories are self-revealing: *Saint Dympna, the First Virgin and Martyr of the Brabantian Kempen: Presented as an Example to the Belgian Youth* (Buelens, 1837) or *Teodoor, or the Virtuous Schoolboy: Useful to Teach Young People Politeness and Good Morals* (Behaegel). Play is hardly accommodated either in stories or in poetry. In line with the Enlightenment ideas, the child is only allowed to play after learning or working:

> Though I was sweating all over my body,
> Writing, doing sums, learning hard,
> As soon as one has done one's duty
> Play comforts head and heart.

(Waterkeyn 14)[2]

If a playing child exceptionally figures in a poem, it serves to illustrate a moral lesson. In a poem by Andries Van Hasselt, a child who flies kites learns the following lesson, formulated as a generic sentence: "Nothing can stay up high by its own strength alone" (16).

An exceptional voice in the 1840s is that of the poet Prudens van Duyse. He is considerably more attentive to and appreciative of the playing child than his contemporaries. In his *Poems for Children* (1844), play is still clearly subordinate to learning. Noteworthy in the following lines is the point of view of the child, who cites his father's teachings:

> My father says: "Do what you do,
> Don't play while you study.
> You will progress twice as fast,
> And everyone will honor you
> When your task is ready."
>
> (Van Duyse, *Gedichtjes* 40)[3]

However, in some of Van Duyse's later poems, the idealization of childhood displaces or affects morality. The tension between the progressive and the regressive child images is reflected most straightforwardly in "Soap bubbles" from his collection *Last Poems for Children* (1883). The I-speaker first describes children playing, then begins to preach a moral lesson but immediately retracts it, only to end on the note of nostalgic longing:

> Life, children, is a bubble.
> It grows, swirls and disappears.
> But what am I saying? How sad it would be
> If you already understood this. . . .
> Let me too blow a bubble, indeed.
> See, there it swells . . . O, I succeed.
> How happy is he who still may
> Find joy in the child's sweet play.
>
> (*Laatste* 32–33)[4]

The first children's books written by liberal authors appear after 1850. Although they expand the thematic spectrum, play continues to receive little attention and remains subordinate to learning in their stories and verses. In the foreword to his *Stories for Children* (1853), Pieter Geiregat assures his young readers that they can play to their heart's content, but he adds that they have to learn studiously in the first place. The playing child remains largely absent from the stories and poems authored by Catholic writers in the 1850s and 1860s. Not much playfulness can be expected of texts whose titles read *Emilia or the Fruits of Irresponsibility* (Anonymous) or "It's good dying a Catholic" (Hahn 137).

1870–1880: From Children May to Children Should Play

The first harbingers of change appear in the 1870s. In the preface to his *Fables and Poems for children* (1870), Napoleon Destanberg calls children "our sweet dictators" (12). The book contains several poems about children's games, some of them without a moral lesson. The final aim of the collection, though, is in line with the enlightened image of the child. In "Children and butterflies," the poet emphasizes that children are allowed to play, like the butterflies, but he concludes that

> Work comes before play.
> That makes us strong every day.
> As such firm we stand
> In the Belgian fatherland.
>
> (108)

The metaphor of the butterfly proves to be ambiguous. In "Being a Butterfly," the child says it prefers being an industrious ant rather than a vain butterfly. Jan Van Droogenbroeck also wants to educate in the first place, as is evidenced by such titles as "Pay Attention" or "The Sluggard." But his collection *These Are Sunrays* (1873) also contains poems without lessons in which children catch fish or long for a bunny to play with. Van Droogenbroeck renews the form too: he plays extensively with sound and rhythmical variations. The wording in his "Butterfly Song" is much more playful than Destanberg's idiom. Moreover, the idealization of the child overshadows all morality:

> On the flower meadow butterflies play,
> happily frolicking together. . . .
> In the green meadow children play,
> happily frolicking together.
>   Watch them jump,
>   Hear them sing
> Sometimes on their own,
> Sometimes together.
>   Or they dance,
>   weave wreaths
> And put them on their curly hair:
> How beautiful is the child's life
> When it is surrounded by
> Flowers, joy and peace!
>
> (37–38)[5]

In prose writings, a new approach to play appears for the first time in the 1873 collection of stories *Three Children's Parties* by G. J. Kroes. The following excerpt captures the transition from "children are allowed to play" to "children should play," although there is a "but":

> Dear boys and girls, you too may be playing mothers and fathers. That is very good; you may do so; there is no harm in that. You should play, and the more you play the better. But if you ever are father or mother, do not do it the way I do.
>
> (23)[6]

Not only is the tone of Kroes's stories more light-hearted than ever before, but his style is more playful, relying on spoken language, dialect, child language, and puns. The book can be viewed as a prelude to his *Children's Games* (1879), the foreword to which starts with "How charming are children's lives with their games! What poetry shines through it." Despite this enthusiasm, the voice of the educator is unmistakable as well: "How important they are for the upbringing of the child, and what influence they will exercise in their later lives as citizens" (4).[7] Kroes blends amusing incidents with information and wise lessons. "Pants-stand-fixed," for example, is an old-fashioned cautionary tale in which a disobedient boy who plays leapfrog falls on his head and dies. At the end, the narrator directly addresses the young reader: "Let this incident be a lesson for you, too." (58). Besides, these teachings are only intended for boys, because "nature has given girls a much gentler temper than boys" (3).[8]

In the 1870s, such cautionary tales were very popular as a matter of fact. In his collection *Children's Treasure* (1873), Polydoor Van Hauwaert seems to adopt a child's viewpoint, but he patently does so from the perspective of an adult educator who corrects children and stresses the differences in our (adults') experience as opposed to their (children's) experience:

> Many children believe that parents and teachers cannot stand that young people have fun. This is wrong. We are convinced that playing is suitable in childhood, and that it is a mark of life and health. What we want to prevent is only dangerous games, and our concern is all the greater as young people are inexperienced and do not look before they leap.
>
> (56–57)[9]

Van Hauwaert dedicates a separate section to "dangerous games." In one of his cruelest stories, a child tosses up a bean to catch it with his mouth. Alas, he chokes when the bean gets stuck in his throat and swells.

1880–1900: A Child among Children

During the 1880s, a new attitude toward children and play incrementally yet irrevocably negotiates its way into stories for children, albeit only those by liberal authors. This tendency is evident in the work of Virginie Loveling. She chooses a child as the main focalizer far more often than her predecessors did. *A St Nicholas Gift* (1889) opens with a description of the toys that Jantje sees in the window of a toy store. The toys are depicted through details that make them attractive to the child. The following sentence makes it clear that the narrator sympathizes with the child: "and who could pass by, without stopping for a while?" (3).[10] As early as the very beginning, play is put on equal footing with learning: "Jantje learned well and loved it, but that did not prevent him from playing just like other boys of his age" (3).[11] However, what the story clearly has in sight is its crowning lesson about the importance of honesty.

A more radical change in the representation of play occurs at the end of the 1880s, with the introduction of a new genre, specifically the boyish story.[12] The protagonist of the boyish story is invariably a mischievous rascal with a heart of gold. This new character type is vividly encapsulated in the description of Jan Vermeulen, a figure in Alexis Callant's short story "Zwarte Willem":

> Jan Vermeulen was ten years old and a really popular boy. He was what one calls "a good one." He ran, jumped, and played as the wildest little rascal of the alley. And there lived many boys over there. Torn pants, through which a "tiny flag" came peeping, and a large black face in no way interfered with his bright happiness.
>
> (Callant, *Zwarte Willem*, 65)[13]

In these "rascal stories," play is an important motif as an integral part of children's lives. It is often described in detail, complete with game rules and specific terms. The genre is suffused with nostalgia and an idealization of childhood. Colored by the regressive child image, mischief is described with gentle humor, and the fun that children enjoy while playing replaces any moral lessons. Since the author tries to write as a child among children, rather than as an adult educator, his diction typically relies on the use of nicknames, dialect, and the language of adolescents. The following passage exemplifies this new attitude toward play:

> Solemn silence. Rik looks up mischievously, Bert smiles, Jantje whispers something into Miel's ear and then laughs out loudly, Blanche looks at her sister questioningly.
>
> And Marie goes again, as if in doubt:
>
> "That three times you will . . . kiss Blanche!"
>
> "Kiss Blanche!"
>
> "Come on, boy!"
>
> "It's cheap!"
>
> "It's for free!"

Flor hesitated one moment and turned as red as a rose. Blanche looked dismayed.

And suddenly, the boy rushed towards the girl, and kissed her – kissed her three times . . .

If ever there was a good laugh, it was now.

(Callant, *Frissche bloemen*, 20–21)[14]

Noteworthy in the book is the reaction of Flor's mother, illustrating a playful relationship between parent and child, which was hardly imaginable a decade earlier: when her son tells her what happened, she reprimands him, but the auctorial narrator adds that she only pretends to be severe.

Leo Van Nerum goes one step further. In one of his stories, the auctorial narrator suddenly intervenes, condemning a father who forbids his child to play: "Unwise father! Forbidding a tender child to play!" (5).[15] The evaluative adjective "tender" is not a random lexical choice. Van Nerum is much more interested in exploring and portraying children's feelings than other authors of his time. The short story "Killemendé, dé, dé" (8) is illustrative of this preoccupation. Little Ernest is never asked by the girls to participate in their circle games until one evening they all ask him at the same time. Eventually, everything is revealed to have been a dream, and Ernest is left alone and sad.

Though the new view on children's play was unstoppable, there were still authors who continued to write cautionary tales. Hippoliet Ledeganck's *Novellen and vertellingen* (ca. 1900) includes a section on "Dangerous children's games." Similarly to his contemporaries, he describes the games with an eye for detail, pithy dialogues, and nostalgia. However, in his role as an adult educator, he puts restrictions on children's play and teaches them lesson after lesson, for example: "Children, never play with guns or gunpowder" (41).[16]

The boyish story is in fact the exclusive domain of liberal authors. Indeed, playing is almost entirely absent in the Catholic stories for children at the end of the century. Nearly all of them continue to present examples to be followed, which is apparent from the titles, such as *Winter flowers: Pleasant and Useful Stories* (Witteryck-Delplace, 1894) or *Edifying Evening Hours* (Gobbers, 1881). In Catholic poetry, too, the traditional view that playing comes after learning still prevails after 1880, with verses such as "It is so that all those nice games/ are a reward for you./ After learning one may play" (De Vreese 106).[17] Remarkable in this respect is Ivo Strobbe's poem "Children and Butterflies." Contrary to Destanberg or Van Droogenbroeck, Strobbe forces the butterfly metaphor into the mold of the morale: the children in the poem want to go to school to be as diligent as butterflies.

In contrast, playing is increasingly experienced from the child's point of view and dissociated from moral teaching in poems by liberal authors.

As a striking novelty, some of these poems depict parents playing with their children. For example, in "Making Pancakes" the eponymous activity turns into an entertainment when the father becomes involved:

> When father joins in,
> Cooking becomes fun:
> A pancake tumbles in the air,
> Tumbling it ends up in the pan again!
>
> (Callant, *Een kransje*, 85)[18]

As the content takes on a lighter tone, the poetic form becomes more playful: poets abundantly make use of neologisms, onomatopoeias, alliterations, assonance and rhythmic variations. This approach is vividly exemplified in "Our Gust," where Theofiel Coopman lists numerous children's games, giving their names in dialect:

> Playing at marbles,
> I'll beat Pol and Piet.
> I play for keeps
> Cause I don't knuckle down.
> I'll teach those little boys
> How I can boss out. I know all hidden corners
> For playing hide-and-seek.
>
> (Coopman 61)[19]

Similarly to all other writers, Coopman's representation of play is clearly gender-related: "Playing cooking-eating/ is no game for boys:/ no boy can cook,/ but eat he surely can!/ Do ask your sister;/ or ask Griet and Claire,/ There!" (82).[20]

In conclusion, it can be stated that, in the course of the nineteenth century, stories and poems for children register a radical change in attitudes toward play, a development that is paralleled by transformations in the images of the child and intergenerational relationships. The role of the adult as an educator who links play to moral lessons competes more and more with that of the adult as an observer or an admirer who associates play with happy childhood. Longing to be a child amongst children, the adult sometimes becomes a participant in the child's game. Moreover, in an effort to bridge the intergenerational gap, the educator becomes milder, faking severity when the playing child gets into mischief. Finally, the increasing attempts to empathize and identify with children affect the style of writing, which becomes more playful, incorporating elements of children's language.

In order to interpret the shift in the representation of play in Flemish children's literature around 1870, particularly in the stories and poems of liberal authors, I examine the educational system of the period.

Play in the Educational System

From the 1880s onward, paying attention to the nature of the child becomes a prevalent preoccupation in pedagogy. It is inspired mainly by the Romantic pedagogies of Rousseau, Pestalozzi, and Froebel, who gain the status of the most popular educators in the late nineteenth century. Friedrich Froebel has the strongest impact on thinking about play. Froebel insists that playing is inherent in the nature of the child, or, in the words of an anonymous contributor to the periodical *The Future* from 1859, "[p]laying is the natural, innate activity of the child. It is out of this activity that the first knowing, the first knowledge stems; it must therefore precede learning, or, rather, learning must happen by its agency" (Anonymous 165).[21]

In Flanders, the interest in Froebel commences in the 1850s, but his ideas only become widely disseminated in the 1870s. This stance is well represented by J Simmer's article "Children's Pleasure," which was printed in *The Future* in 1877. In the article, Simmer encourages parents to let their children enjoy leisure time, because only then will they be able to withstand the storms of life when they grow up (535–38). This text is perfectly aligned with the changing attitude toward play in literature for children in the 1870s.

In the 1880s and 1890s, educational periodicals display a substantially increasing interest in children's play. While some articles only enumerate children's games and toys, most of them have a clear educational purpose. Many papers emphasize that a child's play must be properly managed, and they discriminate between good and bad, dangerous play. Playful learning is placed at the heart of the new way of thinking even more emphatically than in the preceding decades, whereby references to Froebel are frequently made. While liberal magazines underscore learning, their Catholic counterparts stress moral education, a difference that is reflected in children's books.

In educational manuals, too, the educational value of playing is repeatedly highlighted. At the same time, these books show the influence of the regressive child image, which foregrounds the childlike imagination and the importance of children's play for its own sake. In *The Working-class Child: His Upbringing and His Education*, Marie Lievevrouw-Coopman deems playing "just as necessary [for the child] as the air he breathes, as the bread he eats" (35). While for the adult educator children's play is a source of observations, for the learning child it is a welcome break from educational activities, a diversion that in her view has become more indispensable than ever before because of the increase in homework assignments and overloaded school curricula.

This plea for children's play as a defense against burdening children with knowledge is consistent with new teaching ideas, which opposed excessive intellectualism and utilitarianism in education (De Vroede 74).

Just as in children's books, this view leads to an idealization of children and their play: "Let us not deprive young people of their play. As long as one plays, one remains a child, that is, an innocent, happy creature who develops his resources of courage, strength, and perseverance, and who, as a mature man, will live his life with more ease, with more natural orthodoxy" (Lievevrouw-Coopman 41).[22] Noteworthy in this comment is the blending of the regressive image of the child with the progressive one. For Lievevrouw-Coopman, playing is important for moral education as a remedy against "secret passions" and a safeguard against improper involvements. She thus advocates establishing special playgrounds to keep children off the streets. This view is prompted by a mistrust of the street, which the bourgeoisie (liberals and Catholics alike) considered a breeding ground for socialism. This is one reason why more pleas in favor of playing are published in Catholic periodicals at the end of the century.

Catholic educators regarded play as the best remedy against boredom and idleness, which drove children into the streets and, therefore, into the hands of the socialist "devil":

> Playing abundantly satisfies the child's desire to move; it is a powerful antidote against the dangerous idleness and its terrible trail of vices; it prepares the child for a sociable life; it makes the soul cheerful and prepared for new efforts, and frees it from boredom.
>
> (V. T. Karel 244)[23]

The Catholics wanted to promote this "sociable life" especially in the families, as they could control those more easily than the streets: "In our times, complaints are made about the deterioration of family life, about the longing for outdoor pleasures; a major reason for this is that joy, this friendliest housemate, this guardian of family life, has been driven out of doors, and boredom has been allowed to creep into the house" (Van Meurs, 139).[24] This stress on family life, paired with a deep mistrust regarding street life, may explain why the boyish story did not penetrate into the Catholic literature for children at that time.

It may have become clear by now that the changes in the representation of play in children's books were inspired by new pedagogical insights. From the 1870s onward, the attention to children's play in educational periodicals and manuals increased substantially. Parents and teachers were advised to encourage children to play, although at the same time the ultimate educational goal remained very prominent. Play had to be controlled as thoroughly as possible, and playful learning was the cherished ideal. At the end of the century, pedagogues favored intergenerational forms of play within the family, as they kept children off the street, which was considered the "playground" of the socialist movement.

Conclusion

Children's literature clearly reflects the attitude of adults toward children's play, which of course may considerably differ from children's real-life experiences. That attitude fundamentally transformed during the nineteenth century, although the change was gradual. Subversive books that "overturned adult pretensions and made fun of adult institutions" (Lurie x) were not published in nineteenth-century Flanders. This changing attitude was inextricably linked to the evolving images of childhood and the changes in intergenerational relationships, which were inspired by new pedagogical theories. From the 1870s onward, increasingly more authors sought to empathize and even to identify with children at play. They adopted the role of a sympathizing observer, a nostalgic admirer, or a participant. Still, the voice of the educator, which was inspired by the progressive child image, remained dominant throughout the century, revealing what Frost calls "an urge for control and protection" (46). In order to present a complete and nuanced picture of changes in the representation of any cultural phenomenon in children's literature over time, it appears important to study multiple genres. As my analysis shows, approaches to children's play differed materially depending on the genre. The new attitude toward playing was most explicitly conveyed in prose, while poetry for children mostly remained in the service of education.

Noteworthy also are the different attitudes endorsed by Catholic and liberal authors. Given that play carried a heavy ideological load, it was given divergent renderings by Catholic and liberal authors, who associated play with different values. The Catholics insisted that children's literature should first and foremost serve educational ends and that education itself should focus on values, such as piety and obedience. Such imperatives were not accommodating for play. The new attitude toward play was almost exclusively espoused in works by liberal authors. Less inhibited by authoritarian parenting ideas, they wrote about frolics and mischief with gentle humor and nostalgia. At the end of the century, the liberals and the Catholics found some common ground in their fight against socialism, a shared purpose for which they mobilized children's play. In the meantime, as the child's world was becoming more and more restricted, the child itself was increasingly idealized as an unworldly, innocent creature.

Notes

1. It is legitimate to assume that many of the children's authors read these publications. Approximately 70% of the authors whose profession I could trace (91/166) spent (a part of) their careers in education, and about 15% of them were priests. Some of them also published in educational periodicals.
2. For the sake of clarity, I provide all Dutch quotations and titles in my English translation. The original Dutch passages can be found in the footnotes.

"Hebben wy wat moeten sweeten,/ Schrijven, rek'nen, leeren fel;/ Als men heeft zijn pligt gekweeten,/ Dan verkwikt zoo goed het spel."

3. "Myn vader zegt: 'Doe wat gy doet,/ En speel niet onder 't leeren./ Zoo vordert gy met dubblen spoed,/ En ziet, als leerzaem van gemoed,/ Door ieder u vereeren.' "
4. "'t Leven, kindren, is een zeepbel./ Wassen, weemlen en vergaan!/ Maar, wat zeg ik? Hoe beklaaglijk,/ Moest gij dit alreeds verstaan. . . . Laat mij ook een zeepbel blazen,/ Zie, daar zwelt zij . . . O, 't gaat wel/ Hoe gelukkig, die nog vreugd vindt/ In het lieve kinderspel."
5. "Op de bloemenweide spelen vlinders/ Dartlen vroolijk door elkaar. . . . In de groene weide spelen kinders Dartlen vroolijk door elkaar/ Zie ze springen,/ Hoor ze zingen/ Nu weer een alléén,/ Dan te gaar./ Of ze dansen,/ Vlechten kransen/ En sieren er hun lokkig hoofdje mee:/ Hoe schoon is het kinderleven/ Waar het zacht omgeven/ Bloemen, vreugd en vree!"
6. "Kleine lezers en lezeressen, gij ook speelt misschien vaderken of moederken. Dat is heel goed; ge moogt dat doen; er zit daar geen kwaad in. Gij moet spelen, en hoe meer gij speelt hoe beter. Maar als gij ooit vaderken of moederken zijt, doet het dan niet zooals ik."
7. 'Hoe schilderachtig is het kinderleven met zijne spelen! Wat al poëzie straalt erin door! Van hoeveel belang zijn zij niet voor de opvoeding des kinds, en welken invloed zullen zij later op het maatschappelijk leven niet uitoefenen!"
8. "De natuur heeft de meisjes eene veel zachtere geaardheid geschonken dan de jongens."
9. "Vele kinderen denken dat ouders en meesters niet kunnen lijden dat de jeugd zich vermake. Dit is verkeerd. Wij zijn overtuigd, dat het spel der kindsheid past en het een kenmerk is van leven en gezondheid. / Wat wij willen beletten, zijn slechts de gevaarlijke spelen, en onze bezorgdheid is des te grooter, daar de jeugd geen ondervinding heeft en niet verzint eer zij begint."
10. "en wie zou voorbij kunnen, zonder eens te blijven staan?"
11. "Jantje leerde goed en gaarne, dit belette hem niet ook gaarne te spelen als andere jongens van zijnen ouderdom."
12. The genre of the boyish story became popular all over Europe after 1880 (Kuhn and Merkel 91; Avery 143; Ghesquière et al. 32, 269).
13. "Jan Vermeulen was tien jaar oud en een echte volksjongen. Hij was, wat men 'een goede' noemt. Hij liep, sprong en speelde gelijk de wildste bengel van zijn steegje. En daar huisden vele jongens. Een gescheurde broek, waar een 'vaantje' kwam doorkijken, en een groot zwart gezicht verstoorden geenszins zijn helderen gelukshemel."
14. "Plechtig zwijgen. Rik kijkt schalks op, Bert glimlacht, Jantje fluistert Miel iets in 't oor en lacht dan schaterend, Blanche ziet vragend op naar hare zuster. En Marie wêer, wijfelend: Dat ge drie keer . . . Blanche zult kussen! – Blanche kussen! – Toe, jongen! – 't Is goedkoop! – 't Is voor niet! Flor aarzelde een stond en werd rood als eene roos. Blanche bleef beteuterd omlaag zien. En opeens, snelde de jongen op het meisje toe, en zoende heur – zoende heur drie keeren . . . Als er ooit smakelijk gelachen werd, was het wel nu."
15. "Onverstandige vader! Een teer kind verbieden te spelen!"
16. "Kinderen, speelt nooit met vuurwapens of buskruit."
17. "It Is dat al die schoone spelen/ Voor u een belooning zijn./ Na het leeren mag men spelen."
18. "En als vader zich dan moeit,/ Maakt hij er een spelen van:/ Draaiend vliegt een koek omhoog,/ Draaiend komt hij in de pan!"
19. "Met het marbelstekken/ Klop ik Pol en Piet;/ 'k Zal ze rutte spelen/ Want ik kneukel niet./ 'k Zal die ventjes leeren/ Hoe ik putje stuik!/ Hoekjes ken en kantjes/ Voor het piepkenduik!"

20. "Koken-eten spelen/ Is geen jongensspel:/ Koken kan geen jongen;/ Eten kan hij wel!/ Vraag het aan uw' zuster maar;/ Vraag het ook aan Griet en Klaar,/ Daar!"
21. "Het spel is dus de natuerlijke, ingeborene werkdadigheid des kinds. Uit deze werkdadigheid spruit hem het eerste weten, de eerste kennis: zij moet derhalve het leeren vooraf gaen of beter gezegd, het leeren moet door hare vermiddeling geschieden."
22. "Ontnemen wij de jeugd haar spel niet. Zoolang men speelt, zoolang ook blijft men kind, dat is een onschuldig, een blijgeestig wezen dat zijn voorraad van levensmoed, van kracht en volharding opdoet, en later met des te meer gemak, met des te meer ongekunstelde rechtzinnigheid, als volwassen mens in het werkelijke leven optreden zal."
23. "Het spel schenkt een overvloedig voedsel aan de bewegingszucht des kinds, het is een machtig behoedmiddel tegen de vervaarlijke luiheid en haren vreeselijken sleep van ondeugden; het bereidt het wichtje tot gezellig leven; het maakt de ziel opgeruimd en geschikt tot nieuwe krachtinspanning, bevrijdt haar van verveling."
24. "Men klaagt tegenwoordig over den achteruitgang van het familieleven, over uithuizigheid, zucht naar verstrooiing buitenshuis; een voorname reden hiervan is: dat men de vroolijkheid, de vriendelijkste huisgenote, den schutsengel van het familieleven, over den drempel heeft gejaagd, en er de verveling heeft laten binnensluipen."

Works Cited

Anonymus. *Emilia of de vruchten der lichtzinnigheid*. J.-P. Van Dieren, 1853.

———. "Froebels opvoedingstelsel." *De Toekomst*, 3, 1859, pp. 280–88.

Avery, Gillian. *Childhood's Pattern: A Study of the Heroes and Heroines of Children's Fiction, 1770–1950*. Hodder and Staughton, 1975.

Behaegel, Pieter. *Teodoor of den deugdzaemen schoolier: Dienstig om aen de jeugd de beleefdheid en de goede zeden in te boezemen*. C. de Moor, 1834.

Buelens, Jan-Baptist. *De heylige Dympna, eerste maegd en martelares der Brabantsche Kempen; tot voorbeeld voorgedragen aan de Belgische jeugd*. T.J. Janssens, 1837.

Callant, Alexis. *Frissche bloemen*. Brussel, L. Lebègue en Cie, 1886.

———. *Een kransje gedichten voor onze kleinen*. *I*. Vanderpoorten, 1890.

———. *Zwarte Willem en andere verhalen*. *I*. Vanderpoorten, 1893.

Chudacoff, Howard P. *Children at Play: An American History*. New York UP, 2007.

Coopman, Theofiel. *Kinderlust*. A. Siffer, 1897.

Cross, Gary. "Play, Games and Toys." *The Routledge History of Childhood in the Western World*, edited by Paula S. Fass. Routledge, 2013, pp. 267–82.

Destanberg, Napoleon. *Fabelen en kindergedichtjes*. C. Annoot-Braakman, 1870.

De Vreese, Lodewijk. *Dwalende lichtjes*. L. de Busscher, 1890.

De Vroede, Marc, editor. *Bijdragen tot de geschiedenis van het pedagogisch leven in België in de 19de en 20ste eeuw. Volume III: De periodieken, 1986–1914*. Universitaire Pers KUL, 1976.

Even-Zohar, Itamar. "Polysystem Theory." *Poetics Today*, vol. 1, no. 1–2, 1979, pp. 287–310.

Ewers, Hans-Heino. *Fundamental Concepts of Children's Literature Research: Literary and Sociological Approaches*. Routledge, 2009.

Fairclough, Norman, *Analysing Discourse: Textual Analysis for Social Research*. Routledge, 2003.

Fowler, Roger. *Linguistic Criticism*. Oxford UP, 1986.

Geiregat, Pieter. *Verhalen voor kinderen*. L. Hebbelynck, 1853.

Ghesquière, Rita, et al. *Een land van waan en wijs. Geschiedenis van de Nederlandse jeugdliteratuur*. Atlas Contact, 2014.

Gobbers, Hendrik. *Stichtende avondstonden of de kleine godvruchtige verteller*. E.-F. van Velsen, 1884.

Hahn, André Ernest. *De lentekrans*. C. De Backer, 1856.

Huizinga, Johan. *Homo Ludens. Proeve eener bepaling van het spel-element der cultuur*. Met foto's van Vincent Mentzel. Amsterdam UP, 2010.

Joosen, Vanessa, and Katrien Vloeberghs. *Uitgelezen jeugdliteratuur: Ontmoetingen tussen traditie en vernieuwing*. Lannoo Campus, 2008.

Karel, V. T. "Spelen." *De Lagere Onderwijzer*, vol. 3, 1897, pp. 241–47.

Kroes, Willem Jozef. *Drie kinderfeesten*. J. Plasky, 1873.

———. *Kinderspelen*. Brussel, D. Windels, 1876.

Kuhn, Andrea, and Johannes Merkel. *Sentimentalität und Geschäft. Zur Sozialisation durch Kinder- und Jugendliteratur im 19. Jahrhundert*. Basis Verlag, 1977.

Ledeganck, Hippoliet. *Novellen en vertellingen*. J. Lebègue, ca. 1900.

Lievevrouw-Coopman, Marie. *Het volkskind. Zijne opvoeding en zijn onderwijs*. I. Vanderpoorten, 1895.

Loveling, Virginie. *Een Sint-Nicolaas geschenk*. I. Vanderpoorten, 1889.

Luhmann, Niklas. *Soziale Systeme. Grundriss einer allgemeinen Theorie*. Suhrkamp, 1984.

Lurie, Alison. *Don't Tell the Grown-Ups: The Subversive Power of Children's Literature*. Bloomsbury, 1990.

McCallum, Robyn, and John Stephens. "Ideology in Children's Books." *Handbook of Research in Children's and Young Adult Literature*, edited by Shelby A. Wolf, et al. Routledge, 2011, pp. 359–71.

Nikolajeva, Maria, editor. *Aspects and Issues in the History of Children's Literature*. Greenwood, 1995.

Oittinen, Riitta. *Translating for Children*. Garland, 2000.

Sarland, Charles. "Critical Tradition and Ideological Positioning." *Understanding Children's Literature*, edited by Peter Hunt, 2nd ed. Routledge, 2005, pp. 56–75.

Simmer, J. "Kindergenot." *De Toekomst*, vol. 21, pp. 535–38.

Stephens, John. *Language and Ideology in Children's Fiction*. Longman, 1992.

Strobbe, Ivo. *Een bloemtuiltje voor de jeugd*. A.-J. Witteryck, 1896.

Van Dijk, Teun A., editor. *Discourse as Social Interaction*. Sage Publications, 1997.

Van Droogenbroeck Jan. *Dit zijn zonnestralen*. Wed. Nys, 1873.

Van Duysse, Prudens. *Gedichtjes voor kinderen*. No Publisher, 1844.

———. *Laatste kindergedichtjes*. De Seyn-Verhoughstraete, 1883.

Van Hasselt, Andries. *Het Gouden Boeksken*. Jamar, 1845.

Van Hauwaert, Polydoor. *Kinderschat*. I. Vanderpoorten, 1873.

Van Meurs, B. "De vroolijkheid in den huisenlijken kring." *De Opvoeding*, vol. 7, 1892, pp. 138–40.

Van Nerum, Leo. *Bij kinderen*. G. Devreese, 1899.

Vloeberghs, Katrien. "Kindbeelden in de moderne westerse moderniteit." *Literatuur zonder leeftijd*, vol. 70, 2006, pp. 10–23.

Waterkeyn, H. B. *De zangschool*. P.-J. Merckx, 1848.

Weber, Jean-Jacques, "Educating the Reader: Narrative Technique and Evaluation in Charlotte Perkings Gilman's Herland." *The Language and Literature Reader*, edited by Ronald Carter and Peter Stockwell. Routledge, 2008, pp. 177–86.

Witteryck-Delplace, Antoon-Jozef. *Winterbloempjes of aangename en nuttige lezingen*. A. Siffer, 1895.

Zohar, Shavit. *Poetics of Children's Literature*. U of Georgia P, 1986.

3 "When you have said your les-sons well, then you shall go out to play"

Play, Gender, and the Child Addressee in Nineteenth-century Children's Dictionaries

Sarah Hoem Iversen

Introduction: Children's Dictionaries in a Historical Context

Examining ideologies of childhood and the implied reader in children's information books from the 1990s and 2000s, Larkin-Lieffers notes that the information book genre "has often been overlooked in favour of children's fiction" (77). The same could be said for children's dictionaries, which, as Béjoint notes, "have rarely been the object of research" (48). The history of children's literature and the history of lexicography are both large and growing areas of interest in their respective fields. By contrast, the history of children's dictionaries has remained unexplored until recently. Dictionaries for children are not mentioned in Hartmann ed. *Lexicography: Critical Concepts* (2003), edited by Hartman; *Yesterday's Words: Contemporary, Current and Future Lexicography* (2008), edited by Mooijaart and van der Wal; or in the two-volume *Oxford History of Lexicography* (2008), edited by Cowie. This lacuna is unsurprising: In the history of English-language lexicography, children's dictionaries are seen as twentieth-century phenomena, pioneered by the American psychologist Edward Thorndike's *Thorndike Century Junior Dictionary* (1935). Histories of lexicography acknowledge that the original purpose of English dictionary making was pedagogical; the earliest dictionaries were compiled for students (Starnes and Noyes 1; Béjoint 62). The existence of early dictionaries specifically addressed to children, such as John Withals' English-Latin *A Shorte Dictionarie for Yonge Begynners* from 1553, is also well-documented. However, it has been assumed that dictionaries used by children before the twentieth century were simply abridged adult dictionaries, which "made no concession to simplicity" (Landau 25). Contrary to this assumption, I argue that there were several dictionaries in Britain specifically adapted for children already in the nineteenth century.

To demonstrate this, the present chapter analyses entries related to the semantic fields of play and gender in three British children's dictionaries published in the first half of the nineteenth century: Maria Edgeworth's "Glossary" at the back of *Early Lessons. Harry and Lucy*; Anna Brownell Murphy's (later Jameson) *A First, Or Mother's Dictionary for Children*; and Francis Wilby's *Infant School Spelling-Book, And Pictorial Dictionary*. My previous work on eighteenth- and nineteenth-century British children's dictionaries has examined gender-roles in children's reference books, concentrating on works by female codifiers (Iversen, "'To Teach Little Boys and Girls'"), pedagogical uses of nineteenth-century children's dictionaries and evidence of historical users (Iversen, "'Do You Understand This My Little Pupil?'"), and sexuality and taboo in children's dictionaries (Iversen, "Class, Censorship"). By contrast, this chapter draws on narrative theory and the concept of the implied reader to examine the ways in which the child reader is addressed in the text. Drawing on critical discourse analysis methods, I also investigate the ways in which dictionaries reflect and construct ideologies of childhood and gender. This analysis contests the assumption that children's dictionaries did not exist as a distinct genre before the mid-twentieth century. Instead, dictionaries both stylistically and ideologically aimed at child readers existed at least as early as the nineteenth century. These dictionaries aimed not simply to impart the meaning of words but also to provide social and moral education for children. Entries related to play in children's dictionaries demonstrate the power relationship between (adult) narrators and the implied child reader. Moreover, the moral didacticism in children's dictionaries was part of an ongoing construction of gender identities. Entries related to play in children's dictionaries further reinforced this gendered socialization, creating separate roles for girls and boys.

Already in the seventeenth century, Comenius's 1658 *Orbis Sensualium Pictus*, an early example of an illustrated dictionary, had stressed the pedagogical value of enjoyable learning. Comenius argued that children learned words that were accompanied by pictures more efficiently and with more pleasure. However, these ideas did not become truly widespread until after the publication of John Locke's 1693 *Some Thoughts Concerning Education*, in which Locke noted that he had "always had a Fancy, that Learning might be made a Play and Recreation to Children" (141 §148). From the mid-eighteenth century onward, it was increasingly common for reference works for children to be advertised as "pleasurable" and described as "playthings" (Lerer 106–7), which is reflected in such titles such as *The Play Grammar*. Books intended to expand the middle-class market were not only described as playthings but sometimes even sold with toys such as balls and pincushions.

However, dictionaries were not conventionally seen as sources of pleasure for children. In Maria and Richard Edgeworth's 1798 educational treatise *Practical Education*, such works are associated with rods and tears:

> Some people, struck with a panic fear lest their children should never learn to read and write, think that they cannot be in too great a hurry to teach them. Spelling books, grammars, dictionaries, rods, and masters, are collected; nothing is to be heard of in the house but tasks, nothing is to be seen but tears.
>
> (38)

While it was common in this period for children to memorize their dictionaries and spelling books (Iversen, " 'To Teach Little Boys and Girls' " 334–36), Maria Edgeworth did not approve of such pedagogical practices. *A Rational Primer*, which Edgeworth also co-authored with her father, complained that "[f]ew children . . . get through their . . . hy-phen-d spelling books, without sighs and tears," which created an "early association of pain with learning" (Edgeworth and Edgeworth 19).

Theoretical Framework and Methodology: Narrative Voice and Critical Discourse Analysis

In her discussion of nineteenth- and twentieth-century children's fiction, Barbara Wall defines the narrator as the "voice" that "speaks" to the "narratee" or the "reader-in-the-text" (2–4). These terms are seen as distinct from the "implied author," the "authorial presence in the text," and the "implied reader," the "reader for whom the real and implied authors have consciously and unconsciously shaped the text" (6–7). Wolfgang Iser stressed that the "implied reader" concept had both a textual and mental dimension, incorporating not only the pre-structuring of potential meaning in the text but also "the reader's actualization of this potential through the reading process" (xii). This chapter adopts the view that any discourse has a built-in subject position for an "ideal subject" or implied reader that actual readers "have to negotiate a relationship with" (Fairclough 41).[1]

The discussion draws on what Hollindale calls "the three levels of ideology" in children's books: "active ideology" (the individual writer's explicit beliefs), "passive ideology" (the writer's unexamined passive beliefs and values), and "organic ideology" (the dominant ideologies of the society in which a text originated) (36). With the caveat that one cannot discover a historical author's true intention, it is nonetheless worth noting some differences between the "implied" and historical author of a children's dictionary such as Murphy's *Mother's Dictionary*.[2] In general, this work seems to promote ideals of domesticity and motherhood, but it was written by a childless governess who travelled the world, left her husband, and became a women's rights advocate (Johnston 2; Thomas

11). In short, the dictionary may have reflected the "organic ideology" of the Victorian period, but the lexicographer's personal positions ("active ideologies") may also have come into play.

In examining these ideological constructions, this chapter draws on critical discourse analysis, which aims to uncover ideologies and power structures through the systematic investigation of written, spoken, or visual semiotic data (Wodak and Meyer 3). The analysis is influenced by Fairclough's approach to critical discourse analysis, which is rooted in linguistic analysis and social theories of power and discourse. Central to this approach is the assumption that "discourse" – or "language as a form of social practice determined by social structures" (14) – is a fundamental aspect of both institutional and individual power and control. The textual analysis concentrates on pronominal use, word choice, and deontic modality related to duty and obligation (see Simpson 47–48), demonstrating the ways in which the speaker and the implied reader are constructed through these linguistic devices. For example, Murphy's *Mother's Dictionary* sometimes uses the first and second person pronouns. In other words, the (adult) speaker (*I*) directly addresses the child addressee (*you*), as in the dictionary entry for the adverb *solely*[3]:

> [1] I wish you to be good *solely* for your own sake.

For the purposes of this chapter, "intergeneration play" refers to the parameters of play as created and regulated by the adult speaker for the child addressee. A striking example of this is the sentence illustrating the use of the verb *abridge* in Eliza Robbin's 1828 *Primary Dictionary*[4]:

> [2] "I shall *abridge* your play-time," would signify, "I shall not allow you so much time to play" (2).

The speaker in this dictionary example expresses the adult's desire to control the child's play-time, further underscored by the use of deontic modality, realized by the modal auxiliary verb *shall* and the lexical verb *allow*. The implied reader of this dictionary is a child who expects to be regulated in such ways. However, as will be discussed later, the speaker could also invite the addressee to engage in playful experimentation as part of a rational education. As such, these dictionaries reveal an ideological tension between the speaker–educator's desire to separate "pain" from "learning" (*A Rational Primer* 19), whilst simultaneously monitoring the child's "play-time."

Dictionary Examples: Child-centered Didacticism

My analysis of dictionary entries concentrates on illustrative examples, that is, phrases or sentences demonstrating the typical use of a word, as in examples [1] and [2] earlier. The reliance on invented illustrative sentences in nineteenth-century children's dictionaries sometimes generated entries that were not just linguistically instructive but also morally didactic. Murphy's illustration of *ambitious* is an example:

> [3] You should be *ambitious* to read well, means that you should *wish and try* to read well.

This sentence provides a semantic and syntactic context for the term *ambitious*. At the same time, it prescribes conscientious study (seen as the appropriate direction for the implied child reader's ambition) through the use of the deontic auxiliary *should*. In this respect, works such as Murphy's dictionary differ from general dictionaries such as Samuel Johnson's influential 1755 *Dictionary of the English Language*, which, though certainly didactic, was not tailored to children and relied on literary citations from canonical authors.[5]

Other examples of normative messages specifically tailored to the implied child reader can be found in Francis Wilby's *Infant-School Spelling-Book, And Pictorial Dictionary*, as in the entry for *fun*:

> [4] The word *Fun* means mirth, sport. We are fond of *fun*. It is good *fun* to play at hide and seek. *Fun* is not mis-chief (34).

The definition of *fun* as "not mis-chief" is strongly didactic in redefining the parameters of acceptable fun for children. In this way, the writer prioritizes the socializing aspect of the dictionary and creates a specifically child-centered entry, rather than providing a more generally applicable definition of *fun*. In both this example and the following examples, the use of the "inclusive *we*" (Fairclough 106), that is, inclusive of the reader as well as the speaker, presents a world-view shared by the speaker and the addressee:

> [5] When we are *at* school, we must be qui-et and thoughtful. . . . 'We ought to be *at* school by nine o'clock' (Wilby 37).
> [6] We ought *not* to play when we are at school, or when we ought to be learning our les-sons (Wilby 53).
> [7] The word *hush* means the same as *be si-lent*. When we are making a noise, if our teach-er cries out *hush*, he means that we are to be si-lent (Wilby 107).

In other examples, the second person pronoun *you* is used instead, as in the entry for *when*:

> [8] *when* you have said your les-sons well, *then* you shall go out to play (Wilby 107).

Example [8] perhaps evokes an implied reader in Infant School,[6] as these institutions promoted frequent shifts between work and play (McCann and Young 22). Again, as in previous examples, the speaker attempts to demarcate the boundaries between "les-sons" and "play."

Directly addressing the reader (*you*) in this way also creates a friendly style, which Fairclough refers to as "simulated personal address" (106). The use of the first and second person pronoun is a common feature in present-day pedagogical dictionaries. As Berry argues, the inclusive *we* in definitions "attempts to approach readers by suggesting a joint enterprise between them and the writer" and the use of *we* and *you* in definitions is a more user-friendly alternative to "traditional lexicographese" (Berry 3). The previous examples show that such devices were used in children's dictionaries already in the nineteenth century. Although these were factual texts, they employed modes of address commonly found in children's fiction, rather than the dry, quasi-scientific language one might expect to find in dictionaries.[7]

The Implied Child Reader: Class and Gender

The three nineteenth-century dictionaries examined in this study evoke implied readers belonging to different genders and socio-economic classes. For instance, Maria Edgeworth's "Glossary" in the children's book *Early Lessons* addresses the readers as "my little boys and girls," "my little friends," and "my little pupils." Anna Murphy's *Mother's Dictionary*, which, as the author states in her preface, was inspired by Edgeworth's Glossary (Murphy iii), uses a similar mode of address. Both Edgeworth's and Murphy's texts construct an implied child reader from the upper classes, as demonstrated in the verb *condescend* in Murphy's *Mother's Dictionary*:

> [9] You should not *condescend* to make companions of the servants, though you must treat them with kindness and civility.

Example [9] does more than illustrate the typical use of *condescend*. The modal verbs *should* and *must* prescribe a particular reference model of behavior for the implied child reader. Moreover, the example also establishes a frame of reference for a specific readership, namely wealthy children in households with servants. The child addressee (*you*) is told that servants do not make appropriate playfellows. However, children are also reminded to be kind and are clearly required to obey instructions from adult educators. Although governess and writer Anna Murphy was an educator, she also happened to be a servant, if a genteel one.[8] In Gleadle's words, "[g]overnesses were generally thought too lowly to be welcomed as one of the family, but of too high a background to mix on easy terms with the servants" (52).

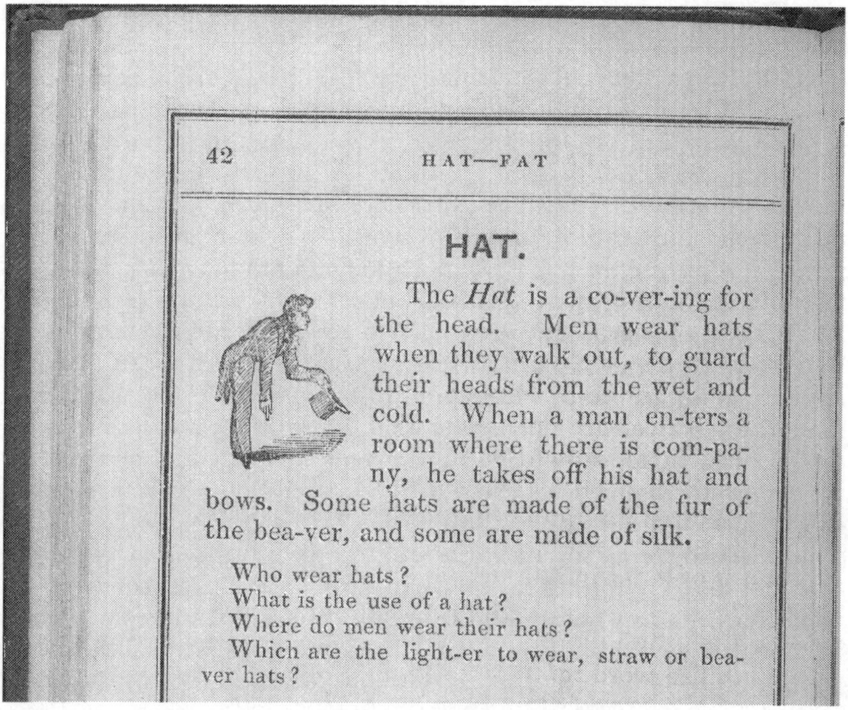

42 HAT—FAT

HAT.

The *Hat* is a co-ver-ing for the head. Men wear hats when they walk out, to guard their heads from the wet and cold. When a man en-ters a room where there is com-pa-ny, he takes off his hat and bows. Some hats are made of the fur of the bea-ver, and some are made of silk.

Who wear hats?
What is the use of a hat?
Where do men wear their hats?
Which are the light-er to wear, straw or bea-ver hats?

Figure 3.1 Entry for *hat*

Source: © The British Library Board. Shelf mark: RB.23.a.1641

Francis Wilby's 1844 *Infant School-Spelling Book, and Pictorial Dictionary* differs from Edgeworth's and Murphy's dictionaries but is no less child-centered, as is illustrated by the following entry for *hat*. In addition to the lexical definition of *hat* as "a co-ver-ing for the head," this entry also functions as a spelling lesson (polysyllabic words are divided into syllables), provides encyclopedic information about hats, and even prescribes a model of gendered conduct; men wear hats and take them off in company.

Visual and Verbal Representation of Gender and Play in Wilby's Dictionary

The preface to Wilby's dictionary emphasizes the importance of pictures and visual learning, as children "very soon begin to employ their ingenuity and skill in copying what they have seen" (Wilby 1). Although the dictionary overtly addresses "the Infant multitude" (Wilby v), the implied reader of Wilby's dictionary seems to be a little boy, as Wilby's entry for *man* reveals:

> [10] I am a *Child*. When I am a few years old-er I shall be a *Youth*. When I am more than twen-ty years of age, I shall be a *Young Man* (20).

Indeed, the dictionary contains entries for *man, men, lad*, and *son* but no corresponding entries for girls or women. Girls are also represented in very few pictures in Wilby's dictionary: Out of thirteen images depicting children, only three are girls, and out of twenty pictures representing adults, six are women. Whenever children are referred to generally, illustrations invariably depict boys. For instance, the entries for *sit* and *mat* are both accompanied by illustrations of schoolboys. The verbal definition of *clap* refers to "children" but is accompanied by an illustration of a boy; similarly, the entry for *shrug* shows a boy shrugging, and the entry for *fit* depicts a boy playing dress-up in oversized clothes. The prototypical child, these images suggest, is a boy.

By selecting gender-specific pictures for otherwise gender-neutral verbal definitions, Wilby further reinforces the gender ideologies conveyed by the dictionary as a whole. For instance, the entry for *bat* does not specify that bats are boys' playthings, but the illustration suggests that they are.

Gendered Representations of Toys

As Jean-Jacques Rousseau claimed in his 1792 treatise *Émile, or On Education*, "[b]oys want movement and noise, drums, tops, [and] toy-carts" (1290). By contrast, Rousseau argued, girls prefer toys "which appeal to the eye," and a girl's fondness for dolls "very obviously shows her instinctive taste for life's purpose" (1290). Similarly, girls' interest in learning is overshadowed by their "natural" vanity: "most little girls only reluctantly learn to read and write," whereas "sewing they learn gladly" since they "take pleasure in believing that these talents will one day serve them for their own adornment" (1290–92). Although Rousseau saw girls' play as a reflection of their innate nature, the toys and activities selected for girls played an important role in the inculcation of appropriate feminine behavior. Langford argues that, throughout the long eighteenth century, "[s]choolgirls exercised as regularly as schoolboys, with due allowance for the requirements of maidenly manners" (41). However, "maidenly manners" could place severe restrictions on girls' choice of activities. Before the mid-Victorian period, advocates of physical exercise for girls were mindful of the need to preserve feminine propriety (Gorham 71). Even after this time, most writers recommended that boys could play active games in public, while girls should play them only in private.

Sit

Clap

Figure 3.2 Examples of boys in Wilby's dictionary

Source: © The British Library Board. Shelf mark: RB.23.a.1641

Mat

Bat

Figure 3.2 (Continued)

It is not surprising that play was gendered in this period or that this gender-segregation was maintained in children's dictionaries, especially considering how gender-specific children's books and toys still are today. However, in the nineteenth century, this segregation of play was closely linked to notions of female propriety. In line with these attitudes, active and noisy toys are associated with boys in nineteenth-century children's dictionaries such as Wilby's. In fact, Wilby's dictionary specifically genders toys even when adult dictionaries, such as Samuel Johnson's 1755 *Dictionary*, do not. Johnson's definition of *top* is gender-neutral: "An inverted conoid which children set to turn on the point, continuing its motion with a whip." By contrast, Wilby explicitly states that "A *Top* is a play-thing for boys," explaining that "There are three kinds of tops; the top that is spun by string – the whip-top, which is spun by whip-ping – and the hum-ming top." The definition is accompanied by an illustration of an elegantly dressed boy playing with a top. Similarly, *trap*, defined by Johnson as "A play at which a ball is driven with a stick," is unequivocally constructed as a boy's plaything in Wilby's dictionary, which specifies that *trap* is "a boy's play-thing, made of wood, in the shape of a shoe; a part of which be-ing struck, toss-es the ball up in-to the air, be-fore it is struck with the bat." The gender coding in the verbal entry is supported by the illustration of a boy engrossed in outdoor play. The boys depicted in the illustrations for *top* and *trap*, respectively, appear to belong to different social classes, with the top being depicted as a plaything for upper-class boys.

The only toys assigned to girls in Wilby's dictionary are skipping ropes. Skipping was appropriate for girls because it was seen as a less energetic and more decorous form of exercise: "To *skip* is to leap or jump light-ly," explains Wilby's entry for *skip*. As the author of *Girls' Games* (1887) observed, "[j]umping games are not well adapted to girls, partly because they are rather boisterous, and partly because the dress of girls is unsuited to the necessary movements," but "[s]kipping is an amusement specially adapted for girls; and it is one of the healthiest kind of exercise they can have" (Bourne 7–6). In Wilby's illustration, the dainty movements of the skipping girl, demurely but attractively attired in an ankle-length dress and a hat, contrast with the livelier movements of the hopping boy. Wilby uses the plural form of the nouns *boy* and *girl* and the declarative mode to construct general statements such as "Girls *plat* their hair" (40), "Boys *hop* o-ver things, to try how high they can *hop*" (70), and "Boys, when they slide, some-times *trip* up each-other" (65).

The "Good Girl" and the "Good Boy"

The moral didacticism in children's dictionaries, then, often manifested itself in specifically gendered ways, constructing prototypical images of the "good girl" and the "good boy" at play. Children's reference

Top

Plat

Figure 3.3 Children at play in Wilby's dictionary

Source: © The British Library Board. Shelf mark: RB.23.a.1641

books addressed to a mixed audience of both genders frequently had to negotiate opposing moral didactic aims. The good boy and the good girl typically defined each other by antithesis: What was expected of the good boy was often inconceivable for the good girl and vice versa. The difference in energy and activity between the "good boy" and the "good girl" is further illustrated by Wilby's pictorial representations of *pat* and *pet* below. While both the boy and the dog are in action, the girl and the lamb are both inactive, and the girl seems to be comforting the lamb. The image evokes the role of females as nurturers and moral purifiers, creating an idyllic tableau reminiscent of religious iconography.

Compilers of children's dictionaries did not promote any single ideal of manliness for boys. They could also use subtle means to discourage what was considered improper conduct. For example, both Wilby and Murphy proscribed boisterous and unruly behavior in boys, encouraging them to be kind and compassionate:

[12] a boy of generous *spirit* never takes pleasure in hurting any thing which is less and weaker than himself (Murphy, *Spirit*).
[13] A good boy will *shun* a-ny play-fel-low who is wick-ed (Wilby 35).

Wilby's dictionary portrays boys playing with pop-guns, "a hol-low piece of wood, from which boys shoot small piec-es of wet pa-per" (70), accompanied by a smiling boy playing with a gun. On closer inspection, however, the speaker in Wilby's dictionary deviates from what Vance refers to as patriotic and military notion of Victorian "manliness," when juxtaposing hunters and soldiers with "cru-el men" and "murderers" in the definition of *gun* (8–10): "A *gun* is not of a-ny real use, it is on-ly used by cru-el men, to shoot birds and beasts with, and by mur-der-ers and sol-diers" (Wilby 36). In other words, while guns are depicted as appropriate toys for boys, considerable unease surrounds the use of real guns by adult men.

These examples demonstrate the extraordinarily precarious balance that needed to be struck in order for the "good boy" to develop into a proper gentleman. Boys had to be active but not boisterous, brave but not cruel. The "good boy" is always in action, pushing the boundaries, hopping "to see how far he can hop" (Wilby 70). Boyish energy had to be channeled through appropriate games and activities so that boys developed "manly" virtues such as strength and courage, whereas boyish vices, such as cruelty and recklessness, were checked. As socially didactic works, children's dictionaries attempted to steer him in the right direction, reining him in or spurring him on as appropriate.

By contrast, the "good girl" was depicted as content to be confined within the boundaries of feminine propriety. The "bad girl," then, was

Pat

Pet

Figure 3.4 Pictorial representations of *pat* and *pet*

Source: © The British Library Board. Shelf mark: RB.23.a.1641

Figure 3.5 Pictorial representation of *gun*

Source: © The British Library Board. Shelf mark: RB.23.a.1641

not rough and cruel but someone who overindulged her "natural" vices, such as vanity. Of course, depicting girls as naturally gentle and vain was a powerful prescription in itself, albeit one that was more covert and insidious than the admonishments directed at boys.

By associating compliance and kindness with girls, lexicographers participated in the construction of the "good girl" as a model for female readers. As Murphy's example for the verb *train* states, "this little girl has been *trained* up in the habits of industry and good behaviour." Murphy's examples praise girls' cheerfulness and kindness, thereby promoting these as particularly feminine virtues, as in the example for the entry *conclude:* "when I see a little girl much beloved by her friends, I always *conclude* that she is very good." At least one of Murphy's examples suggests that little girls can engage in transgressive play too, though the repercussions are terrible:

> [11] a little girl who was playing with fire, was in *imminent* danger of burning herself to death (*imminent*).

Playful Encounters: Parent-Teachers, Child-Pupils, and Rational Play

In contrast to the limited range of activities offered to girls in Wilby's dictionary, Maria Edgeworth, a progressive advocate of "practical education," encouraged "experimental" and active toys for both boys and girls. The 1798 treatise *Practical Education* encouraged parents to let children of both genders examine and play with technical objects such as air-pumps, barometers, microscopes, and orreries. These views are also reflected in Edgeworth's Glossary. For example, the entry for *barometer* reminds the readers that "Little girls and boys may see barometers in many places" (Edgeworth 81). There is, however, evidence of the speaker's ambivalent attitude toward the relationship between children's "amusement" and "learning" in Edgeworth's Glossary. For example, the entry for *diverted* explains that "amusement turns aside our thoughts from applying too closely to any thing" (87). In contrast, the entry for *thermometer* insists that "The thermometer, barometer, orrery, and air-pump, will entertain young people very much when they have knowledge sufficient, to enable them to understand their uses, and the manner in which they are made" (110). In other words, the speaker advocates entertainment that also promotes learning.

Dictionary addressees are encouraged to examine objects such as magnets and perform simple experiments to understand basic laws of physics. For instance, the entry for *attracted* concludes with the following invitation: "My little boy, or girl, when you read this, ask the person who teaches you, to show you a magnet, or to let you try these experiments" (81). Similarly, Murphy's dictionary includes entries for words such as *arithmetic*, *astronomy*, and *botany*, in which children are encouraged to learn more about each topic by carrying out instructive and amusing experiments. The entry for *telescope*, for instance, explains that "[c]hildren, when they grow older and learn more, will understand better the use of a *telescope*, and the manner in which it is made: perhaps they may be allowed to look through one now, and they will observe that objects which are really very far off, appear quite near and plain to the eye." Although such invitations were chiefly relevant to privileged children, whose parents had access to well-furnished studies and laboratories, they were nevertheless extended to both genders.

Conclusion

The three dictionaries examined in this chapter employed different modes of address and evoke different implied readers. The title of Wilby's dictionary suggests that the book was aimed at working-class children attending Infant School, although the images in the book depict people from different social classes. The implied reader evoked by the dictionary is a young boy. The speaker is the benevolent schoolmaster. By contrast, the implied reader of Edgeworth and Murphy's dictionaries is a young person from the upper classes who would have access to servants, tutors, and parents, as well as diverse spaces for learning and play, including well-stocked libraries and laboratories. The speaker in the latter texts is the genteel mother-teacher.

Most aspects of Murphy's *Mother's Dictionary* articulate agreement with the dominant ideologies of motherhood and domesticity, from the title, to the definition of *housewifery* as "those things which women ought to attend to, such as the proper care of the family, &c" and the illustrative examples centering on pleasant little girls. However, both Edgeworth's Glossary and Murphy's *Mother's Dictionary* allocated much more space to girls than Wilby's dictionary, in which girls were all but invisible. Both in their dictionaries for children and in the wider body of their works, Edgeworth and Murphy reiterated dominant domestic ideologies, whilst encouraging both girls and boys to playfully explore the world around them, to perform simple experiments, and to delve into fields such as physics and astronomy. The speakers in these texts evoked the ideals of the enlightened parent-teacher and the rational child and invited the child addressee to engage in educational play and playful learning regardless of gender.

Notes

1. The present analysis concentrates on the implied reader as evoked in the text, rather than on the reader-response aspect.
2. "The implied author" is sometimes defined as the image of the author evoked by stylistic, ideological, and aesthetic properties in the text (Schmid 1). However, as this is a highly contested concept (see e.g. Kindt and Müller 1), the analysis concentrates on the ways in which the "speaker" or "narrator" addresses the addressee or "reader-in-the-text" (Wall 2).
3. Note that Murphy's dictionary is unpaginated (apart from the preface).
4. This dictionary was based on Murphy's *Mother's Dictionary*, with many nearly identical entries.
5. Johnson's first citation for *ambitious* is a Dryden quote: "The neighb'ring monarchs, by thy beauty led, / Contend in crouds, *ambitious* of thy bed."
6. Alternatives to traditional "dame schools," Infant Schools were aimed at working-class children whose parents both had to work (Whitbread 15).
7. Barbara Wall describes the "overt authorial narrator who flourished in the nineteenth century" and addressed narratees as "children," "boys and girls," or "you" (5).
8. Murphy worked as a governess for the Marquess of Winchester from 1810–1825 (Thomas 6–9).

Works Cited

Béjoint, Henri. *The Lexicography of English*. Oxford UP, 2010.

Berry, Roger. "Awareness of Metalanguage." *Language Awareness*, vol. 13, no. 1, 2004, pp. 1–16.

Bourne, E. D. *Girls' Games – A Recreation Handbook for Teachers and Scholars*. Griffith, Farran, Okedan & Welsh, 1887.

Cowie, Anthony Paul, editor. *The Oxford History of English Lexicography*. Oxford UP, 2008.

Edgeworth, Maria. *Early Lessons: Harry and Lucy. Part I*. J. Johnson, 1801.

Edgeworth, Maria, and Richard Lovell Edgeworth. *Practical Education*, 2 vols. J. Johnson, 1798.

———. *A Rational Primer*. J. Johnson, 1799.

Fairclough, Norman. *Language and Power*, 2nd ed. Pearson Education, 2001.

Gleadle, Katherine. *Borderline Citizens: Women, Gender, and Political Culture in Britain 1815–1867*. Oxford UP, 2009.

Gorham, Deborah. *The Victorian Girl and the Feminine Ideal*. Croom Helm, 1982.

Hartmann, Reinhard R. K., editor. *Lexicography: Critical Concepts*, 3 vols. Routledge, 2003.

Hollindale, Peter. *The Hidden Teacher: Ideology & Children's Reading*. Thimble Press, 2011.

Iser, Wolfgang. *The Implied Reader – Patterns of Communication in Prose Fiction from Bunyan to Beckett*. John Hopkins UP, 1974.

Iversen, Sarah Hoem. " 'To Teach Little Boys and Girls What It Is Proper for Them to Know': Gendered Education and the Nineteenth-Century Children's Dictionary." *Proceedings of the 15th EURALEX International Congress*, edited by Ruth Vatvedt Fjeld and Matilde Jule Torjusen, U of Oslo P, 2012, pp. 613–18.

———. " 'Do You Understand This My Little Pupil?' Children's Dictionaries, Pedagogy and Constructions of Childhood in the Nineteenth Century." *'Ye Whom the Charms of Grammar Please': Studies in English Language History in Honour of Leiv Egil Breivik*, edited by Kari E. Haugland, et al. Peter Lang Group, 2014, pp. 331–54.

———. "Class, Censorship and the Construction of the Child Reader in Nineteenth-Century Children's Dictionaries." *Children's Literature in Education*, 2018, pp. 1–16.

Johnson, Samuel. *A Dictionary of the English Language*, edited by Anne McDermott, 1st ed. and 4th ed. Johnson's Dictionary Project, Cambridge UP, 1996.

Johnston, Judith. *Anna Jameson: Victorian, Feminist, Woman of Letters*. Scolar Press, 1997.

Kindt, Tom, and Hans-Harald Müller. *Narratologia: The Implied Author: Concept and Controversy*. De Gruyter, 2006.

Landau, Sidney I. *Dictionaries: The Art and Craft of Lexicography*, 2nd ed. Cambridge UP, 2001.

Langford, Paul. *Englishness Identified: Manners and Character, 1650–1850*. Oxford UP, 2000.

Larkin-Lieffers, Patricia A. "Images of Childhood and the Implied Reader in Young Children's Information Books." *Literacy*, vol. 44, no. 2, 2010.

Lerer, Seth. *Children's Literature: A Reader's History, from Aesop to Harry Potter*. U of Chicago P, 2008.

Locke, John. *Some Thoughts Concerning Education*. A. & J. Churchill, 1693.

McCann, Philip, and Francis A. Young. *Samuel Wilderspin and the Infant School Movement*. Croom Helm, 1982.

Mooijaart, Marijke, and Marijke van der Wal, editors. *Yesterday's Words: Contemporary, Current and Future Lexicography*. Cambridge Scholars, 2008.

Murphy, Anna Brownell. (later Jameson). *A First, or Mother's Dictionary for Children*. W. Darton, n.d., c. 1813.

Rousseau, Jean-Jacques. *Émile, or on Education*, translated by Barbara Foxley. Project Gutenberg EBook, 1762, www.gutenberg.org/ebooks/5427. Accessed 10 Jan. 2016.

Schmid, Wolf. "Implied Author." *The Living Handbook of Narratology*, edited by Peter Hühn, et al. Hamburg UP, 2014, www.lhn.uni-hamburg.de/article/implied-author-revised-version-uploaded-26-january-2013. Accessed 24 Jan. 2017.

Simpson, Paul. *Language, Ideology and Point of View*. Routledge, 1993.

Starnes, De Witt Talmage, and Noyes, Gertrude E. *The English Dictionary from Cawdrey to Johnson 1604–1755*. John Benjamins, 1991.

Thomas, Clara. *Love and Work Enough – The Life of Anna Jameson*. MacDonald, 1967.

Vance, Norman. *The Sinews of the Spirit: The Ideal of Christian Manliness in Victorian Literature and Religious Thought*. Cambridge UP, 1985.

Wall, Barbara. *The Narrator's Voice: The Dilemma of Children's Fiction*. Palgrave Macmillan, 1991.

Whitbread, Nanette. *The Evolution of the Nursery-Infant School: A History of Infant and Nursery Education in Britain, 1800–1970*. First published in 1972. Routledge, 2007.

Wilby, Francis. *The Infant School Spelling-Book, and Pictorial Dictionary*. Darton & Clark, 1844.

Wodak, Ruth, and Michael Meye. *Introducing Qualitative Methods Series: Methods of Critical Discourse Analysis*. Sage Publications, 2001.

4 Transnationalism and Play in Mexican Children's Childhood and Multicultural Children's Literature in the United States

Yoo Kyung Sung

In the United States, transnational Mexican ethnicity is recognized with diverse collective labels. These ethnic identity labels, e.g., "Latino/a," "Hispano/a," "Hispanic," and "Chicano/a," subsume different countries of origin, such as Mexican American (Villarreal and Peterson 304). The familism of Hispanics is culturally specific, and as such it differs from other cultural groups' familism. Significantly, the intergenerational nature of Hispanic familism is its distinctive aspect (Villarreal and Peterson 305). Familism is a cultural value that emphasizes interdependent family relationships of Latinx people, which are characterized by warmth, closeness, and supportiveness (Campos et al. 81). Thus, even long after immigration to the United States and in spite of generational living status in America, familism survives and is even sometimes enhanced as part of the cultural ethos in people's transnational identity. The representations of transnational Mexican childhood in picture books are informed by a pervasive sense of familism, especially in the relationships between grandparents and grandchildren. In this study of selected picture books, I build on the notion of *Hispanicness* in order to refer to possessing Hispanic ethnicity as different from simply being Hispanic (Villarreal and Peter 303). In more precise terms, I do so to identify the specific state of possessing Mexican ethnicity or "Mexicanness." In the studied books, "Mexicanness" is projected through various forms of play in which children interpret storytelling, household goods, traditional activities, and even labor as playful media. In fact, storytelling acquires an especially significant function. As Rudine Bishop states, "[w]hen a group has been marginalized and oppressed, the cultural function of [a] story can take on even greater significance, because storytelling can be seen as a means to counter the effects of that marginalization and oppression on children" (25). Given the meaningful relationship between grandparent characters and storytelling functions, intergenerational relationships are an important aspect of Mexican culture and childhood experience. Mexican children's identities are linked to their grandparents' lives, and these relations are among the most important social bonds and frameworks of reference for Mexican children. To explore the representations of such familial networks and their relation to play, this chapter poses a series of research questions. First, how do multicultural children's books in the U.S. portray play in the context of transnational Mexican childhood? Secondly, do familism and intergenerational relationships have a significant presence in multicultural children's books? Finally, if they do, how do familism and intergenerational relationships around play represent transnational Mexican childhood in these texts?

Multicultural Children's Books and Transnational Identities

Deborah Boehm notes that "Mexican (im)migrant families and communities live within and across two nation-states, and their lives both transcend and are separated by the U.S.-Mexico Border" (778–79). Perceptions of connectedness among the members of and roles within families are affected by transnationalism and by the sense of physical and cultural separation (Orellana et al. 573). For Clare Bradford, "[t]he term 'transnational' refers to duality in the lives of individuals and groups and to textual manifestations of this duality" (23). Like in other national contexts, multicultural children's books in the U.S. include stories of immigrants whose "transnational identities are formed . . . [through negotiations] between and across cultures and languages" (23). The transnational identities of immigrants' children do not cease when joining a new nation but continue through various forms of acculturation. Thus, multicultural children's books in the U.S. include the stories of immigrants and their descendants alike.

Intergenerationality is used as an analytical framework to examine transnational Mexican children's daily practices depicted in the selected texts. Intergenerationality can be understood as the "intergenerational relations" through which "ideas and practices are shared, or not, between and across generations" (Hopkins et al. 315). I also rely on critical multicultural analysis, which, in the context of this analysis, "problematizes childhood, children's literature, reading, and the enterprise of publishing children's books" (Botelho and Rudman 78). Since this approach extends typical notions of multicultural analysis, this framework is an especially relevant tool because "children's literature is a product of culture as well as evidence of power relations" (71). In particular, the cultural experience marked by intergenerational solidarity in transnational Mexican contexts projects Otherness. The "Other" is marked by linguistic, cultural, and/or racial difference from the perspective of the social norm defined by White Anglo-Protestant culture (103). Familism meets the expectations of imagined Mexican cultures as formed by mainstream readers. In this analysis, I want to rethink the social and literary meanings of Otherness in a context where children's texts are a "cultural artifact."

My theoretical framework will help me understand the ways in which multicultural literature has acquired value and status in relation to Mexican and Mexican diaspora childhoods.

This chapter aims to explore the accounts of intergenerational play processes in families that experience the various translocations characteristic of Mexican emigration to the United States. It also examines the role of intergenerational solidarity and its enhancement across transnational Mexican children's experiences in picture books. Finally, it addresses the portrayals of childhood cultures that do not showcase intergenerational involvements but instead focus on children's independent play. As Robin Bernstein explains, "[c]hildren's play is simultaneously compliant and unruly. . . . They play in ways that are socially sanctioned and they play otherwise" (460). Adult family members are not indispensable for children to play, yet the depictions of children's independent play in the texts analyzed herein are not as common as the representations of intergenerational relationships in cultural contexts.

Transnational Mexican Childhood in Children's Literature

The Children's Literature Comprehensive Database (CLCD) was utilized to collect the Mexican and Mexican-American books that are the object of this analysis. The CLCD is one of the few online databases of children's and young adults' literature. It contains over 3,000,000 titles and 50 professional review sources that provide book reviews by children's books experts. The CLCD has identified a large volume of Latinx literature realistic fiction books. I narrowed my focus down to twenty-six books, which included Mexican and Mexican-diaspora stories and were tagged with keywords that are pertinent to childhood cultures (for example, children, family, toys, friends, or movement). I limited my corpus by the nationality criterion. Authors often share their transnational Mexican identities in the biographical notes on book covers. I examined those to remove books by authors who were Latino/a but not Mexican. I scrutinized the copyright pages to select the Mexican-diaspora books that specifically indicated the young protagonists' Mexican identities in the annotations. All these books are works of contemporary realistic fiction. Out of the twenty-six transnational stories with Mexican protagonists, eighteen books emphasize intergenerational connections in their characters' cultural affirmation and celebrations. Six books narrate the stories of their young protagonists without depicting intergenerational solidarity. Two books – *Home at Last* by Susan Elya (2006) and *The Upside Down Boy: El niño de cabeza* by Juan Felipe Herrera (2013) – were chosen for their portrayals of the experiences of being new to the U.S., as selected examples of the second phase of immigration.

In *Toys as Culture* (1986), Brian Sutton-Smith observes that a toy or a tool can serve as a means of identification for children, because the child organizes his or her actions and conceptions of the world through toys (207). In my sample of books, such "play necessities" of children of Mexican origin are often replaced by the time spent with adult family members, specifically with grandparents. In these books, grandparents assume caregiving and other family responsibilities. In reality, after immigration, children evolve into cultural experts faster than adults, and the traditional role differences between adults and children are often reversed in the wake of migration (Sime and Pietka-Nykaza 210). Nevertheless, the images of immigration experiences projected by diaspora authors are often based on their (grand)parents' experiences (Sung 170). It is not uncommon for the authors to employ autobiographical details as the texture of their works so that their childhood memories of the time spent with their grandparents become staple motifs in their stories. Thus, Mexican traditions, foods, and cultural ethos are highlighted in the books. The authors' diasporic backgrounds shape transnational Mexican childhoods through narratives based on memories and family emigration and immigration histories.

Transnational Mexican culture is entwined with the lives of (im) migrants and finds its intergenerational embodiment in two of the most vulnerable family members – the oldest and the youngest – or grandchildren and grandparents. Intergenerational relationships enhance the culturally rich contexts in the stories of transnational Mexican children. Rosalinda Barrera and Ruth Quiora have found that Spanish kinship relations that are most frequently featured in children's books are evoked in the references of Latino child protagonists/narrators to their parents and grandparents by means of terms such as *mama*, *papa*, *abuela*, and *abuelo* and their more endearing or diminutive forms: *mami*, *papi*, *abuelito* (grandpa), *abuelita* (grandma), *tía* (aunt), and *tíno* (uncle) (250). Barrera and Quiora infer that "mama" and "papa" are recognizable and comprehensible to monolingual readers (English speakers) because of their graphic similarity to their English-language equivalents, thereby satisfying the perspectives of implied mainstream readers (250). Through exposing readers to language variations other than English, multicultural books in the U.S. emphasize the diverse voices of people of color as a means of developing sociocultural awareness to address cases of social (in)justice.

My following argument unfolds in two parts. One of them focuses on transnationalism in three different phases of immigration as represented in my sample of twenty-six books. The other examines depictions of intergenerational solidarity in eighteen transnational Mexican children books that foreground two major motifs: heritage celebrations and universal childhood.

Locating Transnational Citizenship Status in Samples of Books

The transnational Mexican-American books analyzed in this section of my study for the most part feature three different phases of transnational citizenship status, which are bound up with their respective themes determined by the distinctive contexts sequentially experienced by immigrants: 1) leaving Mexico and border-crossing; 2) being new to the U.S.; and 3) enjoying stable citizenship. For the sake of clarity, these transnational experiences are identified by consecutive phases.

Phase 1: Leaving Mexico and Border-Crossing

In the stories of border-crossing, California is a recurring location that takes on literal and figurative significance. When a Mexican family suffers hardships in Mexico and finally decides to move to California, a child's space for play becomes circumscribed. In the narratives of Mexican relocators, California geographically symbolizes a better life and even hope, as *Migrant* (2014) by José Manuel Mateo illustrates. Simultaneously, California is often a setting for Mexican-diaspora stories, such as *My Diary from Here to There: Mi diario de aqui hasta allá* (2002) by Amada Irma Perez and *From North to South: Del Norte al Sur* (2013) by René Laínez. In these stories, Mexican children experience relocation to California as a loss. For example, the transition away from their home country may mean giving up their communities and best friends. In *My Diary from Here to There: Mi diario de aqui hasta allá*, young Amanda, who promises her best friend Michi that they will not forget each other, explains dolefully: "I've known Michi since we were little, and I don't think I'll ever find a friend like her in California" (6).

Five books briefly portray the lives of families in Mexico before they head to California. *Super Cilantro Girl: La Superniña Del Cilantro* (2003) by Juan Felipe Herrera presents living in a border area between the United States and Mexico. Additionally, translocating journeys are depicted in *My Diary from Here to There: Mi diario de aqui hasta allá, Home at Last*, *Super Cilantro Girl: La Superniña Del Cilantro*, *My Very Own Room: Mi propio cuartito* (2011) by Amada Irma Perez, and *Two White Rabbits* (2015) by Jairo Butrago. These texts show the experiences of communal practices in Mexico and the border-crossing process. The characters' transnational citizenship is not yet complete, but is emerging in their new home nation. Mexican children are "brought up across borders" (Levitt 75), and transnationality generates new kinship configurations in "transnational spaces" (Boehm 781). Exemplifying "transnational textuality," *My Diary from Here to There: Mi diario de aqui hasta allá* and *Super Cilantro Girl: La Superniña Del Cilantro* conjure up such a "doubleness of transnational identities and lived experiences"

(Bradford 24). For instance, in *Super Cilantro Girl: La Superniña Del Cilantro*, eight-year-old Esmeralda dreams of rescuing her mother, who is stopped at a detention center at the border between Mexico and the U.S. due to an issue with her green card.

In this initial phase of leaving Mexico and crossing the border, grandparents and relatives help young protagonists develop self-confidence in solving urgent problems. Intergenerational solidarity is subtly built in this transnational space. As parents are preoccupied with the actual moving process or border-crossing, young protagonists tend to play supporter roles for their migrating parents. As a result, children's agency is firmly asserted in this first phase of leaving Mexico and crossing the border. Orellana et al. point out that while immigrant children depend on adults for physical, economic, and emotional care, their perceived needs are culturally constructed. Border-crossing or on-the-road status creates a unique transnational lifestyle and culture in which children's play spaces and the nature of childhood culture are formed atypically (587). A child's resources are being reconstructed with tremendous flexibility due to his or her transient circumstances.

Phase 2: Being New to the United States

Another major theme addressed in the books under study is the adjustment of new immigrants to living in the United States. The texts convey their young protagonists' journeys of adaptation to new schools and learning a new language in a new land. Two books, *Home at Last* and *The Upside Down Boy: El niño de cabeza*, portray the consequences of migrating to the United States in a particularly revealing way. In *Home at Last*, Ana learns English faster than her mother does and readily adjusts to her American school, while her mother struggles with homesickness for Mexico and her language barrier grows more difficult to overcome. In *The Upside Down Boy: El niño de cabeza*, Junito's family moves to a big city, and he enrolls at a new school, where he feels frustrated because of the language barrier. Yet, he soon finds a way to regain self-confidence after a teacher recognizes and comments on his artistic talent. Language barriers make for the central obstacle to children's attempts at finding playful spaces. Peer cultures are hardly ever pictured in these books, in contrast to other book categories examined here.

Phase 3: Enjoying Stable Citizenship

The third phase introduces the notion of celebration, addressed by eight books in the corpus. Unlike the works exploring the other two thematic foci, they do not present citizenship concerns as a source of crisis. In this category, most of the protagonists do not refer to their legal status. Rather, the plots afford opportunities for celebrating aspects of the

Mexican heritage through food, symbolic Mexican feasts, and grandparents' storytelling. The transnational legal status of the characters is presumed to be already established. Since this stable phase evokes a long residential history as Mexican-Americans or as Mexicans in Mexico, the characters of these books boast the position of socially and economically secure Mexican or American citizens. Ultimately, Mexican landscapes and the Mexican-diaspora community in the United States are connected through this unarticulated status of legality. In American contexts, many characters are long-time citizens who see themselves as Americans with the Mexican heritage.

Importantly, the books in the thematic category of "enjoying stable citizenship" share the following major motifs: celebrating one's heritage, culture, and pride in Mexican culture. Such celebrations are not limited to special occasions, such as the Day of the Dead and Christmas. Daily rituals, e.g., visiting flea markets and making tortillas, are framed as forms of cultural celebrations. In *Magda's Tortilla* (2000) by Becky Chavarría-Cháirez, Magda makes her first tortilla on her seventh birthday with her *abuela's* help. In *Grandma and Me at the Flea: Los Meros Meros Remateros* (2002) by Juan Felipe Herrera, the grandma wants to sell rebozos (shawls) and shirts from Oaxaca at a flea market to support her family members in Mexico.

Children's playful spaces transform as their citizenship status changes. In other words, the childness of children is sustained, as in this phase their playful contexts are not invaded by the vicissitudes of the major geopolitical relocation. In the second part of my argument, transnationality will only be discussed in terms of the third category of enjoying stable citizenship. Even though some degree of intergenerational solidarity is exhibited across the three transnational phases, intergenerational relationships are richest and culturally most representative within this thematic group. The Mexican value of *familismo* mandates that family members from all generations work together for the family's well-being (Gibbons and Fanjul de Marsicovetere 22). Given this, the theme of established citizenship is perhaps best positioned to highlight this value.

Intergenerational Relationships and Autonomous Childhood

Eighteen books convey the theme of enjoying stable citizenship. In this section, I discuss intergenerational solidarity in Mexican children's spaces and identify two pivotal sub-themes: the sharing of stories to initiate new adventures or to aid in problem-solving and the commodification of intergenerationality in Mexican childhood. Commodification in this context refers to the overrepresentation of intergenerational experiences, which suggests catering to the social expectations toward stories of Mexican-American childhood. It also implies the assumption that the appeal of books would be reduced, if not altogether lost, if they did not revolve around intergenerational plots. As Güç notes, this involves "the reproduction of spaces as a consequence of hegemonic power relations and treats the cultural and historical heritage of a city or a certain location as a cultural commodity which 'one sells and buys'" (644). Crucially, this refers both to physical topographies and to mental spaces. Intergenerational solidarity in transnational texts functions as a literary reproduction of the spaces of young Mexican-American protagonists.

Intergenerational learning shapes post-migration processes for individuals through language or other cultural tools (Sime and Pietka-Hykaza 211). Such activities are portrayed to convey children's Mexican-American identities. Intergenerationality is at the center of childhood culture in many books of my sample, connoting and incarnating family love and Mexican pride so that *abuela* and *abuelito* both serve as the cultural lynchpins of family life. However, six books out of eighteen do not depict intergenerational solidarity in the spaces of young Mexican characters, instead shifting universal childhood and children's agency to the forefront. They present childhood in playful, imaginative, and universal ways with a subtle cultural emphasis.

The twenty-six transnational Mexican picture books analyzed herein depict a range of intergenerational experiences of childhood play cultures. Most of the stories highlight significant intergenerational Mexican connections, especially between the child protagonists and their *abuelitas* (grandmothers). Only three books – *Just in Case* (2008) by Yuyi Morales, *My Little Car* (2006) by Gary Soto, and *Juan and the Chupacabras* (2011) by Xavier Garza – include grandfather figures. The gender roles of *abuelos* either are socially compatible with a particular problem-solving situation (e.g., fixing a car) or are more contingently framed (e.g., the storyteller). It cannot be ruled out that the *machismo* ethos entrenched in Mexican culture contributes to perceiving grandfathers as less heroic, tender, or loving than their female counterparts (Gibbons and Fanjul de Marsicovetere 29). The majority of the books emphasize intergenerational solidarity between *abuelitas* and the young protagonists as they share knowledge and experiences.

Shared Stories for New Adventures and Problem-Solving

In *Juan and the Chupacabras*, *abuelo* (Grandfather) recalls: "I myself once stood face to face with this hideous creature, when I was not much older than you two" (n.p.). In this story about the chupacabras, gruesome creatures known for child-stealing, the grandchildren wonder if the chupacabras are actually real. *Abuelo* insists that they are, and that he has seen them with his own eyes. Not only does *abuelo* recollect his childhood experience from long ago, he also tells the children that the chupacabras still live in the same cornfield. The story profoundly affects the children. They become even more curious about the chupacabras and embark on an adventure to test the veracity of *abuelo's* tale. Mexican and Mexican-immigrant families' storytelling traditions derive from the oral folklore of Mexican culture (Briggs 246). Such storytelling is portrayed in the books as one of the most common media for enhancing intergenerationality in Mexican-heritage children's play cultures. Storytelling transports children to imaginary worlds. When a grandparent adopts the role of a storyteller, the Mexican heritage and the fantasy world intersect and mingle. Grandparents' childhoods are often referenced in ways that expand playful spaces both physically and spiritually.

Storytelling also fulfils important roles in a number of other books. In *Chavela and the Magic Bubble* (201) by Monica Brown, the eponymous Chavela is a young girl who loves to chew *chicle*, chewing gum. Once, Chavela and *abuelita* buy some magic chicle at the market. Chavela later chews several pieces of it, and her enlarged wad of gum transforms into a balloon in which Chavela travels to California, Arizona, Texas, and the white sand beaches of Playa del Carmen. In *Floating on Mama's Song* (2010) by Laura Lacamara, *abuela's* story takes on a rather different dynamic. Family stories told by *mama* and grandma serve as a healing mechanism. The narrative shows how the family comes to recognize *abuela's* talent for singing and to understand that she does not sing to conceal the trauma she has experienced as the victim of community bullying. In *Just in Case*, questions of what Grandma loves most lead to displays of popular Mexican toys and children's play cultures. The spirit of Señor Zelmiro, Grandma's husband, who is the narrator of the story, conjures up a fantastic world, using the famous symbol of the skeleton associated with the Day of the Dead. As these texts reveal, the intergenerational connection is illustrated as central to children's play in Mexican culture.

The Commodification of Intergenerationality in Mexican Childhood

Storytelling is the common medium of children's imagination and emotional exploration, serving to reaffirm their cultural identities. In *Nana's Big Surprise: Nana Que Sorpresa!* (2013) by Amanda Irma Perez, the characters are aware of their Nana's sadness. At the same time, the narrator, a grandchild, confesses that Nana's childhood stories about living through the Mexican Revolution and those about raising her thirteen children are "some of our favorites." The two motifs combined form the affective-cultural nexus of children's storytelling-mediated identities. In *My Abuelita* (2009) by Tony Johnston, the boy character lives with his *abuelita*, who is a storyteller by occupation. Participating in daily rituals with *abuelita* is shown as a magical and formative journey. In *Grandma and Me at the Flea: Los Meros Meros Remateros*, Juanito joins his grandma on an outing to a flea market. Juanito's day is filled with his grandmother's stories about the Mexican-immigrant community. Traditional Mexican games, such as *La Loteria*, which is often referred to as "Mexican Bingo" (Villegas, "History of La Loteria"), also appear in young protagonists' spaces as a medium of intergenerational solidarity. Ultimately, young people's spaces for play are extended and enhanced and their playful objects are multiplied, as familism-underpinned Mexicanness enters the children's cultures. Despite this augmenting potential, intergenerationality in the studied texts actually tends to constrain child-led stories and imagination. The grandparents' expansive interceptive roles often relegate the child characters to passive positions, where the latter cannot be playful or imaginative without intergenerational triggers. The grandparents become protagonists and appropriate the literary spotlight as the child figures become secondary.

The Mexican-American tradition and transnational reality are channeled through intergenerational solidarity. While Bradford's "transnational textuality" (24) does not refer specifically to Mexican immigrants, the texts I have studied do exhibit the duality of the identities of Mexican descendants. The processes of introduction and reproduction affect the cultural commodity exchange between Mexican-American picture books and mainstream readers. U.S.-Mexican cultural traditions are introduced and reproduced through depictions of intergenerational solidarity that do not clearly acknowledge children's unique universal cultures as a part of Mexican childhoods. Intergenerational solidarity turns into a literary commodity that meets aesthetic expectations about certain imagined Mexican cultures. All things considered, the commodification of Mexican culture and its emphasis on intergenerational solidarity evoked in children's books raise a key question: is it possible to depict Mexican childhood cultures authentically, and, if so, how can it be accomplished?

Universal Childhood and Children's Agency

The English and Spanish bilingual book *My Colors, My World: Mis Colores, Mi Mundo* (2007) by Maya Christina Gonzalez shows Maya, a young girl playing alone in her own space. Common daily events and items, such as flowers, cacti, the sky, and even the sunset, become her playmates. She uses her surroundings in creative and explorative ways. Maya says: "I open my eyes extra-wide to find the colors in my world. I invite purple irises to be my guests for tea. Yellow pollen peeks at me" (14). She briefly mentions her father's hair being black, but she says nothing further about him. This method of inviting items from a child's space to have fun together can also be found in *Niño: Wrestles the World* (2013) by Yuyi Morales and its sequel, *Rudas: Niño's Horrendous Hermanitas* (2016). The eponymous protagonist, Niño, plays with several characters that are part of Mexican children's popular culture, including

La Momia de Guanajuato (a zombie), Cabeza Olmeca (a basalt rock sculpture), La Llorona (a Mexican ghost), El Extraterrestre (an alien), and El Chamuco (a devil). These characters exemplify the authentic influences of children's surroundings, including their siblings. Niño's imaginative play epitomizes the ways in which both traditional and popular/contemporary varieties of Mexican culture are absorbed into the culture of childhood. Niño's narratives reflect a young boy's perceptions of zombies, devils, basalt rock sculptures, and Mexican ghosts, all of which have historical currency and import in Mexican culture.

Dwelling on universality in childhood cultures without highlighting intergenerational relationships gives authors a chance to focus on their young protagonists. In this framework, childhood's playful cultures do not have much room to accommodate grandparents and parents. Instead, as the stories focus solely on the child characters, children's agency positions them at the center of playful childhoods. Rather than entailing the pivotal role of Mexicanness in children's lives, traditions and intergenerational narratives revolve around contemporary children and childhood cultures. Hence, children are represented as independent, creative, active, and looking forward to having fun. Importantly, fun experiences ensue from the child character simply being a child. In these stories, the characters do not necessarily need toys, whether traditional or popular, to play; instead, they spin adventures from their own spaces.

Rudas: Niño's Horrendous Hermanitas, a sequel to *Niño: Wrestles the World*, features Niño's twin baby sisters, "Wrestling champions, Lucha Queens!" (n.p.). The sisters make up a considerable part of Niño's wrestling world. Their big brother is portrayed as siding with the fun characters (the devil and the alien) whom he fought previously. This is the only of the twenty-six picture books that have a male protagonist with two baby sisters who are also his playmates. *Niño: Wrestles the World* and *Rudas: Niño's Horrendous Hermanitas* do not feature (grand)parents but instead entirely focus on the siblings and their imaginary wrestling rivals.

Another English and Spanish bilingual book, *What Can You Do with a Paleta?* (2009) by Carmen Tafolla, presents children's playful spaces within their community. Specifically, the protagonist perceives colorful *paletas* (popsicles) as a wonderful invitation to be happy and have fun with all of the members of her community. The colorful paletas (edible paints) turn everyone in her community into her playmate. Just like ice-cream trucks excite other children, the paleta wagon thrills the protagonist, because she knows multiple ways to have fun with the paleta. The sensory descriptions of the paleta serve to cast it as a fun, inclusive, and creative toy. Importantly, *What Can You Do with a Paleta?* proclaims its Mexican-American rootedness in a brief summary on its copyright page: "A young Mexican-American girl celebrates the paleta, an icy fruit popsicle." The location of the community is either close to Mexico or in a "little Mexico" town in the United States. The transnational communal identity of Mexican people is explicitly communicated in the story. The illustrations picture unmistakable roses, crispy tacos, fruits, and the Señora at the fruit stand for the reader. The children in a neighboring yard are playing with colorful paletas. *What Can You Do with a Paleta?* shows the child's territory in the widest-ranging landscape and does not limit her playful spaces to the typical home, school, and familial settings, which recur as children's spaces in most transnational Mexican children's picture books.

Only six texts from my sample convey themes of universal childhood and agency. What, then, do the other twenty books address? Social discourse and transnational Mexican identity remain the dominant paradigms in multicultural children's literature in the United States. These attributes are what mainstream readers look for in children's books featuring the Mexican heritage. Rob Moore and Johan Muller's notion of voice is helpful in understanding how multicultural stories get told for the mainstream audience. They argue that voice involves both the speaker and the hearer, one who is speaking and one who is hearing or, "more accurately, one who is reading" (66). In this light, the limited peer cultures and the dominant intergenerational relations depicted in children's books are an enactment of the hearer's power vis-à-vis the speakers. Hence, the issues of social discourse and transnational Mexican children's cultures call for further epistemological inquiries. Revisiting Maria Botelho and Masha Rudman's notion of children's literature as "evidence of power relations" (71), one can conclude that the internal cultural values of Mexican childhood, with or without intergenerational connections, are a form of cultural ethos. However, such an approach may also entail othering Mexican children, whose childhoods are different in many ways from those of mainstream readers.

Conclusion

The child protagonists in the sample of texts analyzed previously have noticeably confined peer-based social relationships in playful contexts. The stories also insist on the strength of familism in Mexican culture and represent intergenerational relationships as important in Mexican children's childhoods, both culturally and socially. Significantly, the books reflect generational reciprocity in Mexican culture through telling about major events in the lives of families, which require that family members should collaborate, regardless of whether these events are appraised as positive or negative. Simultaneously, the representations of the Mexican cultural experience of exclusion are related to the silencing and suppressing of contemporary children's spaces and cultures. Literary Mexican childhood is a performance that seems to prefigure real children's childhoods. The universality of childhood, however, is rather marginalized when it does not serve as a powerful commodity. Perhaps the still prevalent *cultural* conception of multicultural children's literature does not need universal childhood connections in stories of Mexican-Americans, because universal childhood is preoccupied with and predicated on commonalities in childhood cultures, rather than their exotic heritage-based differences. This explains the overrepresentation of intergenerational solidarity in multicultural children's literature, while the figurations of and links to universal childhood cultures tend to be marginalized in stories of the U.S. Mexicans. Finally, although the bonds with grandparents in the studied picture books would likely have distinct meanings for children of Mexican origin, rethinking the meaning of repetitive grandparent-oriented plots in Mexican childhood cultures may be important, regardless of children's cultural background. Hence, this study may serve as a meaningful gesture acknowledging the need for a wider range of multicultural children's literature that recognizes and asserts the characters' child-identities and their childhood cultures, including intergenerational play.

Works Cited

Barrera, Rosalinda B., and Ruth E. Quiroa. "The Use of Spanish in Latino Children's Literature in English: What Makes for Cultural Authenticity?" *Stories Matter*, edited by Kathy Gnagey Short and Dana L. Fox. National Council of Teachers English, 2003, pp. 247–68.

Bernstein, Robin. "Toys Are Good for Us: Why We Should Embrace the Historical Integration of Children's Literature, Material Culture, and Play." *Children's Literature Association Quarterly*, vol. 38, no. 4, 2013, pp. 458–63.

Bishop, Rudine Sims. "Multicultural Literature for Children: Making Informed Choices. *Teaching Multicultural Literature in Grades K-8*, edited by Violet J. Harris. Christopher-Gordon, 1992, pp. 37–53.

———. "Reframing the Debate About Cultural Authenticity." *Stories Matter: The Complexity of Cultural Authenticity in Children's Literature*, edited by Dana L. Fox and Kathy G. Short. National Council of Teachers of English, 2003, pp. 25–40.

Boehm, Deborah A. "'For My Children': Constructing Family and Navigating the State in the U.S.-Mexico Transnation." *Anthropological Quarterly*, vol. 81, no. 4, 2008, pp. 777–802.

Botelho, Maria José, and Masha Kabakow Rudman. *Critical Multicultural Analysis of Children's Literature: Mirrors, Windows, and Doors*. Routledge, 2009.

Bradford, Clare. "Children's Literature in a Global Age: Transnational and Local Identities." *Nordic Journal of Childlit Aesthetics*, vol. 2, no. 1, 2011, pp. 20–34.

Briggs, Charles L. *Competence in Performance: The Creativity of Tradition in Mexicano Verbal Art*. U of Pennsylvania P, 1988.

Brown, Monica, and Magaly Morales. *Chavela's Magic Chicle*. Clarion Books, 2010.

Buitrago, Jairo, Elisa Amado, and Rafael Yockteng. *Two White Rabbits*. Groundwood Books, House of Anansi Press, 2015.

Campos, Belinda, et al. "Familism: A Cultural Value with Implications for Romantic Relationship Quality in U.S. Latinos." *Journal of Social & Personal Relationships*, vol. 33, no. 1, 2016, pp. 81–100.

Chavarría-Cháirez, Becky, et al. *Magda's Tortillas*. Pinata Books, 2000.

Colato Laínez, René, and Jill Arena. *Playing Lotería*. Luna Ri, 2005.

Colato Laínez, René and Joe Cepeda. *From North to South*. Children's Book Press, 2010.

Elya, Susan M., and Felipe Dávalos. *Home at Last*. Lee & Low Books, 2002.

Garza, Xavier, et al. *Juan and the Chupacabras: Juan Y El Chupacabras*. Piñata Books, 2011.

Gibbons, Judith L., and Regina Fanjul de Marsicovetere. "Grandparenting in Mexico and Central America: Time and Attention." *Grandparents in Cultural Context*, edited by David W. Shwalb and Ziarat Hossain. Routledge, 2017, pp. 17–40.

Gonzalez, Maya Christina. *Mis Colores, Mi Mundo: My Colors, My World*. Children's Book Press, 2007.

Güç, Ayşe. "Commodifying Culture Through Representation: An Analysis of the Intertwined Discourses on Mardin's Urban Space." *Turkish Studies*, vol. 17, no. 4, Dec. 2016, pp. 643–65.

Herrera, Juan Felipe, and Elizabeth Gómez. *The Upside Down Boy: El Niño De Cabeza*. Children's Book Press, 2006.

Herrera, Juan Felipe, and Honorio Robledo Tapia. *Super Cilantro Girl*. Children's Book Press, 2003.

Herrera, Juan Felipe, et al. *Los Meros Meros Remateros: Grandma and Me at the Flea*. Children's Book Press, 2002.

Hopkins, Peter, et al. "Mapping Intergenerationalities: The Formation of Youthful Religiosities." *Transactions of the Institute of British Geographers*, vol. 36, no. 2, 2011, pp. 314–27.

Lacamara, Laura. *Floating on Mama's Song*. HarperCollins, 2010.

Levitt, Peggy. *The Transnational Villagers*. U of California P, 2001.

Johnston, Tony, et al. *My Abuelita*. Harcourt Childrens Books, 2009.

Mateo, José Manuel. *Migrant*. Abrams Books for Young Readers, 2014.

Moore, Rob, and Johan Muller. "'Voice Discourse' and the Problem of Knowledge and Identity." *Social Realism, Knowledge and the Sociology of Education*, edited by Karl Maton and Rob Moore. Continuum, 2010, pp. 60–80.

Morales, Yuyi. *Just in Case: A Trickster Tale and Spanish Alphabet Book*. Roaring Brook Press, 2008.

———. *Niño Wrestles the World*. Roaring Brook Press, 2013.

———. *Rudas: Niño's Horrendous Hermanitas*. A Neal Porter Book, Roaring Brook Press, 2016.

Orellana, Marjorie Faulstich, et al. "Transnational Childhoods: The Participation of Children in Processes of Family Migration." *Social Problems*, vol. 48, no. 4, 2001, pp. 572–91.

Pérez, Amada I., and Maya C. Gonzalez. *My Very Own Room*. Children's Book Press, 2000.

———. *My Diary from Here to There*. Children's Book Press, 2002.

Sime, Daniela, and Emilia Pietka-Nykaza. "Transnational Intergenerationalities: Cultural Learning in Polish Migrant Families and Its Implications for Pedagogy." *Language and Intercultural Communication*, vol. 15, no. 2, 2015, pp. 208–23.

Soto, Gary, and Pamela Paparone. *My Little Car: Mi Carrito*. G.P. Putnam's, 2006.

Sung, Yoo Kyung. *A Post-Colonial Critique of the (Mis)Representation of Korean-Americans in Children's Picture Books*. U of Arizona P, 2009.

Sutton-Smith, Brian. *Toys as Culture*. Gardner Press, 1986.

Tafolla, Carmen, and Magaly Morales. *What Can You Do with a Paleta?* Tricycle Press, 2009.

Villarreal, Ricardo, and Robert A. Peterson. "The Concept and Marketing Implications of Hispanicness." *Journal of Marketing Theory and Practice*, vol. 17, no. 4, 2009, pp. 303–16.

Villegas, Teresa. "History of La Loteria." 2017, www.teresavillegas.com/history-of-la-loteria. Accessed 14 Mar. 2018.

5 Requiem for a Rabbit Scut

The Playful Encounter in Streatfeild and Hutton's *Harlequinade*

Sally Sims Stokes

Dedicated to the memory of my mother, Jean Ashby Johnson Sims (1922–2017), a strong, wise, imaginative, and playful parent, grandparent, and friend.

The Harlequinade was a slapstick theatrical phenomenon with stock characters that originated in Italy's sixteenth-century commedia dell'arte and arrived on British shores in the seventeenth century. During the Victorian period it evolved into a standard afterpiece following the spectacle still known in the twenty-first century as the Christmas pantomime. By the late 1930s, it had faded from the British stage.[1] The last documented performance of a Harlequinade at London's Lyceum had occurred in 1939. On 23 January 1942, Norah Walford, in charge of book design for the London publishing house Chatto & Windus (Warner 23), wrote to the artist Clarke Hutton concerning his proposed new juvenile title.[2] Hutton, best known as a satirist, had illustrated Rodney Hobson's *Caustic Carols*, published by Chatto in 1937. He had recently been moving into the children's realm, having completed the picture book *A Country ABC* for Chatto in 1940. The idea Hutton was floating was for a retelling of scenes, which he would illustrate with lithographs, from the Harlequinade. "The more we think of your idea of illustrating *Harlequinade*, the more we like it," Walford remarked. "Mr. [Harold] Raymond [the boss of Chatto] feels very strongly that an old story re-illustrated has a better future than a modern tale (. . .) (Though stories of battleships . . . sell very well now, they will be dead as mutton after the war)" (CW94/11.17).

Hutton intended his proposed book to convey the nonsense, energy, and 400-year sweep of the Harlequinade. As Walford indicated, she and Harold Raymond preferred that Hutton not relate the book to present times – that is, to World War II. They apparently fancied something that would be retrospective, even escapist, and they concurred with Hutton that the story should not be too whimsical (CW94/11.25). In March 1942, after agreeing to examine Cyril Beaumont's 1926 *The History of Harlequin* and Maurice Sand's 1915 *The History of the Harlequinade*,

Hutton, relying largely on Beaumont, submitted a 4,000-word typescript of stories from a Harlequinade, intertwined with fantastical accounts of the characters' origins. "There is a little sentimental interest between [the lead characters] Harlequin and Columbine," Hutton noted. "[At] the same time I have tried to avoid anything which little boys might think 'soppy'!" (CW/94/11.21). Accompanying Hutton's manuscript were three sample illustrations. Hutton trusted Chatto to identify a children's author to expand his draft to 6,000 words (CW94/11.25).

In April, Raymond would send the Hutton material to a personal friend, Lorna Lewis, for the purpose of expanding Hutton's story (CW94/18.30). Lewis, a sometime member of Virginia Woolf's and E. M. Delafield's circles (Powell 99, 141), had authored several animal-themed children's books but had not published under the Chatto imprint. Over the coming months, Lewis's draft would be abandoned, and Hutton's concept would be entirely transformed. In the final text, published in 1943, the ultimate author, Noel Streatfeild, together with Hutton – the two never had contact, even by mail, until the book was ready for publication – would render a "modern tale" after all.[3] Streatfeild would devise a spirited chance encounter between a group of evacuated circus children and an elderly former Harlequin who welcomes his young fellow performers into his country cottage, "Rabbit Scut." Streatfeild's version would demand of Hutton illustrations of subjects he had never envisioned.

Harlequinade's intergenerational playful encounter depends on the distinctive expression "rabbit scut" for its launch. Thanks to a consequential suggestion from Raymond, Streatfeild builds from "rabbit scut" to an exhilarating intergenerational Harlequinade. Drawing on the publisher's archives and noting trends in social psychological theory of the period, this chapter considers the playful encounter in Streatfeild and Hutton's small volume as a vehicle for relating the Harlequinade's history and for exposing and relieving the stresses of war, separation, and aging. The operating definition of intergenerational play applied here relies on Brian Edwards' inquiry into play as an "enabling factor" that can "coexist with work and seriousness" (70). Intergenerational play in the literary and pictorial place of *Harlequinade* is a cultural activity fostering a bond of delight and consolation between young children and an elder in the appreciation of work-related knowledge through animated conversation and imaginative performance.

The difficulty of explaining a Harlequinade, especially to anyone who had never attended such a performance, was an obstacle to Hutton's proposal. The external readers Chatto engaged to review Lewis's manuscript seemed unsure how to respond to the concept of the Harlequinade or to Hutton and Lewis's presentations thereof (CW94/18.35). Raymond, born in 1887, acknowledged to Streatfeild that he had a "confused memory of" the Harlequinade, not having seen one in forty years: "Perhaps

I should be more exact if I said I have a memory of it as a somewhat confused thing" and "a piece of bathos" (CW97/11.5). Streatfeild, born in 1895, had featured Christmas pantomimes in two books: *The Whicharts*, a 1931 adult novel and its derivative, her best-known children's novel, *Ballet Shoes* (1936). Her impression of the Victorian Harlequinade, though, was in line with Raymond's: "[W]ith its meat shops and sausages, of the London pantomime," Streatfeild wrote, "[it] seems to have been a milk and water affair" (CW97/11.2).

Beaumont and Sand had filled a theatre history gap earlier in the century, but their nonfiction studies were not children's fare. In 1918, Harley Granville-Barker published *Harlequinade: An Excursion*. A boisterous playscript, it has an intergenerational/historical aspect: a teenager and her uncle imagine Harlequinade characters – the sweethearts Columbine and Harlequin; Columbine's father, Pantaloon; Policeman (added to the cast in the nineteenth century); and the doleful Clown – as personages in settings from the River Styx to twentieth-century New York. London publisher Frederick Muller issued Frederick Cowles's *Harlequinade: The Fantastic Story of Harlequin and Columbine* in 1937. Cowles wrote children's wonder tales but was better known for adult horror fiction. Cowles's concoction of Harlequin's adventures, aimed at young readers, apparently did not come to the attention of anyone involved with the Chatto endeavor until close to the 1943 release of the Hutton/Streatfeild *Harlequinade*, when Muller requested that Raymond change the title. Raymond declined to do so (CW97/11.16–17).

Lewis had submitted her work on 12 May 1942 (CW94/18.33). It was not until 17 September, two months after Streatfeild had produced a first draft of an entirely new story, that Raymond wrote to Lewis with the "terrible confession" that her manuscript had been supplanted. "[W]e were beginning to wonder whether we had struck a dud idea, whether it was possible successfully to apply a story for something which had survived through the centuries without a story, or at any rate with the barest shred of one" (CW94/18.35). Lewis replied, "I think you've been very wise. . . . [Streatfeild] will do it well & I hope it goes over Big" (CW94/18.37). The Chatto & Windus archive does not reveal what Raymond or Walford wanted Streatfeild to do to salvage the enterprise. It is evident that by scrapping the Hutton/Lewis typescript she stunned both the publisher and the illustrator. Her vignette of a playful encounter evoking wartime solace and nostalgia, interwoven with the history of the Harlequinade, provided a story where there had been only the "barest shred" of one. She aimed "to take [the narrative] away, as it were, from the strong light of day and give it something of a gas-light quality." Countering objections to her drawing attention the war, she contended that not doing so would "take all probability from the story" (CW97/11.2–3). Raymond gave in (CW97/11.5).[4]

Streatfeild's solution involved setting up the action on a stress point: five unrelated children from the same circus are billeted to a rural village during Britain's scheme to evacuate children from areas vulnerable to air attack.[5] Circuses are nomadic; the children might have been at risk in various parts of the country, wherever their "big top" tent was set up. Streatfeild designates for their billet "a vague town in the West of England"; this lack of specific locale contributes to the "gas-light quality" but may have bemused Streatfeild's biographer Angela Bull, who dismissed *Harlequinade* as a "short, unsatisfactory fantasy" (182). Streatfeild, however, insisted to Raymond that "children are essentially realists and I have tried hard not to produce at any one place an impossibility" (CW97/11.2–3). Her intent was not fantasy but a chronicle of an uncommon – yet credible – playful wartime encounter.

As the story opens, the children are returning to their village because a winter mist has overtaken the field in which all but Nonie, the youngest, have been rehearsing their routines. Nonie is developmentally delayed. In the mist, he becomes separated from the rest. The three other boys – Serge, who is Russian; Andrea, who is Italian; and Nick, who is English (Nonie is adopted; his ancestry is unknown); and the girl, Sadie, who is American, have just worked out an artless plan to search for Nonie when they hear an elderly man call out that if they are looking for a little boy, the child is found. To the relief of his mates, Nonie is safe in the home of the man, whom Streatfeild dubs the "old actor." His house is just steps away, veiled in the vaporous haze.

Nonie's disappearance, designed to grip the reader in momentary unease, is its own mist, obscuring an essential detail: the children's gambol in the field is an activity of enjoyment and recreation that enables work and conserves circus culture. When the mist rolls in, the children are dismayed to have to cease their somersaults and cartwheels. As evacuees, away from parents and their "home" circus environment – now disbanded for the duration of the War – they have been *practicing* their circus techniques while observing circus *practices*. Doing so brings them the satisfaction of maintaining and improving their skills and the comfort of clinging to the customs of their (multi-) cultural group. Streatfeild writes in *Harlequinade*, "[t]he children did not belong to towns, or indeed to houses." They belong to the circus, which at this instant is as an abandoned vessel. They are the "flotsam and jetsam left as the tide goes out" (3–4). As Streatfeild told Raymond, "Circus children . . . are most rigourously trained, day in and day out, by their relatives" (CW97/11.3). The playful activity in the field requires discipline. It acts as a stabilizing emotional connection to those relatives and to work.

Streatfeild had traveled with the renowned Bertram Mills Circus to collect material for her children's novel *The Circus is Coming*, the 1938

Carnegie Medal winner. She was an actress and playwright and had conducted research on children in not only the circus but ballet and theatre as well. Not keen on evacuation out of concern for the effects on children of being separated from their families (Bull 167), Streatfeild understood that no foster parent in the village to which Andrea, Nick, Nonie, Sadie, and Serge have been sent would have known how to help these children conserve their proficiencies. Each of them, most of foreign background and one, Nonie, with a disability, is saddled with otherness greater than the cultural contrasts that urban evacuees presented to their rural hosts. The bond among the five children is their circus work. The apparent playfulness of that work colors their encounter with the old actor.

Streatfeild initiates the encounter between the children and the old actor by implementing the two-word expression "rabbit scut" as a device to establish the story's mood, scene, and intergenerational connection. Romanticizing a country cottage in her own mind, Sadie offers that the house in the mist might be called "Dunroaming" or "Mon Repos."[6] Andrea asks the old actor whether his cottage is indeed called "Mon Repos." The response: " 'No, it is called "Rabbit Scut," but pray come in and see for yourselves.' " Noting that "Rabbit Scut" is painted on the gate, Andrea politely says that he finds the name "very odd" (14). The old actor is proud of having chosen "Rabbit Scut." A residence should indicate the owner's line of work, he declares (16). The children are keen to learn what that work might be.

Once she settles everyone in the cozy sitting room of "Rabbit Scut," replete with its Victorian red plush furniture with the requisite antimacassars (cloths placed over the backs and arms of upholstered sofas and chairs to protect from dirt and grease), Streatfeild lingers over the house's name, allowing the old actor and the children to challenge and savor "rabbit scut" in ways that will coalesce into a mark of attachment between the generations. A scut is a short, erect tail, and Harlequins of centuries past were known to wear a rabbit scut in their hat brims. The children do not learn this immediately, and it is their expanding comprehension of such facts about the Harlequinade that advances the encounter. Streatfeild teases the reader a little longer while the children try to guess why the old actor has so named his abode. As the scene unfolds, harmony and a sense of instructive playfulness take hold.

> Andrea bounced on the sofa.
>
> "Did you dream you'd have a house called 'Rabbit Scut'?"
>
> "Oh dear, yes! I always knew what I would call it."
>
> Sadie put a firm hand on Andrea's knee to remind him people did not bounce on other people's sofas.
>
> "I would say it's a very good idea, calling your house after your business. Now you, I suppose, would be a rabbit breeder."

> The old man's face crinkled and he laughed a thin, gay, tinkling laugh.
>
> "A rabbit breeder! No indeed, my dear. I was an actor."
>
> (16–17)

Sadie thinks "Rabbit Scut" a "silly choice of name," especially for an actor's home. She knows not a thing about rabbit scuts, but she knows what a hare's foot is for: she has seen her mother apply makeup with a hare's foot for circus performances.[7] She informs the old actor that he must have meant hare's foot, not rabbit scut. Her cheekiness threatens to make the encounter confrontational.[8] The old actor, however, takes her pert observation in stride (18). To finesse a rapport with the children, he keeps the conversation agile. He uses Sadie's insistence on a hare's foot to demonstrate that he understands what she is referring to but that the function of the animal's foot in a theatre environment is not the same as that of the scut. Confirming that he did mean "rabbit scut," he introduces the character Harlequin to demonstrate the timelessness of the joy of performing. Speaking the word "Harlequin" will impel the playfulness of the encounter. As to the foot and the scut, "Both wore our badge," the actor explains.

> Nick frowned when he did not understand.
>
> "Badge of what?"
>
> "Harlequin."
>
> . . . They stared at [the old actor], trying to remember what or who Harlequin was. To all of them he was a mere shadow.
>
> (18)

The children will engage more deeply with the Harlequinade – and with its remembrance and memorialization – through their newfound intergenerational affinity, which is aided by the fact that Nick, Andrea, and Serge have faint recollections of pictures of Harlequin. They conjure mental images of his multicolored tights, pleated collar, black mask, and wand. Nonie fixes on the word "Harlequin," repeating it in a whisper. The old actor echoes Nonie. " 'Harlequin. I played Harlequin. We are a great line' " (18–20).

> While he spoke[,] the most glorious feeling of coming home swept over the children. They knew they had not felt themselves since the circus had been disbanded; but they had accepted life as it came and had not analysed their feeling of being strangers. . . . Proper talk was in their ears once more. . . . "I played Harlequin. We are a great line." That was the stuff.
>
> (20)

An edifying scene with the old actor's recounting a textbook history of the Harlequinade might have followed, but it does not. Instead, Nick, ensconced in his sofa corner, urges, "Tell us about being Harlequin" (20). The old actor relates to this attentive audience the evolution of the Harlequinade over four centuries – the characters, their comedy, their costumes – without forgetting Nick's request. He underscores, from the experience of playing him, his impressions of Harlequin, "a creature born of the laughter of the crowd" (22).

> The children sat very still. The old man's words fell like rain into a pond, every drop making its own circle on the water. Each of his words made a circle in their imaginations. . . . If they had found themselves at that very minute at a fair in Italy in the sixteenth century, they would have known what to do with the improvised stage.
>
> (22)

They are children of that stage or any stage. The old actor's account is within and supportive of their cultural perceptions. Their imaginations stretch accordingly as they pepper their host with questions, even as he is rejuvenated by their interest and insight.

As the action proceeds, the old actor happily continues enlightening the eager children. Sadie asks about Harlequin's dress; the old actor reviews how it has changed over time. "One thing is certain," he now avers. "[In] his cap [Harlequin] wore the scut of a rabbit or hare." This statement now orients the children to the rabbit scut's relationship to Harlequin. Andrea likes the rhythmic sound of "rabbit scut," tapping it with his feet (24). Nick presses for the rabbit scut's symbolism. "There's a lot of argument about that," the old actor responds, coming down on the side of "an emblem for speed." The children are starting to admire Harlequin; the old actor corrects them. "[He] is a blackguard, a shocking blackguard. . . . He is more like a piece of quicksilver than a man, a light mocking creature, coarse, I am afraid, but always merry" (28). They hope the old actor has pictures to show them. The old actor declares: "I have better than that. Much better" (34). He lifts the lid of a chest "with such pleasure, and yet with such caution, that it seemed as if whatever treasure was inside had life, and might, if not watched, spring out" (35–36). The treasure consists of props and accessories from a Harlequinade: Columbine's dancing shoes, a string of faux sausages, a poker painted to look red hot, a white satin blouse, a rose, and the *pièce de résistance*: the old actor's Harlequin clothes, with the remains of forty-eight thousand sequins to "shimmer in the firelight" (42). There is no more mention of a rabbit scut. It has performed its role and figuratively exited. The name of the old actor's house – and the encounter within it – have done their part to recall the mythos.

One deduces that Streatfeild originally intended the encounter to conclude after the children had had the opportunity to exclaim over the props and accessories. Her intentions will perhaps never be known. Only correspondence and editorial notes offer clues about Streatfeild's earlier draft or drafts, none of which has been discovered in the Chatto & Windus archives, in Streatfeild's papers, or in her agent Audrey Heath's records. Heath had submitted Streatfeild's manuscript on 7 July 1942; on 16 July, Streatfeild responded to a suggestion from Raymond. She wrote that she was "delighted with [Raymond's] idea of the children acting some kind of version of Harlequinade the old actor played in" (CW97/11.2). She promised a new scene, delivering it within ten days. Streatfeild's complete overhaul of Hutton's story caught the illustrator off guard, but he recovered quickly. Not apparently having had any prior notice whatsoever about Streatfeild's concept for *Harlequinade*, even of the penultimate version of Streafeild's text, he wrote to Raymond on 25 July 1942:

> I like [the manuscript] very much & if you had sent it to me as an uncontemplated story for me to illustrate I would not have any mixed feelings about it. The point is that for some time I have been thinking of the "Harlequinade" along certain lines. I hope you don't get the impression I am disgruntled & am going to be difficult – I am only surprised.
>
> Actually I think Miss S's story is charming.
>
> (CW94/11.34, .37)

Hutton had a dummy of the book ready by mid-September to be sent to Chiswick Press (CW94/11.40). In addition to his images evoking the historical Harlequinade, there were new lithographs. One features an eighteenth-century audience booing a 1761 play whose intent, the old actor tells his young friends, was to "kill Harlequin" (30). The children are suitably appalled. Another shows a twentieth-century audience; one theatre-goer dominates the picture as he dons his overcoat. This lithograph supports the old actor's telling the children that, in recent years, after the pantomime, " '[when] the curtain rose on the Harlequinade, the audience considered the entertainment over, and put on their coats' " (34). Both lithographs represent Streatfeild's leitmotif of Harlequin as perpetually at risk but still breathing. Hutton thus intensifies Streatfield's escalating implication that the children and the actor must reclaim the Harlequinade.[9]

In Streatfeild's new sequence, the old actor, having assigned roles to the children according to their talents and personalities, is in his element among a new generation to which the experience of being coached by an expert has enormously positive associations.

> Tea was over. The curtains were drawn and the lights turned on. The children were playing a Harlequinade. The old man . . . had disinterred from his memory the "business" that each child should be at, and was now sometimes spectator, sometimes prompter, and sometimes compère, having a glorious time at all three.
>
> (40)

The children throw themselves into laughter, dancing, tumbles, acrobatics, and chases over stolen sausages, immersed in their parts with, excepting Serge as Harlequin in the captivatingly too-big authentic garments, only the simplest of costumes. "Sadie had the rose in her hair, and an antimacassar pinned round her to look like an apron" (40). Old and young are playing; they are performing a play; they are enlivening their own spirits while reviving the spirit of the Harlequinade. It is, for all, a "glorious" and psychologically vital achievement.

The psychological element of Streatfeild's narrative can be discerned from the start of *Harlequinade*. Introducing the children in the first pages of the book, Streatfeild describes Nick as old enough "to miss the free and easy laughing life of his own world, to suffer at the lack of training. . . . Gone was the practise with his father. . . . [H]e was also old enough to know that . . . a world at war had no time for circuses" (4). During the climactic Harlequinade at "Rabbit Scut," Streatfeild writes, "Andrea tried to perform all the funny things he had seen his father do" (44). British psychiatrist John Bowlby's work in maternal attachment theory would become more prominent after World War II, but views he expressed in the 1930s are pertinent to the *Harlequinade* children's emotional states. In 1939, Bowlby and colleagues remarked on negative effects upon children under age five of "separation from their mothers and familiar environment" (1202) through evacuation. These experts were less worried about evacuees six and older, as Nick, Andrea, and the rest presumably are.

Another British psychiatrist, Jeremy Holmes, proposed in 2000 that Bowlby's work might have resonated with Streatfeild. Holmes, in his afterword to her 1945 adult novel *Saplings*, finds Streatfeild "in tune with the zeitgeist" of Bowlby's writings (whether she read them is unknown) on the "impact of war on child mental health" (364). Streatfeild's sensitivity to her *Harlequinade* characters' situation bestows resolve on children old enough to "stand separation and even benefit from it" (Bowlby et al. 1202). This does not preclude a yearning for an opportunity like playing a Harlequinade with – and under the guidance of – an adept, indulgent (grand)father figure for whom the rewards of this winter afternoon are immeasurable. It does raise the issues of evacuation's toll on a child such as Nonie, whose developmental age is in question; the Harlequinade's benefit to Nonie; and whether Nonie can "attach" to the old actor.

The work of Romanian-American psychiatrist Jacob Levy Moreno is also pertinent to *Harlequinade*. Moreno is known for having founded the psychodrama, a role-playing therapy. Moreno maintained in 1940 that an earlier concept, the "impromptu play," was his brainchild and that between 1911 and 1930 he was "practically alone in using the principle" (242). Without presuming to address here the complexities of Morenean psychiatry, and with no evidence that Streatfeild knew of Moreno, briefly mapping some of his theories to *Harlequinade* may spur further exploration of how Moreno's perceptions of human interaction and response apply to Streatfeild's Harlequinade performance scene. In his 1940 recollections of how he used the impromptu play in his therapy work, Moreno observed, "I assisted the children in putting together a plot which they were to act out, spontaneously, with the expectation that this impromptu play would . . . produce in its participants a mental catharsis" (242). There is no evidence that Raymond encouraged Streatfeild to tie the scene to the characters' emotional needs, but she did so, and it teems with meaning.

Moreno might have considered the Harlequinade at "Rabbit Scut" to be outside his definition of an impromptu play. The Harlequinade was not a new plot. Rather, it emanated from what he would have termed the "cultural conserve" (210) of the old actor and the circus children. Still, the similarity is evident. "Mental catharsis" and "encounter," key to Moreno's work, apply as well. Moreno defines "mental catharsis" as "relief from grief or fear without changing a person's overall situation" (228). The children and the old actor may be said to have gained a mental catharsis from the "Rabbit Scut" Harlequinade, if one accepts that all are grieving a separation from what has previously brought them gladness and satisfaction (Huse 77) and that any may be fearing the war's possible outcome. The old actor may be fearing death. The Harlequinade does not change any character's "overall situation," but it delivers relief. As to "encounter," in this chapter the term has carried the unstated received meaning of an unexpected meeting that, in this instance, becomes playful. Moreno in about 1914 put forth what he saw as the connotations of "encounter," the foundation of post-1940 group therapy. Adam Blatner describes Moreno's concept of encounter as requiring a degree of maturity and going "beyond empathy, as there is an associated opening of one's heart, an act of will, an exercise of imagination and an expanding of one's perspective" (212). Blatner's interpretation of the Morenean encounter characterizes the depth of communication that Streatfeild achieves between the old actor and the children.

The profoundness of this cross-generational connection is consistently infused with both seriousness and humor. Noel Streatfeild was an Anglican clergyman's daughter. Money was tight, and she and her siblings often devised their own amusements, which included staging funerals "with solemnly hilarious rites" for dead creatures found in the garden (Bull 36). Funerals were a commonplace for an Edwardian vicarage family. Macabre connotations of these mock processions and burials must be measured alongside this fact, as well as against Streatfeild's own youthful sense of mischief (Bull 26). Streatfeild's emphasis in *Harlequinade* on dead rabbits' body parts, then, may be less relevant to the demise of the Harlequinade and more relevant to the catchiness of "rabbit scut," which must have captured Streatfeild's attention when she, like Hutton, was reading up on Harlequinade history (CW97/11.2). To Sadie, the term is silly, to Andrea, odd. To the old actor, it is fulfilling. Streatfeild's use of it to enable the encounter, to make the term the foil of "hare's foot," to have it co-occur in the environment of "Rabbit Scut" – the old actor's home – with, as Edwards directs, "work and seriousness," is playful. "Seriousness" can be taken to mean "urgency," and Streatfeild recognizes the urgency of the old actor's taking advantage of the moment – and of the cultural inclinations of the children – to imbue the next generation with the life-force of the Harlequinade.

A dangling question is whether Streatfeild intended her readers to understand the encounter – not just the impromptu Harlequinade but the entirety of the engagement of the children and the old actor – as a memorial service for the repose of an obsolete performance genre or as a renascence of a dormant one or as both. The book concludes on a sentimental note. As the children prepare to return to their village, the old actor, depicted in the final Hutton lithograph (framed within a circle, suggesting a view through a long lens), cocks his head, his hand at his ear, listening to the "rippling, merry wind" coming through the chimney. He had earlier described Harlequin as merry. He and the children all understand the wind to represent "the laughter of nearly four hundred years." Serge exclaims, "We've made the wind laugh." In the last line, the old actor affirms this: "Never forget it is there, yours for the catching. Swell its volume. Bring it back" (46, 47). Streatfeild scholar Nancy Huse sees the narrator's (Streatfeild's) voice merging here with that of the old actor (77). Through a playful encounter, the children and the old actor have revived the Harlequinade, and the old actor has briefly relived it. They bid a collective tacit farewell to the Harlequinade but not a farewell to the children's future in bringing laughter to their souls and to circus audiences yet to come, when the war is over at last. Nor do they bid adieu to the old actor's agency in bringing about these future possibilities. The Harlequinade is dead. Long live the laughter.

Before the *Harlequinade* project first got under way at Chatto & Windus, Norah Walford predicted that stories of battleships would be " 'dead as mutton' after the war." She was referring to children's books focusing on wartime topics. *Harlequinade* was a limited-run publication. It has been all but forgotten for decades, perhaps not so much for its association with World War II as for its intense reach back in time to relate a story already difficult to convey to a 1940s readership and with the added distance, at this writing, of seventy-seven years since Hutton first submitted his idea to the publisher. Huse in 1994 captured the essence of *Harlequinade's* intergenerational encounter of the playful kind. She wrote that it "[links] the children's remembered arts with a past much older than they, and vital to the present" (77). That continuum of remembrance will remain vital to "the present" as part of the linked heritage of performance and playfulness.[10]

Notes

1. For an overview of the pantomime, see Davis.
2. Walford was married; she was also known as Norah Smallwood.
3. In 1948, Clarke Hutton would illustrate a new edition of Streatfeild's *The Circus is Coming*.
4. Attitudes to wartime background were perhaps influenced by individuals' circumstances and outlook: Raymond's sons Tony and Piers were deployed in Libya and India, respectively. Walford's husband was serving in the RAF. Streatfeild was operating a mobile canteen in London. Her flat had been hit by a German bomb in 1941. Hutton was with the Royal Observer Corps (a civil defense organization) in Kent. Lewis seems to have been working in a munitions factory in or near London. These facilities were especially susceptible to airstrikes.
5. For one overview of the scheme, see Welshman.
6. "Dunroaming" ("done roaming": arrived home) and "Mon Repos" were popular British house names and would have been understood by adults and some children in the 1940s. Streatfeild's use of these terms and such words as "antimacassar" exemplifies her not writing down to children.
7. Hare's feet had been used by entertainers as far back as the 1820s.The pseudonymous Haresfoot and Rouge authored an 1877 stage makeup guide. Hare's feet are mentioned as makeup tools in *Community Drama*, a 1921 community players' handbook.
8. Streatfeild child characters whose know-it-all posturing advances a plot include Jane Winter in *The Painted Garden* (1949).
9. In July 1943, as the book neared release, Streatfeild wrote to Raymond that she was "absolutely enthralled" with Hutton's illustrations (CW97/11.20).
10. Many thanks to the following for expediting access to the Chatto & Windus *Harlequinade* files: Penguin Random House UK; the Special Collections staff, University of Reading Library; and, most especially, Ellen Gartrell McGeorge.

Works Cited

Unpublished correspondence

Archives of Chatto & Windus, Special Collections, University of Reading, UK.
Key to correspondents:

CH:	Clarke Hutton
C&W:	Chatto & Windus
FML:	Frederick Muller Ltd.
HR:	Harold Raymond
LL:	Lorna Lewis
NS:	Noel Streatfeild
NW:	Norah Walford
CW94/11.17	NW to CH, 23 Jan. 1942.
CW94/11.21	CH to NW, 18 Mar. 1942.
CW94/11.25	CH to NW, 30 Mar. 1942.
CW94/11.34	CH to NW, 25 July 1942, p. 1.
CW94/11/37	CH to NW, 25 July 1942, p. 4.
CW94/11.40	CH to NW, 14 Sept. 1942, p. 2.
CW94/18.30	HR to LL, 13 Apr. 1942.
CW94/18.33	LL to HR, 12 May 1942.
CW94/18.35	HR to LL, 17 Sept. 1942.
CW94/18.37	LL to HR, 21 Sept. 1942.
CW97/11.2	NS to HR, 16 July 1942.
CW97/11.3	NS to HR, 16 July 1942, p. 2.
CW97/11.5	HR to NS, 17 July 1942.
CW97/11.16	FML TO C&W, 8 July 1943.
CW97/11.17	HR to FML, 14 July 1943.
CW97/11.20	NS to HR, 19 July 1943

Beaumont, Cyril W. *The History of Harlequin*. The Author, 1926.

Blatner, Adam. "The Dynamics of Interpersonal Preference: Tele." *Psychodrama Since Moreno*, edited by Paul Holmes, et al. Routledge, 1994, pp. 201–15.

Bowlby, John, et al. "Evacuation of Small Children." *The British Medical Journal*, vol. 2, no. 4119, 1939, pp. 1202–3.

Bull, Angela. *Noel Streatfeild*. Collins, 1984.

Community Service, *Community Drama*. Community Service, Inc., 1921.

Cowles, Frederick Ignatius. *Harlequinade: The Fantastic Story of Harlequin and Columbine*. Frederick Muller, 1937.

Davis, Jim, ed. *Victorian Pantomime*. Palgrave Macmillan, 2010.

Edwards, Brian. *Theories of Play and Postmodern Fiction*. Garland, 1998.

Granville-Barker, Harley. *The Harlequinade: An Excursion*. Little, Brown, 1918.

"Haresfoot and Rouge." pseud. *How to 'Make-Up'*. S. French, 1877.

Hobson, Rodney. *Caustic Carols*. Chatto & Windus, 1937.

Holmes, Jeremy. "Afterword." *Saplings*, edited by Noel Streatfeild. Persephone Books, 2000, pp. 363–77.

Huse, Nancy. *Noel Streatfeild*. Twayne's English Authors Series. Twayne, 1994.

Hutton, Clarke. *A Country ABC*. Chatto & Windus, 1940.
Moreno, J. L. "Mental Catharsis and the Psychodrama." *Sociometry*, vol. 3, no. 3, July 1940, pp. 209–44.
Powell, Violet. *The Life of a Provincial Lady: A Study of E. M. Delafield and Her Works*. Heinemann, 1988.
Sand, Maurice. *The History of the Harlequinade*. Martin Secker, 1915.
Streatfeild, Noel. *Ballet Shoes*. Dent, 1936.
———. *The Circus Is Coming*. Dent, 1938.
———. *Harlequinade*. Chatto & Windus, 1943.
———. *The Circus Is Coming*, new and revised ed. Dent, 1948.
———. *The Painted Garden*. Collins, 1949.
———. *Saplings*. 1945. Persephone Books, 2000.
———. *The Whicharts*. Heinemann, 1931.
Warner, Oliver. *Chatto & Windus: A Brief Account of the Firm's Origin, History and Development*. Chatto & Windus, 1973.
Welshman, John. *Churchill's Children*. Oxford UP, 2010.

6 Girls, Boys, Bombs, Toys[1]

Terror and Play in Contemporary Children's Fiction

Blanka Grzegorczyk

The contemporary terror threat reverberates beyond the collective adult psyche to the child's play. Among the resonant media images of those caught up in current wars of terror are portrayals of Western children reenacting scenes from the 9/11 attacks on America – and later the November 2015 Paris shootings – with their Lego toy bricks and figures, as well as pictures of Syrian children splashing in a swimming pool created in a bomb crater amid the rubble of their Aleppo homes or holding up posters of Pokémon mascots in the hope of drawing international attention to their plight. Photographs of improvised explosive devices hidden in brightly colored children's toys as part of Islamic terrorists' military strategy, together with stories of children playing border guards and asylum seekers in actual refugee camps in Greece, give a further indication of how precarious young people's lives have become. With the transnational threat of terror affecting whole cultures and societies, terroristic violence is witnessed, appropriated, and reimagined by Western and non-Western children who are trying to grasp – and to take control of – the difficult realities shaping their social experience. The profusion of children's fiction written in response to the events of 9/11 and 7/7, as well as to the declaration of the US-led "war on terror" and its global repercussions, likewise suggests that terrorism and counter-terrorism have inscribed themselves in the contemporary imagination and discloses some significant intellectual common ground in the broader scope of children's literary culture. Perhaps most strikingly, many of the children's novels that comment on the re-ordering of the world around the battle lines drawn after 9/11 and 7/7 seek to demonstrate how real world and fantasy, fact and imagination, violence and play seem to collapse into one another through terror effects.

This chapter examines representations of play in several recent British children's novels, which reveal how it has been used as an intellectual, rhetorical, political, and military tool by the victims and witnesses of terror and its effects, as well as by participants in conflicts linked to terrorism. Contemporary children's fiction is thus shown as capable of offering powerful imaginative interventions in post-9/11 social and political culture. With its commitment to challenging the binaristic "us vs. them" thinking, it can be said to complicate the politics of terror and counter-terror and to guide younger audiences to think about complex questions of humanity, mortality, and moral agency in the ethical context of acts of terrorism and violence. At the same time, such writing seeks to drive home the impact on children of the lived experience of terror or the threat of terrorist attacks, while considering the erosion of particular communities as intricately bound up in the personal and political need for vengeance in response to terrorism. Children's writers, through their focus on the practices of play, find ways of registering the transformed political and social conditions of post-9/11 life. Paying particular attention to how some British writers for the young extend an understanding of violence, victimization, and trauma, I look at how they deal with the psychological aftermath and ethical implications of terrorist attacks and their global consequences.

Ashes, Absences, and Acting Out

Catherine Bruton's *We Can Be Heroes* (2011) and Annabel Pitcher's *My Sister Lives on the Mantelpiece* (2011) make for particularly good examples of novels depicting play practices to frame, within a narrative of social and familial rupture, the child protagonists' responses to their own traumatic experiences of losing family members in terrorist episodes. In *We Can Be Heroes*, this is done through the perspective of twelve-year-old Ben, whose father was killed in the 9/11 attacks when Ben was a toddler and who sees fear of terrorism disrupt the mundane lives of the multi-ethnic community of Birmingham a decade later. Of particular importance is how the novel broadens its poignant treatment of the manner in which the attacks on the Twin Towers are related to the lives of Ben's family to embrace a more general atmosphere of racial tensions and anti-Muslim hostilities in post-9/11 and post-7/7 Britain. Within the dominant racist structure of his immediate community – in which a biker gang jeer and throw bottles at British Asian children playing in the park but "won't bother with a white kid" (346) and Ben's own grandfather responds to the boy's growing friendship with Priti, their eleven-year-old British Muslim new neighbor, by asking him if he is "sure [he] wants to get pally with that lot," that is, the "sort that killed [his] dad" (29) – Ben struggles to make sense of events that remain more complex than a rhetoric based on the cultural clash of East and West allows. A similarly damaging internal conflict is evident in Pitcher's *My Sister Lives on the Mantelpiece*, a novel set in the Lake District, where an unstable, alcoholic father takes ten-year-old Jamie and his teenage sister, Jas(mine), for a "Fresh New Start" (5). Overcome with grief, Jamie's father understands the move as getting away from all Muslims in Britain – 'None of that foreign stuff in the Lake District,' he says. 'Just real British people minding their own business' (26) – whom he blames for the killing of his other daughter, Rose, in a bombing in Trafalgar Square five years before. The father's problematic honoring of the urn that contains Rose's ashes makes the healing process particularly difficult for the two surviving siblings, as does their absent mother's indifference to their plight. Even more confusing from Jamie's point of view, however, is the friendly welcome offered to him at his new school by Sunya, his only British Muslim classmate. Worried that his sympathetic connection with Sunya constitutes a betrayal of his father and dead sister, Jamie begins to spend his playtime in the school toilets, "respecting Dad" and "put[ting his] hands under the dryer, pretending it was a fire-breathing monster" (112), rather than playing with a Muslim girl. His resolve to "follow The Ten Commandments. . . . [i] ncluding number five" holds until he realizes that his father has been "giving False Evidence" when saying that "[a]ll Muslims are murderers. . . . Make bombs in their bedroom" (112, 117). The point that the two novels make repeatedly is about the contaminating effects of terror on the workings of the child's mind and imagination and about extracting from ethical discourse a way to negotiate the ideological fault lines created by the family and society in the aftermath of terrorist attacks.

The bringing together of the adult-controlled world of war violence and the world of children's games and toys is certainly not new in the children's literature tradition, as demonstrated, for instance, in Margaret R. Higonnet's important articles on the narrative functions of play in books about war and trauma (1998, 2005, 2007). Writing for the young, Higonnet argues, has the power to draw attention to game-playing as an "instrument of therapy" ("Time Out" 157), to supply a better understanding of how painful wartime losses can be acknowledged and contained through the child's play. Novels like *We Can Be Heroes* and *My Sister Lives on the Mantelpiece* provide a contemporary slant on young people's responses to loss of life caused by violent actions, expanding the category of childhood processes interrupted by the destructiveness of war to encompass the damage inflicted on children by terror and its repercussions. However, these novels do so by employing similar strategies of representing play to those adopted by writers of children's war narratives. One such strategy is to imagine what scenarios are likely to dominate children's play choices after a terror-related trauma directly experienced by themselves or the larger society within which they move. In the two novels discussed here, the main characters constantly rehearse scenarios that revolve around saving other people's lives and confronting villains, whether as undercover agents in *We Can Be Heroes* or superheroes in *My*

Sister Lives on the Mantelpiece. While Pitcher's book reveals little about the specifics of the evil plans that are thwarted by Jamie and Sunya – or "Spider-Man" and "Girl M" – in their numerous imaginative performances, the young protagonists of Bruton's novel, we learn, are busy tracking and eliminating terrorists, with Ben depicting the role play activities in which he engages with Priti and his cousin, Jed, in comic strips about Ben-D, Lil' Priti, and Jed-eye. Offering more of a cathartic release from horrifying events rather than simply a rehearsal of adult roles in the wars against terror (see also Higonnet, "War Games," "War Toys"; Agnew and Fox), playtime in these novels alerts us to their child characters' desire for control and power over the fates of themselves and others within these broken communities. Here, as Higonnet would have it, the work of play can be seen to focus on "re-establishing channels of communication and freedom from fear" ("Time Out" 161). And if, at first, these play practices seem to replicate the reductionist "good versus evil" thinking that responses to terrorism have often invited, each book shows how shared playtime gradually helps the protagonists to question the generalizing assumptions behind narratives based on cultural or religious clashes. The characters' growing subjectivity can be read in ethical terms, I would submit, insofar as it is predicated on a recognition that responsibility for the other, what Emmanuel Levinas describes as "answering for everything and for everyone" (Levinas, *Otherwise Than Being* 114), is essential to one's engagement with the world. Importantly, then, in *We Can Be Heroes*, Ben's cartoon ends with a vision of a world in which "Da Hona Killaz and Da Bikaz make up and become best of friends" and where it is the right-wing radicals who "turn out to be the real baddies, so they get arrested for perverting the course of justice" (470); in *My Sister Lives on the Mantelpiece*, Jamie commits himself publicly to his friendship with Sunya when he reacts violently against the racist abuse screamed at her by school bullies (which leaves open the question of violence breeding violence).

While Bruton's and Pitcher's characters fantasize about saving the lives of others, these fantasies, together with Jamie's real accomplishments in football and Ben's talent for drawing, frame their actual successes in helping to heal others' wounds. *My Sister Lives on the Mantelpiece* is particularly good in reflecting on the role played in this healing process by children's toys. On hearing his sister's story of how, when she was little, she lost her favorite (tatty) teddy bear but was then "relieved to get back to [her] other bears," whom she loved more than ever because "there was one less" (151) – an obvious reference to their parents' hurtful rejection of the siblings' needs after Rose's death – Jamie presents Jas with a gift of a brown, fluffy, tattered bear ("I pulled his eyes off and everything" (221)) and is rewarded with a rare smile. That the bear is already damaged can itself be seen as a means of acknowledging and domesticating loss; the displacement of physical injuries onto a toy helps, in Higonnet's words, to "bring the experience of destruction close to a child's world, while it diminishes its impact" ("War Games" 8), perhaps even suggesting that "deconstruction may be a first step toward reconstruction" ("Time Out" 163). From the last section of the novel – a first-person narration, which, unlike the earlier chapters, is focalized through Jas – we learn that another toy, a walkie-talkie, allows Jas to negotiate her needs in relation to those of others and to regain some control over her own narrative in the wake of the trauma of her twin sister's death: "soon I was speaking to Rose for an hour a night as if we were still young, hiding under duvets either side of a wall, giggling into walkie-talkies in the darkness" (222). Viewed from this perspective, the walkie-talkie – or a "half broken two-way toy radio" (222) – becomes what D. W. Winnicott would call a "transitional object" – even though Winnicott's interest lies in the use of special objects by children in general, not just those who have experienced trauma (1951/53; see also Kuznets 1994) – that comes to represent Rose as well as herself to Jas. The girl's conversations with her dead twin by means of a toy radio typify only one transitional stage of psychological healing – with her leaving of the walkie-talkie on Rose's grave – and a final reassertion of an independent sense of identity on the way back from the cemetery ("in a shop window. . . . I recognise the pink-haired girl staring back at me. I whisper *I am Jasmine* before walking home" (226)) epitomizing a significant step toward recovery. The resolution of *We Can Be Heroes* is similarly optimistic in tone, showing that Ben is finally able to stop thinking of his father as a "stick man falling out of a tower." Rather, thanks to Priti, who urges him to collect family stories in a memory box, Ben now sees his father through the eyes of others, as a "smiling man playing football with a little boy on his shoulders" (465), an image that, for him, clearly holds a regenerative power but that nonetheless reminds the reader of the carefree joys of play – be it children's or intergenerational – that might be lost as a result of terroristic violence.

Refugees from Childhood

The issue of what is lost or suspended in the contemporary child's everyday experience in the aftermath of terror has also been raised by children's novelists with regard to the trauma-like effects of the recent wars around terror on those affected by or engaged in these conflicts. Sumia Sukkar's *The Boy from Aleppo Who Painted the War* (2013), Elizabeth Laird's *Welcome to Nowhere* (2017), and Pooja Puri's *The Jungle* (2017) stage the effects of terror on their non-Western child characters in war-torn cities and bleak refugee camps, showing how comfortable domestic routines are wrecked and social and familial structures are tested when the experience of war and dislocation begins to define individuals, communities, and nations. Sukkar's and Laird's novels present the Syrian conflict through the eyes of Adam – a fourteen-year-old boy with Asperger's syndrome who grounds himself by translating his own and other people's feelings, moods, and intentions into paintings – and Omar, a twelve-year-old with entrepreneurial ambitions who is profoundly uninterested in politics, respectively. While both novels follow the protagonists and their families as they move through Syria struggling to escape violence, the second part of *Welcome to Nowhere* sees Omar's family flee their homeland altogether and seek refuge in a Jordanian camp where "nothing felt the same. [They] were at the bottom of the heap. . . . Nobody saw [them] as real people, who had had lives. [They] were just . . . refugees" (205). The characters in *The Jungle* are similarly displaced and dehumanized, but most of the children in its fictionalized Calais camp are unaccompanied, and Mico, the main protagonist, finds himself slowly forgetting his family (but not the violence that he left behind) and navigating this inhospitable environment with the help of a new family unit that comprises himself, Hassan, and Sy(ed), two older boys from Syria and Afghanistan respectively. All three novels establish the intimacy of and trust in family only to then put those close relations in suspension. For these writers, the malfunction of family life is attended by disruptions of the domestic order which manifest themselves in discarded opportunities for play; on the other hand, play also functions as a form of escape from the burdens of despair, anguish, and anger about living in these degraded circumstances, as well as a sign of a self able to go on hoping for a better future.

At least initially, then, family games in these three books provide temporary relief from the horrors and uncertainties of Adam's, Omar's, and Mico's new realities. In an early scene from *The Boy from Aleppo Who Painted the War*, Adam is delighted when his father offers to play games with him, and after they are joined by his brothers and sister; with the whole family playing cards and having tea together, he feels that he can "almost forget about the bombing" (44). In another passage, Adam's family are shown playing ball games on a short visit to the seaside, and the boy can momentarily dismiss from his mind the war raging back home, but on their return to Aleppo "a dark square rests on [his] heart, pushing it down" (65). A similar moment of family intimacy is presented in *Welcome to Nowhere*, in which Omar's family – having already fled their home in Bosra and then their grandmother's house in Daraa, for a farming village – are enjoying a summer picnic during which the children are chasing each other and playing football: "[T] here was something golden about that afternoon," Omar says. "I felt – don't know why – a rush of love for all my family, and . . . looking round at all of them, it was as if I was noticing things I'd never noticed before" (157). That the togetherness offered by play can provide a useful, if often illusory, safety net for a traumatized child still experiencing conflict is also true for *The Jungle*'s Mico, for whom getting together with Hassan and Sy for games such as dominoes, cards, or *carrom* in their shared tent makes it possible to "forget the world that was waiting outside to swallow him up" (61). These and similar episodes ensure that readers are aware of the depth of the bonds that are endangered by the violent conflicts these families are trying to escape. At the same time, if we accept Levinas's assertion, made in his *Totality and Infinity* (1961/1991), that the child's introduction to ethical responsibility for the other comes through family, then the intimacies thus constructed take on an ethical meaning.

To assert the ethical importance of familial intimacies is not to say that the family bonds referred to in such passages stand out symbolically against the surrounding violence (and counter-violence) throughout these novels. These devotions and intimacies are nowhere to be found, for instance, in the scene in *The Boy from Aleppo Who Painted the War* in which Adam and his sister, Yasmine, ask their father to play a board game with them, but the now mentally unstable and physically deteriorating Baba becomes confused by their questions and acts violently toward the boy, hurting Adam's hand (91); that the experience of war is starting to define this family is also evident when Adam hears his older brothers talking about the turbulent political atmosphere in Syria in voices that "sound like bullets," their words causing him physical pain (56). *Welcome to Nowhere*, too, offers a portrait of a "family . . . falling apart" during their first few weeks in Za'atari refugee camp (220) and with his parents and older brother, Musa, crippled by feelings of pity, anger, and pain, Omar is left running errands and taking care of other family members while looking on enviously as his six-year-old brother Fuad roams around the camp with other young children. As *The Jungle* progresses, Puri presents a similarly fractured family: increasingly desperate and bitterly disillusioned with the French police, lawyers, and authorities, Hassan and Sy quarrel over the government's response to the refugees' plight and start to avoid each other; Mico now finds the atmosphere in their tent to be "hot as a rocket, fully charged and ready to explode" (60) and learns that Sy sold the football with which they all used to play (67–68), a move that could be seen as foreshadowing Sy's subsequent readiness to betray the other boys' trust.

Yet the ethical significance of the family, according to Levinas, lies in the "infinity of responsibility" for the other that emerges primarily from one's relations to family members (244). For Levinas, family is not just a "step toward the anonymous universality of the State"; it "[i]dentifies itself outside of the state," which reduces the other to the same and allows one's own subjectivity to be "for others" (Levinas,

Totality and Infinity 306, 46, *Otherwise Than Being* 107). Levinas thus posits a model of a sociality that arises from filiality. That is what the characters in Sukkar's, Laird's, and Puri's novels ultimately gain from the intimacy of the family: an infinite world of possibility that comes with responsibility for others' lives and often involves what Higonnet reminds us are "peaceful games" ("War Games" 13). As we consider the possibilities inherent in Adam's recording of – or bearing witness to – the lives and deaths that he sees ("One day, when the war finishes, I'll have my paintings to show people what was really going on. My paintings don't lie" (Sukkar 191)) and his family's efforts to look out for their neighbors and, later, for the people they meet on their journey from Aleppo to Damascus or Omar's new role as the "big daddy of the Hooligans, a bunch of fatherless brats" running wild in the camp and Musa's storytelling sessions for these children (Laird 264, 325) or else Mico's continued attempts to help the most vulnerable inhabitants of the Jungle and Hassan's plans for a little theatre for the camp's younger children (Puri 212), we will keep in mind how children's novels about recovery from traumas caused by terror can also transform the child reader's mental landscape, opening it up to ethical awareness and consideration.

A Game of Soldiers

The impact of terrorism and counter-terrorism upon the preoccupations of children is also addressed in Kerry Drewery's *A Brighter Fear* (2012), David Massey's *Torn* (2013), and Phil Earle's *Heroic* (2013). The three novels are focused through adolescent protagonists caught up or participating in the wars in Iraq or Afghanistan and register these young people's reactions to the violations of childhood that they witness. Set in Iraq during the early stages of its invasion, *A Brighter Fear* tells the story of Lina, a teenage girl growing up in US-occupied Baghdad in which, "where the children used to play, [there were] now . . . piles of soil and dust in rows," and where "trigger-happy soldiers . . . looked like school children" (210, 174). *Torn* and *Heroic* allow a glimpse into the West's military decisions and strategic considerations in the current Afghan conflict: the former adopts the perspective of Elinor, a young medic learning to cope with the exigencies of war on her first tour of duty, whereas the latter alternates between the viewpoints of Jammy – a soldier in his late teens whose first tour is also his best friend Tommo's – and Sonny, Jammy's younger brother who is shown trying to come to terms first with his brother's absence and then with his war-scarred presence back in England. On the one hand, the teenage characters in these books have clearly been deprived of the normal preoccupations of adolescence: Lina wishes she could go to classes, see her friends, and do "[n]ormal, everyday, ordinary things" instead of learning "what gun makes what kind of noise," "what IED and RPG stood for," or "what the stripes on soldiers' uniforms meant" (Drewery 97–98); Elinor finds it "hard seeing what [Western] bombs have done" to civilians' lives and worries when her fellow soldiers, many of whom joined the army straight out of school, turn the daily experiences of war into jokes ("the more extrovert you are, the more you internalize the bad stuff. In training they said guys like [that] go home and get hit by post-traumatic stress") (Massey 16, 34); in *Heroic*, we are told that Jammy and Sonny's town "had been ordinary," but "everything changed when the Twin Towers came down" and "[s]uddenly, there were more people in uniform than ever . . . on the estate: flyering, persuading, filling shaven heads full of dreams," so now what "gave everyone a purpose" were the numerous funeral parades for young soldiers killed in action (8, 9). On the other hand, affecting these characters especially powerfully are cases of younger children being, to use Lisa Sainsbury's words, "denied childness" (79; see also McMahan 2006), cases which depend for their power on the incongruity between innocence and experience, children's play and terror. Indeed, the wars around terror are presented in these novels as wars on childhood, as we see children being injured, killed, or themselves acting as frontline fighters as a result of such conflicts; these children are offered as victims (or, in the case of the child soldier, as what Sainsbury describes as the "ultimate victim-perpetrator" (71)) whose rights to learn and play have been taken away from them and whose quests for stability or redemption are deferred indefinitely (Walsh 192).

It is worth noting that the three writers make the figure of the child soldier embody terror's contaminating effects more generally, as they are not interested in the extent to which children might incorporate extremist ideology when they are forcibly drawn into the war machine. Rather, the image of a child with a gun arising in their works has very much the same shock value as that used by UNICEF and other international child protection agencies to highlight the problem of child recruitment by terrorist groups (see, for instance, Rosen 2005); such images are of particular interest insofar as they bear on other characters' perspectives on the war. In *A Brighter Fear*, Lina's father, Joe, a local interpreter for the US troops occupying Baghdad, is killed in an exchange of fire between the American soldiers and a young boy with a "full-sized gun, not a toy," who is only "playing at being a soldier" (67). Ironically, this happens mere moments after one of the soldiers "showed [Joe] a photo of his little brother playing in the Texan desert with a toy rifle" while longing to be a soldier himself (65), and later on, Lina is thinking of how modern-day American soldiers have "made their nationality and their patriotism seep down their arms to their hands holding their weapons and their fingers resting on their triggers," the word "terrorism" now "draw[ing] breath deeper and quicker than any four-letter word could" (74). On the other side of the conflict, *Torn*'s Elinor finds that child soldiers stir up memories of her younger brother, which adds to her confusion about "this stupid war [in which] . . . nothing is simple, nothing is black and white" (161), while Jammy in *Heroic* is unable to shoot at a "a kid, [his] age, [his] height, a shaking pistol in his hand and two semi-automatic rifles slung across his back" because he reminds him of a local boy about whose death he feels guilty (264), the moment of hesitation resulting in his friend Tommo's death. And while the Western soldiers in Massey's and Earle's novels are concerned with restoring the opportunities for innocent play to the vulnerable children around them as part of a wider campaign to secure the local people's trust, such efforts only end up putting them in even greater danger, as when Jammy and his fellow soldiers decide to teach the local boys some football tricks, with Jammy bringing them a brand new ball from the camp ("Fills me up to see them acting like they should be," one of the more experienced soldiers tells him after a game kicks off, "It's them who misses out in all this mess. . . . But all it takes is one pair of eyes to notice, and it could all get messy" (114)), only to witness a little boy being blown apart a few weeks later by a bomb hidden in the football by Afghan terrorists.

Viewed from this perspective, *A Brighter Fear*, *Torn*, and *Heroic* provide an understanding of what is at stake for the different parties in the wars around terror. Without sidestepping the suffering and damage that the terrorist aims to inflict, these texts raise important questions about the presence of Western armed forces in countries like Iraq and Afghanistan. Thus, if the books register the young soldiers' need for the "goodness promised by political ideology" (Sainsbury 71), they also show that goodness being repeatedly denied to them in reality. In *Heroic*, for example, being able to connect to Afghan children through football, Jammy feels that he is "finally making a difference": "If this was what being a soldier meant," he thinks, "then maybe I could hack it after all" (111). Later, however, "with the events of the bombing looped in [his] head," he finds himself telling the army doctor that the little boy's death "reminds [him] why we're here. Sharpens the resolve. . . . There's so much still to do" while realizing that he is, in effect, telling lies (242). Elinor has a similarly violent reaction to a child's death in Massey's *Torn*; she deems the "contrast between innocence and the wild reality of war" to be "sickening" (69), and even though she complies with a senior officer's request to win the trust of an Afghan boy found with an AK-47 (and, to that end, promises to play football with him), we also see her wondering "if they'll even hear about [children dying in the war] on the news back home" and doubting that this is the case (85). In parallel with these young recruits' loss of confidence in what is advertised as the West's "virtuous militancy" (Houen 574), the civilians in these texts are shown to question the rightness of the actions and motives of foreign military operating in their countries: "[S]o much had been promised for our futures: freedom, democracy, a better life," reflects Drewery's Lina (139), yet she herself no longer believes that Western soldiers "have any answers for [the Iraqi people]" or that "they know what to do" (170); *Heroic*'s soldiers who attempt to collect intelligence about the drugs trafficked by the Taliban are asked by the locals why they "didn't . . . concentrate on rebuilding houses flattened by [their] air strikes" or "[b]ring medicine for the kids hit by [their] shrapnel" (43). Readers are thus encouraged to work thoughtfully and critically to pull together Western and non-Western perspectives on the wars on terror rather than unquestionably support these wars and the policies that attend them. The novels' repeated association of terror, soldiering, and suspended or disrupted play ultimately attests to the precarious character of a child's life and turns the reader's gaze toward the human cost of these conflicts.

Conclusion

What happens to children in the sample of texts considered here serves to underscore their increased vulnerability in an age of terror. In these recent novels, children's writers have variously explored terrorism's effects by relating the traumas inflicted by terrorism and the wars against it to matters of intimacy, responsibility, play, and imagination. By narrating hardship and pain – but also recovery and resistance – these texts envision a better future for the futureless yet prompt us to bear witness to both their past and present. Their engagements with terrorism and play offer ways of working through and thinking beyond terror while encouraging a more critical response to its operations and repercussions. Direct accounts from either the families of terrorism's victims or participants in the wars linked to terror are often missing from narratives of counter-terrorism, but writing for children can become an aesthetic means of investigating the experience of terror and of representing complex socio-political and ethical issues to a young audience.

Note

1. A reworked version of Blanka Grzegorczyk's chapter appeared as chapter 1 in her monograph *Terror and Counter-Terror in Contemporary British Children's Literature* (Routledge, 2020).

Works Cited

Agnew, Kate, and Geoff Fox. *Children at War: From the First World War to the Gulf*. Continuum, 2001.

Bruton, Catherine. *We Can Be Heroes*. Egmont, 2011.

Drewery, Kerry. *A Brighter Fear*. HarperCollins Children's Books, 2012.
Earle, Phil. *Heroic*. London: Penguin Books, 2013.
Higonnet, Margaret R. "War Games." *The Lion and the Unicorn*, vol. 22, no. 1, 1998, pp. 1–17.
———. "Time Out: Trauma and Play in *Johnny Tremain* and *Alan and Naomi.*" *Children's Literature*, vol. 33, 2005, pp. 150–70.
———. "War Toys: Breaking and Remaking in Great War Narratives." *The Lion and the Unicorn*, vol. 31, no. 2, 2007, pp. 116–31.
Houen, Alex. "Reckoning Sacrifice in 'War on Terror' Literature." *American Literary History*, vol. 28, no. 3, 2016, 574–95.
Kuznets, Lois R. *When Toys Come Alive: Narratives of Animation, Metamorphosis, and Development*. Yale UP, 1994.
Laird, Elizabeth. *Welcome to Nowhere*. Macmillan Children's Books, 2017.
Levinas, Emmanuel. *Otherwise Than Being, or, Beyond Essence*, translated by Alphonso Lingis. 1974. Kluwer Academic Publishers, 1991.
———. *Totality and Infinity*, translated by Alphonso Lingis. 1961. Kluwer Academic Publishers, 1991.
Massey, David. *Torn*. Chicken House, 2012.
McMahan, Jeff. "Child Soldiers: The Ethical Perspective." 2007, https://www.files.ethz.ch/isn/45682/2007_Child_Soldiers_Ethical.pdf. Accessed 25 May 2017.
Pitcher, Annabel. *My Sister Lives on the Mantelpiece*. 2011. Indigo, 2013.
Puri, Pooja. *The Jungle*. Ink Road, 2017.
Rosen, David M. *Armies of the Young: Child Soldiers in War and Terrorism*. Rutgers UP, 2005.
Sainsbury, Lisa. *Ethics in British Children's Literature: Unexamined Life*. Bloomsbury, 2013.
Sukkar, Sumia. *The Boy from Aleppo Who Painted the War*. Eyewear Publishing, 2013.
Walsh, John. "Coming of Age with an AK-47: Ahmadou Kourouma's *Allah n'est pas oblige*." *Research in African Literatures*, vol. 39, no. 1, 2008, pp. 185–97.
Winnicott, D. W. "Transitional Objects and Transitional Phenomena: A Study of the First Not-Me Possession." 1951. *International Journal of Psycho-Analysis*, vol. 34, 1953, pp. 89–97.

Part 2

Constructs of Children's Agency in Representations of Childhood and Play

7 Branching out from the Family Tree

Fairy Tales, Imaginative Play, and Intergenerational Relations in Works by the Brothers Grimm, Ludwig Tieck, and Hans Christian Andersen

Elliott Schreiber

The first half of the nineteenth century witnessed the flourishing of the genre of the fairy tale for children in German-speaking Europe. The most famous compilers of such fairy tales are, of course, the brothers Jacob and Wilhelm Grimm, the first edition of whose *Children's and Household Tales* (*Kinder- und Hausmärchen* [*KHM*]) appeared in 1812 (volume 1) and 1815 (volume 2). Their collection built on the interest in *Volkspoesie* generated by Johann Gottfried Herder's anthology of folksongs at the end of the eighteenth century, and by Achim von Arnim and Clemens Brentano's own folksong anthology, *Des Knaben Wunderhorn* (The Boy's Wonder Horn, 1805–8), to which the Grimms contributed significantly. While all of these early folkloric projects engage critically with the literary, intellectual, and social transformations wrought by modernity, the Grimms' collection further responds in an implicit way to Napoleon's invasion and occupation of German lands, including the Grimms' native Hesse. With the publication of their tales, they attempted to safeguard a cultural legacy that they claimed had been passed down through the generations and subtended German national identity (Schreiber 23–27; Tatar 392).

The Grimms' fairy tales gradually attained wide popularity over the course of their lifetimes. However, their contemporaries such as Ludwig Tieck and Hans Christian Andersen also incisively challenged their understanding of fairy tales as a form of cultural patrimony requiring faithful conservation. Tieck and Andersen, two of the most revered authors of their day, instead emphasize the way in which fairy tales originate from children's capacity for imaginative play. As a result, these two authors embrace, rather than resist, radical transformation as central to the evolution of fairy tales. Despite this commonality, Tieck and Andersen each draw different conclusions about how fairy tales and imaginative play relate to one another. An important consequence of this divergence is that they also have very different visions of how older and younger generations interrelate. While Tieck, in his fairy tale "The Elves" ("Die Elfen" 1812), regards these relationships in terms of contestation, Andersen's "The Elder-Tree Mother" ("Hyldemoer" 1844) underscores their playful reciprocity. Andersen thereby prefigures an important paradigm in today's understanding of intergenerational imaginative play and storytelling, Dorothy and Jerome Singer's concept of a partnership in play between children and adults.[1] In tracing the genealogy of this paradigm, I attend to a prominent image that recurs in the texts of the Grimms, Tieck, and Andersen, namely that of the tree. I aim to elucidate how these authors use the motif of the tree to explore the nexus of fairy tales, imaginative play, and intergenerational relations. Further, I locate these authors themselves within a kind of family tree, a discourse across generations that branches out in unexpected directions.

Intergenerational Continuity and Discontinuity in the Grimms' *Children's and Household Tales*

The title *Children's and Household Tales* draws a close connection between fairy tales on the one hand and the familial realm on the other. The paratextual material with which the Grimms preface the first edition of their collection stresses how fairy tales reinforce ties within families between generations. This is already evident in their dedication:

An
die Frau
Elisabeth von Arnim
für
den kleinen
Johannes Freimund.
(To Mrs. Elisabeth von Arnim for the young Johannes Freimund. [*KHM* 1: III]; translation mine)

Ingeborg Weber-Kellermann has argued that the Grimms' collection appeared at a juncture in history when "a bourgeois sense for family had been developed" and that it became "the book read to children by mothers and grandmothers" (14; quoted in Zipes, *Fairy Tales* 60). I would push this argument a step further: beginning with their dedication to the wife of their friend and mentor and their young son, the Grimms offer their collection as a medium that strengthens the bond between mother and child, and they thereby actively contribute to shaping a bourgeois sensibility for intergenerational family relations.

The preface that follows the dedication in the first volume suggests that fairy tales are so well suited to forging intergenerational bonds because these tales themselves retain a living connection with their own distant ancestry. The Grimms trace this connection all the way back to a timeless, quasi-divine source, "the eternal wellspring that bedews all life" (*Annotated Brothers Grimm* 402). They further maintain that their tales preserve this source, "even if it is only a single drop enclosed by a small, protective leaf" (402). A year later, in their preface to the first volume of a compendium of scholarly writings on old German literature, *Altdeutsche Wälder* (Old German Forests, 1813), the Grimms return to this metaphor, depicting such literature as a "dew-wet tree" (III; translation mine). Indeed, the image of the tree, which they inherit from Herder, assumes a paradigmatic function both in their theoretical writings as well as in many of their fairy tales such as "The Juniper Tree." Just as the leaves of a tree are connected via branches, stem, and roots to water and earth, so the tales in their collection maintain a living connection with their "eternal wellspring" or what the Grimms also refer to as their ancient "ground" ("Grund" [*KHM* 1: XIII-XIV]; translation mine). The Grimms' conception of the precise nature of this source varies: while in the previously quoted passage they refer to it as the universal source of all life, toward the end of their preface they draw a distinction between specifically German and "foreign sources" (406). What remains constant, however, is the notion of this tradition as a kind of family tree that grounds the present form of fairy tales in a distant past.

The Grimms perceive the continuity of this lineage to be under threat. They open their preface with another organic metaphor that draws attention to this threat, comparing their fairy tales with ears of grain that have survived a ravaging storm and that poor peasants gather "ear upon ear, carefully bound" (*Annotated* 401). Although the Grimms never spell out the precise significance of the image of the storm, it invites association with modernity's winds of change, as well as with the transformations effected in their day under Napoleon's occupation, such as efforts to impose the Code Napoleon, which the Grimms' mentor at the University of Marburg, Karl Friedrich von Savigny, claimed "still devoured German institutions like a cancer" (cited in Sheehan 549). Despite such onslaughts, the continuity of tradition is maintained with the help of those who collect and cherish fairy tales. Even in modern times, then, fairy tales continue to connect generations past, present, and future: in the Grimms' formulation "ear upon ear, carefully bound" ("Aehre an Aehre gelegt, sorgfältig gebunden" [*KHM* 1: V]) can be heard the homophone "Aera an Aera," or "era upon era." However, fairy tales can only forge such a connection across generations if they have active recipients, that is, if they are cultivated, collected, and passed down to future generations, just as a peasant works the land, harvests a crop, and sets aside "perhaps the only seed for the future" (401).

The Grimms style themselves as just such custodians:

> We have tried to collect these tales in as pure a form as possible. . . . No details have been added or embellished or changed, for we would have been reluctant to expand stories already so rich by adding analogies and allusions. They cannot be invented. A collection of this kind has never existed in Germany. The tales have almost always been used as the stuff of longer stories, which have been expanded and edited at the author's pleasure. To be sure, they had some value for that purpose, but what belonged to children was always torn out of their hands, and nothing was given back to them in return.
>
> (*Annotated* 406)

The Grimms thus claim that their collection preserves fairy tales in their pure, original form, without transforming them in any way, unlike previous collections that, by altering the tales through "analogy and allusion" ("Analogie oder Reminiscenz" (*KHM* 1: XVIII), deprive children of their just inheritance.[2] Two years later, in the preface to the second volume of their tales, they further underscore their fidelity to their sources by recounting the way in which they transcribed verbatim the tales related to them by a peasant woman, Dorothea Viehmann, who herself "preserves these stories firmly ["fest"]in her memory" and can repeat them without altering them in the least (*KHM* 2: V; translation mine). They reinforce this firmness by further describing Viehmann as having "a

Figure 7.1 Frontispiece to vol. 2 of the second edition of *Kinder- und Hausmärchen* (1819) with an etching of Dorothea Viehmann by Ludwig Emil Grimm

firmly set, pleasant face with bright, clear eyes" (408), characteristics that their brother Ludwig Emil Grimm highlights in his etching of Viehmann for the frontispiece of the second edition of their fairytales (1819; see Fig. 1). In her firm "[d]evotion to tradition," Viehmann is portrayed by the Grimms as representative of the peasantry as a whole (408).[3]

Despite upholding Viehmann as their model storyteller, the Grimms also recognize that the German fairy tale tradition cannot entirely avoid change. Indeed, they painstakingly record numerous variants of their tales. However, they regard supposedly "natural" variants, unlike modern, "artificial" renditions, as retaining the core of the tradition: "Never fixed and always changing from one region to another, from one teller to another, they still preserve a basic core ["Grund"]" (*Annotated* 404; *KHM* 1: XIII). In other words, to return to the guiding metaphor of the tree, German fairy tales may indeed evolve over time, comprising "a constantly branching tradition" (Bottigheimer 5), but each branch still preserves a vital, common connection with its original "ground."

Intergenerational Contestation in Tieck's "The Elves"

Among the likely intended targets of the Grimms' critical remarks about modern fairy-tale collections was Ludwig Tieck's *Volksmährchen* (Folktales, 1797–98). Tieck reissued a number of these earlier fairy tales in modified form, along with three new ones, in the first volume of his collection *Phantasus* (1812). In 1811, when he wrote these new tales, including "The Elves" – his "most child-friendly fairy tale," in the words of Manfred Frank (1327) – Tieck would almost certainly have been familiar with the Grimms' views on folklore.[4] He shared their reverence for old Germanic literature and lore, which "The Elves" and many other texts in *Phantasus* tap into. However, as Thomas Meißner argues,

> [i]t is ultimately not without literary-historical significance that Grimms' *Children's and Household Tales* and Tieck's *Phantasus*, the most important collections of fairy tales by the younger and older Romantics, appeared in the same year and with the same publisher. One could see both works as fundamentally contrasting with one another.
>
> (295; translation mine)

While Tieck's "The Elves" draws on a rich European tradition of stories about elves (Frank 1328), it highlights the importance of a very different point of origin for fairy tales, namely each child's capacity for imaginative play. As a consequence, Tieck's tale departs from the Grimms' portrayal of the relation between older and younger generations, which in Tieck's view are no longer necessarily bound by a common fairy tale tradition.

Before engaging with Tieck's tale, it is helpful to have a sense of the broader discourse of children's play around 1800. The Enlightenment thinkers John Locke, Jean-Jacques Rousseau, and their pedagogical disciples in Germany developed a keen appreciation for many forms of children's play. However, it was not until the close of the eighteenth century that the particular form that the twentieth-century psychologist Jean Piaget termed imaginative or symbolic play came to be conceptualized and recognized as integral to children's development. Johann Wolfgang Goethe evokes this type of play especially vividly in *Wilhelm Meister's Apprenticeship* (*Wilhelm Meisters Lehrjahre*, 1795), in which Wilhelm remarks, "[w]hen playing, children know how to make everything from everything: a staff becomes a rifle, a little piece of wood a rapier, every little bundle a puppet, and every corner a hut" (14).[5] Wilhelm makes these remarks while recounting the story of his childhood passion for theatrical play, beginning with puppet play. In the second book of *Poetry and Truth* (*Dichtung und Wahrheit*, 1811), Goethe uncovers the autobiographical basis of Wilhelm's infatuation. Goethe credits his own puppet play as a child with exercising his capacity for invention and representation as well as his imagination (48). Precisely in this context, he relates a fairy tale, entitled "The New Paris" ("Der neue Paris"), that he claims to have composed as a seven-year-old (49–59). This autobiographical framing suggests that his so-called boyhood fairy tale (49) arose out of his imaginative play, as does the fact that such play figures centrally within the fairy tale itself. In short, Goethe suggests the birth of the fairy tale from the spirit of imaginative play.[6]

Tieck published "The Elves" a year after the appearance of the first volume of Goethe's autobiography. Play is at the heart of Tieck's fairy tale, as intimated already in its opening lines:

> Where is Marie, our child? asked the father.
>
> She is playing outside on the green with our neighbor's son, replied the mother.
>
> ("Die Elfen" 306)[7]

Already in the second sentence of the text, then, the central character, Marie, is associated with play. Significantly, her play does not involve her parents, who are separated from her in two ways: at first they are inside the house while she is playing outside, and after her mother brings out an evening snack, she and her husband leave to inspect the fields that they farm, working while their daughter plays with another child, Andres, the son of a neighbor.

After her parents leave, Marie and Andres agree to race to the top of a hill. Marie decides to cheat and take a shortcut through a "fir-tree dell" ("Tannengrund") that both her father and Andres believe to be inhabited by "gypsies and thieves" (310) and that her parents have declared off-limits. Marie is astounded to find a realm of brightness and abundance, and a kind child named Zerina who invites Marie to join her in play. Marie and Zerina's "beautiful game" (311) is characterized by numerous magical transformations. Zerina strews grains of "gleaming pollen" onto the ground:

> Instantly the grass began to stir, as in waves; and, after a few moments, gleaming rose-bushes shot up from the ground, grew rapidly, and suddenly unfolded, while the sweetest perfume filled the place. Maria, as well, took a little of the dust, and when she scattered it, she saw white lilies, and the most colorful carnations, pushing up. At a signal from Zerina, the flowers disappeared, and others rose in their place.
>
> (311)

Their game grows even more wondrous as Zerina places pine seeds into the ground, and pine trees shoot up and lift her and Marie into the clouds, until the trees sink into the ground again and set the children back down. This entire passage detailing Marie and Zerina's play contains a rich variety of metamorphoses. Of these, the most apparent are the almost instantaneous transformation of grains of pollen into rose bushes; the vanishing of one set of flowers and the appearance of others in their place; and the immediate growth of the tall pine trees out of the seeds. In addition, there are several metamorphoses that occur on a more subtle textual level: the transformation of Marie into Maria; the interchangeability of dust ("Staub") and pollen ("Samenstaub"); the metaphorical transformation of grass into waves; and the anthropomorphosis of the pine trees, which pick the children up and set them back down on the ground. This imagery recalls the metaphor of the tree as used by Herder and the Brothers Grimm. However, there is no hint in Tieck's tale that trees symbolize the continuity of an ancient folkloric tradition. Rather, in their constant state of change, they suggest the child's capacity "to make everything from everything," to transform the surrounding world through imaginative play. Tieck stresses that such play is the province of children, not adults. Thus, when Marie first enters the elves' realm, her parents' domain becomes concealed: "and now she stood in the dell ["Grund"], and the fir trees all around hid her parental home from view" (309). The trees in this passage, then, form a barrier between Marie and her parents. To the extent that Tieck's use of tree imagery retains the Grimms' association with a family tree, it shifts the emphasis away from the intergenerational axis and onto the intragenerational, uniting the children whom Marie refers to as "my sisters" as they all play on the trees: "the other little children climbed up and down the tree trunks with quick dexterity" (311).

After playing with Zerina and the other children, Marie is taken on a tour of the elves' bountiful domain that lasts all day and night and into the next day. Before she returns home, the elves ask her "not to tell anyone about us, for otherwise we will have to flee this region, and everyone around, and you yourself, will lose the fortune and blessing of our being close by" (317). When Marie arrives home, she finds out that she has, in fact, been away for a full seven years. She marries Andres, her playmate from childhood, and together they have a daughter, whom she names Elfriede in memory of the elves. The village prospers. One day, though, Marie discovers that Zerina has been playing with her daughter, which she decides to keep a secret from Andres. But when he expresses the wish that the inhabitants of the fir-tree dell be driven away, Marie feels she has no other choice than "to tell him the story of her youth" (324). Her broken promise triggers catastrophe: the elves take flight, and the bounty of the village and its surroundings vanishes, along with the health and good fortune of Marie and her family.

What, then, does Tieck's tale tell us about the relationship between imaginative play and the genre of the fairy tale, and how does this relationship impact the dynamic between younger and older generations? I would like to argue that the tale's main character, Marie, embodies the genre of the fairy tale. Hence, the diminutive form of her name, Mariechen, which appears twice in the tale (314, 318), closely resembles the German word for fairy tale, *Märchen*. Given the importance of names in Tieck's work generally and in this story in particular, this resemblance is unlikely a mere coincidence. After all, it is Marie who narrates "the story of her youth," and I would like to suggest that this story should be seen as a fairy tale. For Tieck, as for Goethe, then, the fairy tale emerges out of imaginative play and harkens back to it. However, Tieck perceives a fundamental dilemma: in disclosing the transformative power of imaginative play, the fairy tale disrupts this very power. Though born of imaginative play, the fairy tale also breaks with it, betraying its very source, its *Grund*.

Why the fairy tale should break with its source in imaginative play becomes clear when one considers the second account given of the inhabitants of the fir-tree dell, namely the story told by Marie's father, by Andres, and by several other members of their village. Six times throughout Tieck's tale, these characters refer to the inhabitants as gypsies (307, 308, 310, 320, 325), and in three of these instances, they also refer to them as robbers (307, 310, 320; see also 324). Thus, in the opening scene of the story, Marie's father calls them "gypsy people who rob and swindle in distant places, and perhaps have their hideout here" (307). This account involves a transformation, the fabrication of "gypsies and thieves" out of the precious little information that the villagers have gleaned about those living within the fir-tree dell. As such, imaginative play underlies this account, too. The problem for Tieck lies not with this transformation as such but with the fact that the story told by Marie's father, Andres, and the other villagers fixes this transformation in place; hence, the story's stubborn continuity both longitudinally (across generations, from Marie's father to Andres) and latitudinally (across the village), a continuity that strongly resonates with the way the Brothers Grimm conceive of the transmission of fairy tales, particularly among the peasantry, in whose milieu Tieck sets his story. Tieck critiques precisely such continuity, for it freezes transformation in place, thereby bringing the process of imaginative play to a standstill. In other words, the fairy tale uproots imaginative play in the act of conserving it. It is thus fitting that, at the end of the tale, the narrator notes that "the woods died away, and the springs ran dry" (327).

In sum, Tieck points to conflict as marking the relationship between the fairy tale and imaginative play, as well as between older and younger generations. On the one hand, his tale displays the manner in which a child's imaginative play can contest the stories she inherits: "So you are no gypsies and thieves," a surprised Marie tells Zerina upon first meeting her, challenging the prevailing narrative (310). By the same token, fairy tales, though they arise out of imaginative play, rupture such play. In so doing, they can arouse animosity on the part of children, as happens with the eternally young Zerina, who, upon being interrupted by Marie and Anders as she plays with their daughter Elfriede, suddenly "grew pale, and trembled violently; not with friendly, but with indignant looks, she made the sign of threatening" (324). In contrast to the Brothers Grimm, then, fairy tales, far from mediating between generations, can generate resentment on the part of children. In an ironic role reversal, this is the very attitude that Tieck, a founding member of the older generation of Romantics, appears to take regarding the conception of fairy tales propagated by the Brothers Grimm, members of the new Romantic generation.[8]

Intergenerational Reconciliation in H.C. Andersen's "The Elder-Tree Mother"

Tieck's critique of the fixity of fairy tales raises the question of whether another type of fairy tale might be possible, one that promotes rather than arrests the transformation inherent in imaginative play and that thereby also heals the intergenerational divisions that Tieck's tale exposes. Approximately three decades later, Hans Christian Andersen takes up just this question. In his German autobiography, *Das Märchen meines Lebens ohne Dichtung* (The Fairy Tale of My Life without Poetry, 1847) – a title that clearly alludes to Goethe's autobiography – Andersen describes how he met Tieck during his first voyage to Germany in 1831. It was Tieck, he writes, who gave him "in my second fatherland the consecrating kiss," thereby ordaining Andersen as poet (1: 82–83). In Andersen's recollection, then, Tieck assumes a distinctly fatherly persona. Andersen goes on to praise Tieck's "The Elves" as "perhaps the most beautiful fairy tale that has been composed in our time" (2: 112). Three years earlier, Andersen already formulated a response to Tieck's fairy tale in one of his lesser-known, albeit most fascinating, fairy tales, "The Elder-Tree Mother." Perhaps the most obvious allusion to Tieck's tale is its mention of "fairy tales of elves and goblins" ("The Elder-Tree Mother" 202). But Andersen does not merely rehearse Tieck's tale; instead, he playfully – but no less radically – subverts it, re-envisioning the relationship between imaginative play and fairy tales as symbiotic rather than antagonistic.[9]

Andersen's fairy tale is composed of three intertwining stories that revolve around imaginative play. The first of these, the frame story, features three characters: a young boy who is sick in bed; his mother, who makes him a pot of elder tea; and an old neighbor who is a storyteller – a multi-generational cast of characters bound by mutual affection, as conveyed by Lorenz Frølich's illustration accompanying the first appearance of the tale, which has the distinction of being the first Danish illustration of one of Andersen's fairy tales (see Fig. 2).[10] The boy asks the old man for a story, remarking, "Mother says that everything you look at can be turned into a story, and that you can make a tale of everything you touch." The mother and son, then, credit the storyteller with an ability that is very much akin to imaginative play: "everything you look at can be turned into a story" recalls Goethe's notion that "[w]hen playing, children know how to make everything from everything." This is a first signal that the dichotomies set up by Tieck in "The Elves" – between the fairy tale and imaginative play, between children and adults – have begun to dissolve.

Rather than offer a story straightaway, the old man instead empowers the boy with creative agency, asking him to "[l]ook! There's one [a story] in the teapot now!" (199). At this injunction, the boy looks toward the teapot and sees

> the lid slowly raise itself and fresh white elder flowers come forth from it. They shot long branches even out of the spout and spread them abroad in all directions, and they grew bigger and bigger until there was the most glorious elder bush – really, a big tree! The branches even stretched to the little boy's bed and thrust the curtains aside – how fragrant its blossoms were! And right in the middle of the tree there sat a sweet-looking old woman in a very strange dress. It was green, as green as the leaves of the elder tree, and it was trimmed with big white elder blossoms; at first, one couldn't tell if this dress was cloth or the living green and flowers of the tree.
>
> (199)

The bed-ridden boy, then, beholds a series of transformations: the elder flowers emerge from the teapot; these in turn shoot out branches;

Figure 7.2 Illustration by Lorenz Frølich from 1845 (Andersen, "Hyldemoer" 204)

Source: Courtesy of the Hans Christian Andersen Museum (Odense, Denmark) which in turn become an elder bush; which in turn becomes a big tree; in which, finally, the Elder-Tree Mother appears. These transformations closely resemble those experienced by Marie while playing with Zerina in "The Elves." They also take these transformations a step further: thus, Andersen fully develops the anthropomorphism subtly implicit in Tieck's description of the magical pine trees such that the figure of the Elder-Tree Mother materializes in the tree.

In describing this series of transformations, Andersen accomplishes a complex feat. On one level, he celebrates the child's potential to engage in imaginative play with minimal adult guidance: the old storyteller merely directs the boy's gaze toward the teapot and suggests that it contains a story. But on another level, of course, Andersen's story performs this imaginative play for its own young audience, recounting for the reader or listener the transformations that the boy witnesses (and presumably initiates) as he gazes at the teapot. The picture is further complicated when we take into account that his story evokes these transformations by means of allusion in the strongest sense of the word, whose roots reach back to the Latin *ludere*, "to play": Andersen's story plays with Tieck's, continuing the series of transformations that Tieck's tale describes. In so doing, Andersen further erases the dividing line drawn by Tieck between imaginative play and the fairy tale. Rather than freeze such play in place, his tale sets it in motion, exemplifying Johan de Mylius' assertion that "[t]o Andersen the fairy tale . . . was an open playground" (173).

Andersen's fairy tale goes on to play not only with Tieck's but also with its own transformations. The transformations in the frame story thus become the jumping-off point for the tale that follows, which begins with the analogy, "A great blooming tree exactly like that stands in New Town" (199). This second story-within-a-story goes on to tell about an old sailor and his wife sitting beneath the elder tree in New Town on their golden anniversary and recollecting how they played together as children: " '[D]o you remember,' said the old sailor, 'when we were very little, how we ran about and played together? It was in this very same yard where we are now, and we put little twigs in the earth and made a garden' " (199). An act of imaginative play, then – the transformations that occur when the sick boy looks at the teapot – grows into a tale which itself begins with a description of imaginative play: the creation of a (living) garden out of (inanimate) twigs.

This second tale, in turn, serves as the seed for the third tale-within-a-tale. In the latter, the Elder-Tree Mother transforms into a young girl, and together she and the sick boy experience an adventure that resembles both Marie's play with Zerina as well as the imaginative play recollected by the old sailor in the second tale. Just as Marie and Zerina are lifted up into the air by the pine tree, so the Elder-Tree Mother "took the little boy out of his bed and laid him against her breast, and the blossoming elder branches wound close around them so that it was as if they were sitting in a thick arbor, and this arbor flew with them through the air!" (200). And like the second tale within Andersen's fairy tale, the third one proceeds with a description of imaginative play:

> Hand in hand they went out of the arbor, and now they were standing in the beautiful flower garden at home. Near the green lawn, the walking stick of the little boy's father was tied to a post, and for the little children, there was magical life in that stick. When they seated themselves upon it, the polished head turned into the head of a noble neighing horse with a long, black flowing mane. Four slender, strong legs shot out; the animal was strong and spirited; and they galloped around the grass plot!
>
> (201)

Much as the second of the three intertwining tales begins with an account of children at play transforming twigs into a garden so the third tale commences with a description of children playing with a stick that metamorphoses into a horse.

Andersen's fairy tale thus not only alludes to (and in so doing plays with) Tieck's tale; it also alludes to its own narrative strands. In so doing, it enacts a shift away from Tieck's notion of the fairy tale and toward one that conceives of the fairy tale as endlessly transformative, not only emerging out of imaginative play but also perpetuating such play. Furthermore, its concatenation of allusions suggests that it is up to the reader or listener, once the fairy tale closes, to pick up the thread and spin it in a new direction, that is, to engage in further playful storytelling.

Andersen's fairy tale, whose frame story depicts a mother's effort to heal her sick son through the restorative properties of elder tea, itself attempts to heal two kinds of division exposed in Tieck's critical response to the Brothers Grimm: the differentiation between imaginative play and fairy tales and the rift between younger and older generations. In Andersen's attempt to reconcile these divisions, his use of the curative elder tree (together with botanical imagery more generally) plays a vital function. As in Tieck's tale, the elder tree, in its constant metamorphosis, attests to the child's ability to transform the surrounding world through imaginative play. At the same time, echoing the Grimms' remarks on fairy tales, the tree and its personification in the character of the Elder-Tree Mother symbolize an ancient and still vibrant folkloric tradition. Thus, the Elder-Tree Mother declares toward the end of Andersen's tale: "Some people call me Elder-Tree Mother, and some call me the Dryad, but my real name is Memory. It is I who sit up in the tree that grows on and on, and I can remember and I can tell stories" (203). In synthesizing the perpetual transformation of imaginative play with the continuity of the fairy tale tradition, Andersen also bridges the generational divide. Whereas the Brothers Grimm view intergenerational relations as grounded in a continuous tradition that, at its core, remains unchanging, Andersen regards such relations as invigorated precisely by dynamic change, as one generation playfully, allusively, transforms the tales of its predecessors.

The debate involving the Grimms, Tieck, and Andersen that I have traced in this chapter continues to ramify into our present day. Consider, for instance, the influential work of psychologists Dorothy and Jerome Singer, who for more than forty years have been at the forefront of research into children's imaginative play. Much like Andersen, the Singers emphasize the importance of adults as "partners in play," to borrow from the title of one of their books. As such partners, adults' most important role consists in creating an environment conducive to children's imaginative play, and the Singers point to storytelling as an integral part of such an environment. As Dorothy Singer noted in a recent interview in *The American Journal of Play*, "[r]eading to children, telling stories, and tolerating or encouraging pretending games will influence constructive play in children" (7). This play, in turn, gives rise to further stories:

> Once the game or activity is started . . . the adult should step back somewhat and allow the child to pursue his own direction. What emerges is likely to be an exciting and lively interchange between them around an increasingly imaginative and complex storyline.
>
> (*Partners in Play*, 13)

Figure 7.3 Drawing by Sandy Rabinowitz in Singer and Singer, *Partners in Play* (90)
Source: By permission of the estate of Dorothy Singer

In short, then, the Singers argue that adult storytelling can set the scene for children's self-directed imaginative play, which itself develops storylines propelled by the child with the gentle participation of the adult caregiver (see Fig. 7.3).

In support of this model, the Singers cite a wide range of literary accounts of children's play such as Goethe's (*House of Make-Believe* 1–18). According to the Singers, these accounts "hold up mirrors to our own lives;" they are "a reflection of our common humanity" (*House* viii). What is missing from the Singers' important studies, though – and what I hope the present contribution has conveyed – is a sense of the historicity and diversity of these literary reflections: literature – even texts produced in a single literary period, such as Romanticism – offers very different reflections of imaginative play in its relation to storytelling and of the effect of this dynamic upon intergenerational relations. Put differently, the Singers' work appears as one more branch on a generations-old discursive tree rooted as much in dissensus as in common ground.

Notes

1. After completing this chapter, I learned of Dorothy Singer's passing at age 90 and would like to dedicate it to her memory.
2. The Grimms did in fact introduce numerous changes to the tales they collected, both the first edition of their collection, as well as in the subsequent six editions. See Zipes, "Introduction," xxviii, xxxvi–xlii.
3. Ironically, she was not a peasant but rather the widow of a tailor. See Rölleke and Schindehütte 116–17.
4. For instance, Tieck would very likely have known Jacob Grimm's essay "Gedanken: wie sich die Sagen zur Poesie und Geschichte verhalten" (Thoughts on How Legends Relate to Poetry and History, 1808), published in Achim von Arnim's short-lived *Zeitung für Einsiedler*, which two months previously had published a work by Tieck.
5. I have amended Eric A. Blackall's translation to more closely reflect the original.
6. For a fuller account of Goethe's genealogy of the fairy tale from imaginative play, see Schreiber, "Narcissus at Play."
7. Translations from "The Elves" are my own, and all references are to the German edition edited by Manfred Frank. I have consulted and borrowed from the classic translation by Thomas Carlyle.
8. On Tieck's general dismissiveness toward members of this generation, see Roger Paulin, "Tieck finds most of the younger generation intolerable" (190).
9. Zipes usefully places Andersen in a lineage with German Romantic fairy-tale authors including Tieck and the Brothers Grimm, but in stressing the derivative quality of his fairy tales, he tends to minimize Andersen's interventions in this very lineage ("Critical Reflections" 226).
10. I would like to thank Dr. Ane Grum-Schwensen of the Hans-Christian Andersen Museum in Odense, Denmark, for providing a copy of the illustration and for confirming its status as the first Danish illustration of a tale by Andersen.

Works Cited

Andersen, Hans Christian. "Hyldemoer." *Gæa, æsthetisk Aarbog*, 1845, pp. 204–13.
———. *Das Märchen meines Lebens ohne Dichtung. Eine Skizze*, 2 vols. Carl B. Lorch, 1847.
———. "The Elder-Tree Mother." *Hans Christian Andersen's Complete Fairy Tales*, translated by Jean Hersholt. Canterbury Classics, 2014.
Bottigheimer, Ruth B. *Grimms' Bad Girls & Bold Boys: The Moral & Social Vision of the Tales*. Yale UP, 1987.
de Mylius, Johan. "'Our Time Is the Time of the Fairy Tale': Hans Christian Andersen Between Traditional Craft and Literary Modernism." *Marvels & Tales*, vol. 20, no. 2, 2006, pp. 166–78.
Frank, Manfred. *Commentary*. Tieck, 1985, pp. 1145–520.
Goethe, Johann Wolfgang. *From My Life: Poetry and Truth. Parts One to Three*, translated by Robert R. Heitner, Suhrkamp, 1987.
———. *Wilhelm Meister's Apprenticeship*, edited and translated by Eric A. Blackall in Cooperation with Victor Lange. Suhrkamp, 1989.
Grimm, Jacob. "Gedanken: wie sich die Sagen zur Poesie und Geschichte verhalten." *Zeitung für Einsiedler*, 4 June and 7 June 1808, columns 152–56.
Grimm, Jacob and Wilhelm Grimm. "Preface." *Altdeutsche Wälder*, edited by Jacob and Wilhelm Grimm, vol. 1, Thurneissen, 1813, pp. I–VI.
———. *Kinder- und Hausmärchen gesammelt durch die Brüder Grimm*, 2 vols. 1812 and 1815. Vandenhoeck & Ruprecht, 1986.
———. *The Annotated Brothers Grimm*, edited by Maria Tatar. W.W. Norton, 2004.
Meißner, Thomas. *Erinnerte Romantik: Ludwig Tiecks 'Phantasus'*. Königshausen & Neumann, 2007.
Paulin, Roger. *Ludwig Tieck: A Literary Biography*. Clarendon Press, 1985.
Piaget, Jean. *Play, Dreams and Imitation in Childhood,* translated by C. Gattegno and F. M. Hodgson. W.W. Norton, 1962.
Rölleke, Heinz, and Albert Schindehütte. *Es war einmal . . . Die wahren Märchen der Brüder Grimm und wer sie ihnen erzählte*. Eichborn, 2011.
Schreiber, Elliott. "Tainted Sources: The Subversion of the Grimms' Ideology of the Folktale in Heinrich Heine's *Der Rabbi von Bacherach*." *The German Quarterly*, vol. 78, no. 1, 2005, pp. 23–44.
———. "Narcissus at Play: Goethe, Piaget, and the Passage from Egocentric to Social Play." Forthcoming in *Play in the Age of Goethe: Theories, Narratives, and Practices of Play around 1800*, edited by Edgar Landgraf and Elliott Schreiber. Bucknell University Press, 2020.
Sheehan, James. *German History 1770–1866*. Clarendon Press, 1989.
Singer, Dorothy G., and Jerome L. Singer. *Partners in Play: A Step-by-Step Guide to Imaginative Play in Children*. Harper & Row, 1977.
———. *The House of Make-Believe: Children's Play and the Developing Imagination*. Harvard UP, 1990.
———. "Reflections on Pretend Play, Imagination, and Child Development: An Interview with Dorothy G. and Jerome L. Singer." *The American Journal of Play*, vol. 6, no. 1, Fall 2013, pp. 1–14.
Tatar, Maria. *The Brothers Grimm: Biographical Essay*. Grimm, 2004, pp. 386–96.

Tieck, Ludwig. "The Elves." *German Romance: Specimens of Its Chief Authors; with Biographical and Critical Notices*, edited and translated by Thomas Carlyle, vol. 1. C. Tait, 1827, pp. 118–47.

———. *Die Elfen*. Tieck, 1985, pp. 306–27.

———. *Phantasus*, edited by Manfred Frank. Deutscher Klassiker Verlag, 1985.

Weber-Kellermann, Ingeborg. "Preface." *Kinder- und Hausmärchen gesammelt durch die Brüder Grimm*, edited by Jacob and Wilhelm Grimm, vol. 1, 1974, pp. 9–18.

Zipes, Jack. *Fairy Tales and the Art of Subversion*. Routledge, 1991.

———. "Critical Reflections About Hans Christian Andersen, the Failed Revolutionary." *Marvels & Tales*, vol. 20, no. 2, 2006, pp. 224–37.

———. "Introduction: Rediscovering the Original Tales of the Brothers Grimm." *The Original Folk and Fairy Tales of the Brothers Grimm: The Complete First Edition*, edited by Jack Zipes. Princeton UP, 2014, pp. xix–xliii.

8 Language Play in Adult-Child Relationships

Gianni Rodari's Pedagogical and Literary Concepts

Ilaria Filograsso

Play and Education

Still widely read today, Gianni Rodari's most famous works date back to the 1960s, when the author gained a wide readership and focused on language and techniques for stimulating creativity of his readers. The writer's springboard to fame was the 1960 Einaudi edition of *Filastrocche in cielo e in terra* (*Nursery Rhymes in the Sky and on Earth*), an incredibly successful collection that marked the start of a highly productive decade, correcting and developing on his earlier experiments. In the 1950s, a turbulent political and cultural period in the midst of the Cold War, Rodari wrote for *L'Unità*, an important Communist daily newspaper, and from 1950 to 1953 he served as an editor of the children's weekly magazine *Il Pioniere*. In this decade, his work was marked predominantly by neorealist choices, linked to his Communist militancy and anti-Fascist civil battles. In the 1960s, Rodari began to explore fields beyond left-wing publishing: with *Filastrocche in cielo e in terra* and *Favole al telefono* (1962), followed by *Il libro degli errori* (1964), *Il pianeta degli alberi di Natale* (1962), and *La torta in cielo* (1966), he chose to address "all" children in "all" Italian families, not only those of the working class (Boero 170; Argilli 95). 1969 saw the beginning of the last decade of Rodari's life and work. Having been awarded the Andersen Prize in 1970, he shifted the focus of his works onto the issues of writing, narrative technique, and linguistic invention in various educational contexts, in particular in schools.

Between the late 1950s and the early 1960s, Italy went through a process of economic development and social modernization that other countries had already experienced but in less turbulent rhythms. The rapid industrialization was accompanied by a profound weakening of the agricultural sector. Moreover, massive migration from the South to the North and abroad contributed to the social disintegration in Southern Italy, where state funding could not guarantee autonomous growth. The bourgeoisie from the towns, the urban proletariat and the farming communities fell in step with increasingly standardized consumer models, shifting toward an indistinct middle class. In 1962, the Italian national education system introduced the single middle school reform, with mandatory education increased to the age of fourteen. Schools were greatly affected by the social changes and subjected to huge pressures. Families saw school as a channel for social promotion for themselves and their children, and throughout the 1970s the demand for education increased at such a rate that new teachers had to be urgently recruited. School was assigned the task of supporting the nation's economic and civic growth, which transformed its entire organization, teaching practices, and teacher training to enable it to respond to the needs of the new social composition of the student population.

Emblematic of the cultural and social tensions of the time, *The Grammar of Fantasy* (1973) traces Rodari's cultural and pedagogical itinerary across his stories and his books: in pages packed with scientific and scholarly references, ranging from linguistics to anthropology, the writer became his own critic, reflecting on the inventive processes through which children learn and enjoy all uses of language. For Rodari, the capacity to use words was a cornerstone of democratic education. He believed that all citizens had the right to understand and acquire the power of the word in order to express themselves, communicate, understand others, and establish positive, reciprocal relations with the world. Rodari's pedagogical agenda combined Marxist ideology and its call for a radical transformation of society with proposals clearly inspired by educational movements that promoted a new idea of education and school,[1] where children played the lead role in their own learning and the school was a place of liberation from social and cultural subordination. Stimulated and educated by language play, children's imagination was to become the first weapon against all forms of passiveness and conformism while childhood's creative potential represented the foundation of a new, liberated humanity (Cambi 125).

In Rodari's theories, which grew more systematic in the 1970s and were expressed above all through his writing for *Paese sera* and *Il Giornale dei Genitori*, children needed support to develop multidirectional thinking. Such support was to be provided by an intentional commitment from an adult, theory and practice implemented by society and institutional settings, including children's literature, families, libraries, etc.:

> What children learn at school is only a hundredth part of what they learn from their parents, relatives, friends, the physical and social environments they are raised in, from television, games, objects, everything and everyone. They learn by absorbing words and notions, images and values; and certainly not passively, but always by responding with the strength of their personalities, integrating the new within the previous patterns and constantly changing these patterns.
>
> (*Il Giornale dei Genitori* 46)

Rodari encouraged all adults to take responsibility for an entirely renewed educational relationship based on listening, mutual respect, and the many unforeseeable possibilities of exchange between generations. Every child represented a novelty the adult – whether parent or teacher – was called on to dialogue with, all the while being open to the child's specific needs and interpreting his/her spontaneous culture. The adult must be committed to being "the hundred things [the child] needs – a playmate, a companion in adventure, an entertainer, an expert, a power figure that procures him the instruments he needs, an adult who provokes, shows new horizons and new directions in which to move" (46).

Rodari lucidly describes this process in "Brif Bruf Braf," one of the *Favole al telefono* (*Telephone Tales*) (1962). Two children are playing in the yard, using an invented language that nobody can understand. A lady "neither good nor bad" (28) who is looking out of the window listens to them and states that their game is silly. A man watching from his balcony responds, smugly, that he disagrees because he has understood the mysterious words spoken by the children. Apparently, the old man has "entered the game," sharing the fun and interpreting the hidden meanings with joy and optimism: "One of them said: 'How happy we are to be in the world.' And the other replied: 'The world is beautiful.' " The man answers the lady's final, skeptical question in the same fantastic language: "Brif, bruf, braf" (28). It is a celebration of the creative force of language that "makes" a world that is purely imaginary for the casual, detached observer yet absolutely "real" for the child involved in the playful act of creation and for the adult who is able to share the game and tune in with the paths of childhood imagination.[2]

In several chapters of *The Grammar of Fantasy*, Rodari suggests that to understand how the imagination works we have to start by observing children in their context of interaction, as they play in the woods, read or listen to others reading, look at comics, or watch television. Observing children enables adults to follow the formation of their imagination processes and knowledge development. As such, observation represents a precious instrument for adults, helping them to support children's learning processes and to develop a relationship with the child that is both respectful of the child's world and fruitful in terms of his cognitive-social development. In an educational setting that promotes creative thinking and active, autonomous knowledge construction, where the objectives and processes are not predetermined and automatic, continuous dialogue between the adult mind and the child mind is a fundamental factor.

This chapter aims first of all to identify aspects and purposes of language play that are central to Rodari's theoretical reflection and the educational role Rodari assigns to adults in the context of an education focused on the child's capacities and discoveries. While play, enjoyment, and the unexpected are the foundations of education, the role of the children's writer must be rethought along anti-authoritarian and anti-rhetorical lines: the educational role of children's literature is indeed expressed in writing, which directly engages with children, responds to their desire to grow, and follows and enhances the many paths of their imagination. The conclusion underlines how, over the years of his advanced theorizing, Rodari's pedagogical insights translated into literary experimentation designed to involve the reader. The central focus of this new concept of children's literature was on the child-reader as a creative, critical, and competent interlocutor. The concept of childhood developed by Rodari broke down the barriers between adult culture and children's culture that had prevailed in Italy throughout the nineteenth century (Califano 155), creating a perfect alchemy of pedagogy, writing, ideological commitment, and creativity.

Word Play as an Educational Responsibility

Necessary for understanding Rodari's poetic concepts and pedagogical commitment, play is a recurrent keyword in many of his theoretical works. All his poetic and narrative texts experiment with new techniques and combinations geared to the characteristics of the child's mind, which is structured to process experience creatively. The objective of such experimentation is enjoyment and, through enjoyment, the development of flexible and versatile thinking, i.e. education of the mind's cognitive and creative faculties. In the chapter on "Imagination, Creativity, School" in *The Grammar of Fantasy*, Rodari explains how play, with its inventiveness, freedom, and joy, has a crucial role in children's experience: it springs from the need for control and appropriation of experience and proceeds from the known to the unknown by analogy, movement, and contamination, opening up to unique and unexpected forms of knowledge. Rodari is particularly interested in the translation of meanings of the symbolic dimension of play: objects become "signs," leading to the creative transformation of reality. Underlying play, the imagination is a faculty governed by mechanisms we must understand and enhance as they help to free the mind, making it agile and ready not only to cope with but also to generate change.

At the heart of Rodari's fantastic world lies precisely the continual blending and mutual stimulation of "imagination" and "reason." The theoretical starting point for Rodari is the notion of the complete, whole child, for whom "magic and logic are two poles of the same functional process. . . . Playful creativity and cognitive creativity proceed hand in hand, influencing each other and strengthening each other in the unity of the child-person" (*Esercizi di fantasia* 76–79). In light of Rodari's approach, language play is configured as an extraordinary learning device that fosters not only the child's cognitive and logical skills – which are themselves linked to the ability to explore reality, name things and classify them – but also the child's creative and communicative capacities, instrumental to free self-expression and to thinking outside the box. Rodari explains that play is a full-fledged device that contributes to learning, communication, liberation of the mind, and personality construction:

> Speaking playfully is no less important than speaking seriously, above all at an age in which play is one of the essential means used by children to establish relations with others, with the environment and with reality. . . . Speaking in order to laugh, invent and vent aggressiveness externalises what has been repressed. Yet, it above all helps to feel free or to find the strength and impetus to act, learn, discover, measure oneself against reality, move forward and grow up. (*Scuola di fantasia* 35)

The language games proposed by Rodari are thus intended for adults and children who are inclined to put images and sounds into play in a process he describes as transformational of themselves and of reality. In "Games in the Pine Forest," a chapter of the *Grammatica della Fantasia*, based on his direct notes, Rodari comments on the spontaneous play of two children and proposes "a 'reading' of the game as if it were a 'story in action' " (109). In the game, the children transform themselves, time, and the natural space around them: they proceed by trial and analogy, adding personal emotions, experiences, and the subconscious to the game. The process abounds in the same "fluctuation of meaning" (110), which occurs when they tell stories or invent word games because the imagination in the game follows the same rules as in any other creative activity. Play and poetic creation are triggered by the same stimuli: randomness, variation, association, reversal, and transformation. Play does not reproduce reality but represents its symbolization. In this sense, for Rodari, as for Winnicott (79), play frames a transitional space, a frontier and liminal experience: the threshold between the real and the unreal, in which there is no evasion but rather preparation and the passage – at times indeed difficult – toward the principle of reality. Like all symbolic language, Rodarian play is a precious form of knowledge enabling, rather than denying, life.

The semiotic and linguistic dimension of children's play is underlined in another chapter of the *Grammatica*, "The Toy as Character": the toy becomes the lead character in the story the child tells as he plays while the use of words serves as the first rationalization of the play experience and an initiation toward abstraction because "the story is nothing more than an extension, a development, a joyful explosion of the toy" (69). As children instinctively give a voice to the toy, play becomes a shared process of storytelling (Lawson Lucas 111) and an exercise in sociability. The adult interacts with the child in an empathic, reassuring context and is responsible for arranging the relational, dialogic, and collaborative conditions for the exchange to take place. In his depiction of the specifics of the adult role, Rodari underlines how important it is to watch the child at play and accompany him/her without controlling his/her creative process:

> When adults play with a child, they have an advantage because they have a wider field of experience. Therefore, they can create more space with their imaginations. This is why children like to have parents as playmates. . . . The point here does not concern playing in place of the child, who becomes relegated to the humiliating role of spectator. But it concerns how an adult can place himself at the child's service. It is the child who commands. The adult plays with children in order to stimulate their capacity to invent things, to place new instruments in their hands so that they will use them when they are alone, and to teach them how to play. There is talk during the game. One learns from the child to speak to the pieces of the game, to assign the names and roles, to transform an error into an invention, a gesture into a story. . . . But also one learns – just as the child does – to entrust the pieces with secret messages because they tell the child how much we love him or her, that he or she can count on us, that our strength is theirs.
>
> (*Grammar* 69–70)

Thus, play involving words facilitates communication, encourages dialogue, and promotes "the process of breaking the chains that keep the mind enslaved" (Salvadori 180). In his article "Appunti per un minimanuale del dialogo fra padri e figli," published in 1970, Rodari explains how language play, fueled by an active imagination, effectively produces children's joy and laughter – "that extra thing, the unexpected gift," which involves both the adult and the child in a democratically coordinated experience (*Il Giornale* 30). The child can laugh at the adult's mistakes and experience the pleasure of correcting him/her, responding with surprise to his/her inventions, and creating new and original language games and verbal connections in response. Play, therefore, naturally transforms into language learning through playful experimentation with multiple uses and possibilities of words.

Rodari reminds adults that listening is also a form of dialogue. In the child's very early months, the still internal reactions to the words spoken by the adult form an immense, unexpressed cognitive and emotional process, which represents the child's "part" in the dialogue. The first moment of playful interaction around words occurs when the mother sings a lullaby and the child listens in a non-artificial situation: the meaning of the words tends to disappear while the affectivity of the context prevails, along with the music and the sound, whose functions are not merely reassuring and consolatory. The child lives that moment to the full, which also contributes to forming his/her mind and sensitivity. The playful discovery of rhyme and rhythm, which parents offer by singing or reading out loud stories and nursery rhymes, above all those of popular tradition, represents a liberating experience in which language is enjoyed for its own sake, self-reflectively and independently of the intentions of communication (*Il cane* 162).

In early childhood, the child needs an attentive and judicious parent who realizes that the child's imagination requires at least as much care as his/her scientific curiosity does; at school, the child needs a competent teacher who is a "promoter of creativity" by building interactions based on dialogue and choosing cultural objects that help children to grow. Even when poetry enters children's experience via school, this encounter must remain a personal adventure or a vital and profound discovery, which is not a scholastic reflex but rather the experience of a shared moment. School should simply foster the recapturing of the child's earlier, oral discoveries – the rhythm, the rhyme, and the pleasure of the word for the word's sake – in the realm of the written word.

Rodari particularly values experiences similar to those elicited in primary school pupils by Mario Lodi, a teacher from the Movement of Educational Cooperation. The child becomes a "producer of culture," and the teacher "is an adult who is with the children to express the best in himself or herself, to develop his or her own creative inclination, imagination, and constructive commitment as well" (*Grammar* 116). The children and their teacher are a "small community that was being built" (116) by composing poetry together, inspired by observations and impressions on a topic linked to their concrete, common experience (fog, Christmas, etc.). The class is framed as a learning community in which group work multiplies and expands on individual resources, and the construction of meaning is the result of social negotiation. The importance of the teacher as an "animator" of the setting and a stimulator of creativity is one of the aspects of Rodari's theoretical legacy, which was later picked up and developed, particularly in the Reggio Emilia approach to early childhood education.[3] In this framework, the central focus on viewing

> children and teachers as endowed with a strong potential, ready to enter into relationships, ready to be listened to, and eager to learn. Once we value children and teachers this way, teaching cannot be done only through imparting information, but rather, it has to be an experience in which teachers and learners construct learning together.
> (Gandini 2)

Playful Meetings of the Author and His Readers

The undisputed distinctive feature of all Rodari's works and particularly his poetry is the playful spirit that animates them. Literature is play both in that it is a work of complex, combinatorial engineering of words and in that it is used by a readers who are free to decipher, interpret, and modify what they are reading and use it as a tool for growing and facing up to the world. As Rodari explains in a speech from 1967,

> there is no more ambitious objective for children's writers than this: to write books that are capable of engaging a child in the same way as he uses – and I mean 'use' in a moral rather than superficial sense – a good toy; books which trigger physical and mental energies, inspire a desire to do things and involve the child's entire personality.
>
> (qtd. in Argilli 110)

Rodari's most effective pages are rich in irony and abound in clever metaphors and paradoxes. They include play on words and on situations, creating fantastic, wild, and surreal atmospheres. Through his verses, the writer builds toys to teach readers how to use language and thought freely. He also reveals himself as an authentic person listening to the reader's imagination with a *green ear*, an ability some adults have to see and listen to the world and nature with a child's creative and free eyes and ears (Zipes 426). Rodari thus accounts for his approach to writing literature: "Writing these stories, I always had the idea that each one is a toy in which, like in a game, new combinations of words, behaviours and ways of seeing things are attempted. . . . I am myself, I have my own way of thinking, living, my way of relating to the world, and this will come through in anything I talk about" (qtd. in Argilli 113). The writer places his knowledge and poetic laboratory "at the service of children," inscribing himself into a considerable tradition of writing as play, nonsense, and paradox and tracing his sources back to French and Avant-Garde surrealist poetic experimentation and, first of all, to the transgressive movement in Victorian literature epitomized by, for example, Edward Lear and Lewis Carroll.

Children's literature becomes a form of "user friendly" communication (Salvadori 178) and an open laboratory made available to apprentices. Rodari exemplifies this process in "Autointervista" (1982), included in the collection *Il cane di Magonza*, an atypical and at times romanticized text that tells of the complex production of *La torta in cielo* (*A Pie in the Sky*). The experience is associated with the writer's habit of meeting pupils and teachers to talk with them about creative processes involved in the writing of his stories. In this way, he could verify the effectiveness of his stories, watching the children's reactions and opening up to a game of mutual stimulation. These precious encounters enabled him to discover that "children do not suffer from schematisms, they ignore the official rules of literary genres, they appreciate the humour, adore word games and clearly distinguish full images from empty ones and fantasies well-fed by reality from those that are purely automatic" (*Il cane* 186–87).

By Rodari's report, *A Pie in the Sky* emerged from the orality and playful involvement of the pupils of Maria Luisa Bigiaretti, a teacher at the "Collodi" Primary School in the suburb of Trullo in Rome. The writer encouraged the children to invent a story starting from a visual image conveyed by the English idiom "pie in the sky," which is in itself an authentic and fantastic combination able to spark children's imaginations. The story created with the class features the pupils' names and experiences: as a giant pie lands on a hill next to the school, the population flee fearing a Martian invasion. The children run around the inside of the pie, literally eating its edges, exploring its caves, and coming across strange and funny characters. Rodari describes his and the class's deep involvement in the joint construction of the story:

> The narrator did not read, but spoke, gesticulated and performed the scene before them. An exciting but very particular situation. The story developed among us like "a familiar lexicon," to steal a magnificent expression from Natalia Ginzburg. This is how many stories are born between mothers and their children.
>
> (*Il cane* 187)

In one of the meetings following the first, very provisional draft of the story, a pupil asked Rodari for news about the "atomic" pie (189), and that totally unexpected choice of the adjective led the writer to review the entire plot with the class. To the children's delight, the flying pie became an error of a foreign scientist who had been designing an "atomic flying mushroom" (189) but created a giant chocolate cake by mistake. The text was then published in episodes in the *Corriere dei piccoli*. In "Autointervista," Rodari illustrates his strategy for the final version of the story published in the book format: *A Pie in the Sky* exemplifies the technique of "recasting fairy tales," which is described in *The Grammar of Fantasy* (39). The writer relies on a special narrative device aimed to recover at least a part of the direct involvement and entertainment of the pupils of the Trullo school. In every chapter, he scatters references to stories with which the reader is already familiar because

> meeting situations, characters and movement of the classic fairy tale, whether declared or hidden, the child would perceive an echo behind the words, a denser sound; in a single fairy tale, he would experience the atmosphere of many tales; behind the corridors of the pie, he would see other, far more mysterious ones.
>
> (*Il cane* 192)

The reader's participation in the inventive mechanism of the story, the possibility to choose from a number of inferential paths and autonomously enter the folds of the story and the layers of meanings, following many clues and suggestions: these are a priority for Rodari, who offers more or less explicit practical clues about playing, disassembling, upturning, and alienating words and narrative forms in each of his works.

Earlier, in *Filastrocche in cielo e in terra*, Rodari provided rhymed suggestions for rewriting stories. The traditional fairy tale material can be used to create *Favole a rovescio* (*Backward Tales*), reversing the usual point of departure (Once upon a time/there was a poor wolf/who took his grandmother/her dinner wrapped in a bundle) or *Storie nuove* (*New Stories*), by introducing even slight variations. As can be seen in Rodari's introductory note to the 1971 edition, *Telephone Tales* are also "stories born from the occasional collision of two words, stories created by reworking, or upturning, other stories, stories for playing, etc." As they represent a catalogue of creative methods to be used by the reader, the book can indeed be employed as a "manual for inventing stories" (x–xi). Starting from the fairy tale *A sbagliare le storie* (*Getting Stories Wrong*), which anticipates a chapter in *The Grammar*, Sandra L. Beckett convincingly explains how the game between the grandfather who tells a bizarre version of the tale of Little Red Riding Hood and the girl who listens, disoriented, ultimately illustrates the game Rodari wants to play with the reader, who is stimulated to deal with a "fractured fairy tale" (71).

The creative mechanisms theorized in *The Grammar of Fantasy* were to become particularly clear in *Novelle fatte a macchina* (*Tales Told by a Machine*) (1973), Rodari's mature narrative experimentation. Every story in the collection corresponds to a specific creative solution: "what would happen if" ("Coccodrillo sapiente"), reworked fairy tales ("Padrone e ragioniere," "Miss Universo dagli occhi color verde-venere"), fantastic character analysis ("Trattato della Befana"), animation of the metaphor ("I maghi del calcio" etc.), etc. As Rodari explains in the introduction to each story in the 1977 edition of the volume, each text is based on a particular mechanism that the author wishes to reveal to the reader "so that they may grasp a minimum of the 'grammar of fantasy'" (ix). For example, "Trattato della Befana" is accompanied by a Note that alludes to the plot structure and its consequences:

> With a little time available . . . I could have woven the three stories together, the three strands, to make a single story. But in this way I would have done all the work. Perhaps it is worthwhile to make the reader work a little too, if he wants to.
>
> (204)

After the publication of *The Grammar of Fantasy*, Rodari did not abandon his research into the laws of creative invention. He was collecting materials for another work, entitled *Esercizi di fantastica* (*Exercises in Fantasy*), to be released between 1980 and 1981. Unsurprisingly, the planned work included a chapter dedicated to an envisioned sequel, created and imagined by readers, of *C'era due volte il Barone Lamberto* (*Lamberto, Lamberto, Lamberto*). Rodari's last novel, published in 1978 and set on Lake Orta, the place of his childhood, is a dense and complex work that revolves around the motif of death and the need to exorcise it. Serious though the story is, it is founded on an ingenious game of narrative artifices that elaborate on the topic of the reversibility of existence with lightness and without didacticism (Rossitto 199–200), in contrast to other great authors whom Rodari admired, including Twain and Fitzgerald, who reflected on similar concerns in a far more dramatic fashion. The old, sick Baron Lamberto is rejuvenated to become a child again and obtains the gift of being able to live another life, which means that the reader is given an opportunity to start the story over and over again in a kind of perpetual circular motion. The open ending satisfied Rodari not only because of the hope that the power of "surviving death" would become real but also because of the infinite possibilities of re-invention offered by the motif. The last lines of the novel vividly and emphatically reveal the sense of Rodarian research into children's literature, understood as open experimentation, relinquishing moralistic intentions and addressed to a competent and curious reader who willingly embraces the invitation to play, which Rodari never tired of offering to his readers:

> Not everyone will be satisfied with the way this story ended. Among other things, no one knows exactly what becomes of Lamberto and what he does when he grows up. There is, however, no remedy for that. Readers who are dissatisfied with the ending are free to change it to suit themselves, adding a chapter or two to this book. Or even thirteen. Never allow yourself to be frightened by the words: THE END.
>
> (*Lamberto, Lamberto, Lamberto* 185)

Notes

1. Freinet and the French tradition of active education, Bruno Ciari, Mario Lodi and the Movimento di Cooperazione Educativa (Educational Cooperation Movement), and Don Lorenzo Milani and the Barbiana School are the major sources of Rodari's theoretical inspiration, especially in *Giornale dei Genitori*, where he served as Editor-in-Chief from 1968 until his death.
2. The quotations from *The Grammar of Fantasy* and *Lamberto, Lamberto, Lamberto* come from the published English translations (Zipes; Shugaar). All other quotations from original Italian texts are given in my translation.
3. *The Grammar of Fantasy* is dedicated to the city of Reggio Emilia, where Rodari held a series of meetings with fifty teachers from different schools between 6 and 10 March 1972. Loris Malaguzzi, an educational psychologist who inspired the Reggio Emilia approach, had already met Rodari several times in the editorial offices of *Paese Sera*. The invitation to Reggio Emilia attests to the profound harmony between the two intellectual

figures, who shared the belief in essential pedagogical principles: the power of the imagination, the right to creativity for all and the importance of free expression and of all languages for communicating and interacting with the world.

Works Cited

Argilli, Marcello. *Gianni Rodari: Una biografia*. Einaudi, 1990.

Beckett, Sandra L. *Recycling Red Riding Hood*. Routledge, 2002.

Boero, Pino. *Una Storia, Tante Storie: Guida all'Opera di Gianni Rodari*. Einaudi, 1992.

Califano, Francesca. "Political, Social and Cultural Divisions in the Work of Gianni Rodari." *Divided Worlds*, edited by Mary Shine Thompson and Valerie Coghlan. Four Courts Press, pp. 149–59.

Cambi, Franco. *Collodi, De Amicis, Rodari: Tre Immagini di Infanzia*. Edizioni Dedalo, 1985.

Gandini, Lella. "Play and the Hundred Languages of Children: An Interview with Lella Gandini." *American Journal of Play*, vol. 4, no. 1, 2011, pp. 1–18.

Lawson Lucas, Ann. "Blue Train, Red Flag, Rainbow World: Gianni Rodari's 'The Befana's Toyshop'." *Beyond Babar: The European Tradition in Children's Literature*, edited by Sandra L. Beckett and Maria Nikolajeva. Scarecrow Press, Inc., 2006, pp. 101–26.

Rodari, Gianni. *Filastrocche in Cielo e in Terra*. Einaudi, 1960.

———.*Telephone Tales*, translated by Patrick Creagh. Harrap, 1965. (A selection of stories from *Favole al telefono*).

———. *La Torta in Cielo*. Einaudi, 1966.

———. *Esercizi di Fantasia*, edited by Filippo Nibbi. Editori Riuniti, 1971.

———. *A Pie in the Sky*, translated by Patrick Creagh. Dent, 1971. (Translation of *La Torta in Cielo*).

———. *Grammatica della Fantasia: Introduzione all'Arte di Inventare Storie*. Einaudi, 1973.

———. *Novelle fatte a macchina*. Einaudi, 1973.

———. *C'era due Volte il Barone Lamberto*. Einaudi, 1978.

———. "Appunti per un Mini-manuale del 'Dialogo' fra Padri e Figli." *Il giornale dei genitori*, no. 58–59, 1980, pp. 28–32.

———. "Dalla Parte del Bambino." *Il giornale dei genitori*, no. 58–59, 1980, pp. 46–47.

———. *Il Cane di Magonza*, edited by Carmine De Luca. Editori Riuniti, 1982.

———. *Favole al telefono*. 1962. Emme Edizioni-Einaudi, 1990.

———. *Tales Told by a Machine*, translated by Sue Newson-Smith. Abelard and Shulman, 1976. (A selection of stories from *Novelle fatte a macchina*).

———. *The Grammar of Fantasy: An Introduction to the Art of Inventing Stories*, translated by Jack Zipes. Teachers & Writers, 1990. (Translation of *Grammatica della Fantasia*).

———. *Scuola di Fantasia*. Edited by Carmine De Luca, Editori Riuniti, 1992.

———. *Lamberto, Lamberto, Lamberto*, translated by Antony Shugaar. Melville House Publishing, 2011. (Translation of *C'era due volte il Barone Lamberto*).

Rossitto, Mariarosa. *Non Solo Filastrocche: Rodari nella Letteratura del Novecento*. Bulzoni, 2011.

Salvadori, Maria Luisa. "Apologizing to the Ancient Fable: Gianni Rodari and His Influence on Italian Children's Literature." *The Lion and the Unicorn*, vol. 26, no. 2, 2002, pp. 169–202.

Winnicott, Donald. *Gioco e realtà*, translated by Giorgio Adamo e Renata Gaddini. Armando, 1974. (Translation of *Play and Reality*).

Zipes, Jack. "The Incomprehensible Gianni Rodari." *Marvels & Tales: Journal of Fairy-Tale Studies*, vol. 28, no. 2, 2014, pp. 424–32.

9 Recollecting Childhood

Writing the Child at Play

Elizabeth L. Nelson

This chapter aims to explore how the intergenerational divide characterizes play through a nostalgic lens. Ideas of play are constructed at a generational level. As the current player learns to play, they associate their ideas of play with a correct form of play, which leads to intergenerational differences in understanding play. In this way, perceptions of play are generationally bound. This chapter argues that play anthologies function like literature to create and present an image of childhood and play that, though rooted in the actions of real children, is in part fictional. Anthologies of play are not the unadulterated artefacts of play they strive to be but are necessarily interpretations of play mediated through multiple degrees of removal. Cliff contends that the anthologist's view "can influence [the anthologist's] collection" (142). I extend this notion, arguing that the anthologist's view *necessarily* influences the anthologist's collection. The adult anthologist's understanding of childhood, children and play always influences their depictions of play. How they recognize children playing is based on their own experiences and understanding of play. Children's literature anthologies present observed and remembered moments of play for adult reading. In this way, they narrate children's activities through an adult lens, thus presenting an adult understanding of childhood and play.

In order to demonstrate how play anthologies function like literature to characterize childhood and play, I offer a reading of two important British play anthologies: the first is a two-part collection, *The Traditional Games of England, Scotland, and Ireland* by Lady Alice B. Gomme, published in 1894 and 1898; the second is the 1959 collection *The Lore and Language of Schoolchildren* by Peter and Iona Opie. While honoring the enormous contribution of both the Opies and Gomme, I cast a critical eye at their collection methods, problematizing the ethnographic assumptions that underlie these methods of collection. This chapter examines both Gomme and the Opies' opposing methods of collecting children's games in relation to the concept of intergenerational play. These anthologies can be positioned alongside many classic children's literature texts to be read both as non-fiction counterparts and, critically, as constructions of childhood and play. Nostalgic characterization of play can be evidenced throughout children's literature from J. M Barrie to Roald Dahl; childhood is characterized by adults rather than children. "Recollected" moments of play verge on the imaginary, and even if they are rooted in experience, they are nonetheless romanticized and dated through nostalgia. The common adult lament that children have forgotten how to play reflects an understanding of play that does not coincide with actions of the current generation of players. Play is felt to be a remembered phenomenon rather than a malleable construct, which creates intergenerational tension in discussions of what play ought to be.

Intergenerational Play

Rather than focusing on the action of play between adults and children, I explore the ways in which ideas of play and childhood are constructed intergenerationally or between generations. Bishop and Curtis state that "[c]hildren create and pass on their rhymes for their own enjoyment as they play. They are a living, active art, made by children for their own purposes, their content to be taken in at the children's own level, and that is how they are best understood" (8). Hardman further argues that "children's thoughts and social behaviour may not be totally incomprehensible to adults, so long as we do not try to interpret them in adult terms" (513). Yet this is exactly the role of children's game and lore anthologies. The intergenerational divide is textually represented by play anthologies through the act of recording play. These are acts of translation where the motion of play becomes written text, and the resulting anthology is a version of play that is translated both from action to word and from child to adult. The observed player (child) becomes separate from the observing recorder (adult). Davis refers to this phenomenon as the " 'haunting' of ethnography by the 'secret' of its own epistemological incoherence" (1416). He argues that the ethnographer, no matter how integrated, can never fully map the insider's perspective, for once they start mapping, they step outside of their role as insider. The act of transcription creates the dichotomies of insider/outsider, player/anthologist, child/adult; simply the act of recording separates them. Ethnographies are thus collections of games and iterations of play perceived through at least one generational lens. However, in acknowledging these lenses, we are able to gain insight into past understandings of play and childhood. These ethnographies can be positioned next to contemporaneous fictional texts to provide insight and understanding of past intergenerational representations of play.

Games as Text

Understanding the role of children's agency in play is crucial in recognizing that ideas of play are constructed at a generational level. Children's playground games are multimodal codified utterances that can be recognized as texts of childhood. This chapter offers an enhanced perspective of children's literature that extends traditional meanings by including agentive play. Players of children's games are multiple agents of construction whose agentive roles in creating, curating and sharing these texts continue centuries old traditions of childlore. This agentive element of children's play sets these games apart from all other forms of children's literature. Children's ownership of these texts means that they can represent children in a way that adult-produced literature cannot. Texts of childhood demonstrate agentive play with language and movement that is not concerned with adult understandings. Bishop argues that "[l]ike all play, clapping games are multimodal. Most obviously, they incorporate verbal text, music, movement and touch but other modes, such as proxemics and gaze, are also important" (54). I would extend that definition to include not only "clapping games" but also all singing and rhyme games. The linguistic play occurring in these texts requires sophisticated abilities of decoding. Learning to decode and participate in the play activity involves a multi-layered and complex understanding of rhythm and timing, words and wordplay, and social hierarchy and social positioning in the playground. These texts "challenge a traditional focus on the written, print mode" (Carrington and Marsh 1). Recognizing such games as texts of childhood means accepting the concept of a text as something more fluid than printed media. These are oral and physical iterations of childlore, and I have chosen to understand them as texts.

Grenby and Reynolds provide a generous description of children's literature as a category that "encompasses every form, format, genre and medium," making it "perhaps the largest and most varied area of literacy research" (4). This definition allows for games as texts to be included in the children's literature category. Yet it is the essential ownership of these texts by children that fits these texts so comfortably in a category calling itself *children's* literature. Play anthologies are collections of these multimodal children's texts. Exploring how these texts are depicted through adult lenses raises questions pertinent to children's literature, childhood and intergenerational play. Anthologies of play are arguably children's literature but not in the traditional sense. Rather than being composed of writing by adults for children, play anthologies are collections of texts that are created by agentive child players and printed for adult readers. The texts that make up these collections are made *by and for children*:

> [c]hildren's traditional culture is an expression of their own beliefs and values, not isolated from contact with the adult world, but specific to themselves. Rhymes and other linguistic play are created and reproduced for children's own purposes, not those of folklorists, the educational system or publishers.
>
> (Bishop and Curtis 8)

The creation, curation and dissemination of these games belong to the children in a way that other texts cannot. Texts of childhood are not tied to traditionally published children's literature or publishing culture and are not bound to adult involvement. In many ways, this chapter participates in the discussion of the "impossibility" of children's literature echoing "[Jacqueline] Rose's recognition of the gap between the adult producer of children's literature and the children who are its audience" (Rudd and Pavlik 225). Play anthologies turn this concept on its head though the intergenerational gap remains: children produce texts that are appropriated into adults' literature (for children are not the intended audience of anthologies). This is the case for all child-produced texts that are appropriated for adult use.

In calling these games texts of childhood, it can be acknowledged that childhood is experienced by every child in a different way and that these texts are not equally experienced by or known to all children. However, as the play anthologies show, these texts are shared by children of similar ages that attend the same social spaces such as playgrounds, schools and churches. These games are linked geographically and contextually to times and spaces of play. Childhood games and methods of play are as unique as each childhood; the content, how they are played and by whom tell a different tale for each new set of players generationally, geographically and otherwise. Each new generation of players become what Carrington and Marsh term "produsers" – both the users and producers of the text (6). As produsers, players determine "correct" and consequently "incorrect" ways to play. These definitions continue as new generations of players become produsers. This is how intergenerational understandings of play are formed. Play is a malleable construct for each set of new players, but then once defined, it loses that flexibility. Each generation's role as produsers signifies what play means, how to perform play and therefore how a child ought to play.

Gomme: Remembering Play and Looking Back on Play

Early folklorist Lady Alice B. Gomme's two-part anthology, *Traditional Games*, "based on information from 76 correspondents, relating to 112 locations . . . detailed descriptions of around eight hundred games and their variants" (Marsh and Bishop 14). Gomme worked with educators and folklore enthusiasts, asking them to send in recollections of games played in their youth. A "Memoir" of this immense project "was read as a paper at the evening meeting of the Folk Lore Society, on March 16th, 1898" (Gomme vi). In this collection Gomme first identified "singing games" as a form of game, coining the term for what has gone on to be a rich area of folklore study (Cliff 131). Gomme was an academic and intellectual in her time, yet as Boyes points out, "[i]n the past seventy years, the theory and methods of Alice Bertha Gomme have been widely criticized by folklorists and writers working within the field of childlore" (198).

Looking Back on Childhood

Many folklorists have characterized Gomme as a distinctly Victorian woman in her methods and her apparent temperament as that of "a Victorian pedant who could discern a meaning" not quite nice "in every item she collected" (Boyes 198). However, many of her concepts of childhood and the overall impression and feel of the text is characteristic of her time and is distinctly Edwardian in its purpose and outlook. Critiques of her work often focus on Gomme's collection methods, arguing, as the Opies in 1959 claimed, that her collection was "out of date before ever it was published" (6). Gomme's focus on recording recollections of games played "probably forty or fifty years earlier" (6) is not a unique method and was used by many other play anthologists of the time (Allen 1882; Newell 1884; Udal 1889). While the majority of her two anthologies do appear to be made up of recollections, there is also evidence that Gomme herself participated in early fieldwork, collecting

> a great deal of material as she went around London. Children playing in Regent's Park are given as the source of numerous versions of common games, while a newspaper boy at Barnes Station was clearly buttonholed on the spot to give a demonstration of 'Dabs', a version of Fivestones.
>
> (Boyes 202)

However, her focus on the adult recollections is clear in her short Preface to Volume Two, in which she thanks her "many kind correspondents" but does not acknowledge any children's roles in the collection (Gomme vi).

This lack of registering children's agency in games is further evidenced in her analysis of the games. Typically, anthologists from the turn of the 20th century, Newell (1884), Udal (1889), Nicholson (1897) and Gomme (1898), all look to history in order to understand and represent their findings. They attempt to historicize the games in order to root them in tradition. They trace the actions and words of the games back to early times, arguing that "these games are of interest to the folklorist, as showing connection with early custom" (Gomme 471). Children's games are separated from the child players and, as a result, from childhood as it is being actively experienced. When considering what these texts mean, Gomme turns to the past to decipher actions, stating, "[i]t becomes important, therefore, to work more closely into the details of these games, to ascertain if we can what customs are preserved, to what people or period of culture they might have belonged" (474). Here is a clear example of not seeing children's agency in these games. There is no question of asking the children about where or how these games came about. Instead there is a recognition of the importance of these texts and that in isolating and capturing the text one can isolate the childhood and history it contains. The roots of the text are all in the past, the mystery to be solved without children's help.

These texts are so disassociated from the actual players that any reference to children's role as "produsers" of the texts becomes a discussion of corruption. Children are doubly positioned: first as cultural vessels preserving "some of the oldest historical documents belonging to our race, worthy of being placed side by side with the folk-tale and other monuments of man's progress from slavery to civilization" (Gomme 531) and second as a threat to the texts "due to corruption and the marked decadence now occurring in these games" (63).

Edwardian Ideas of Play

For an academic who is so often characterized by her Victorian ideals, there is a definite Edwardian character to Gomme's play anthologies. These ideas characterize childhood in a way that is similar to the literature of the time and to other play anthologists of the time. W. W. Newell (1884) celebrates the essence of childhood in his editor's forward to *Games and Songs of American Children*, stating that he was "unwilling to overcloud with cumbrous research that healthy and bright atmosphere which invests all that really belongs to childhood" (v). Here Newell positions himself within the Edwardian cult of childhood in a departure from Victorian fiction wherein "childhood is often a time of powerlessness, trial, and emotional (and often physical) pain" (Gavin and Humphries 11). Gomme participates in the celebration of childhood in her publications of games anthologies. She sentimentalizes past play – "I remember well being shown how to make a peep or poppet-show" (44) – and is part of the movement portraying children playing in "groups and [with] siblings," moving away from Romantic and Victorian focus "on the solitary child figure" (Gavin and Humphries 11).

Literary representations of solitary children finding communities through play and creative narrative play include Frances Hodgson Burnett's *A Little Princess* (1905) and J. M. Barrie's play, *Peter Pan* or *the Boy Who Wouldn't Grow Up* (1904) and the subsequent novel *Peter and Wendy* (1911). The children in these texts are like the children's games in Gomme's anthologies: they are in touch with both reality and magic. Gomme refers to the pagan characteristics of games and their origins in children's "belief in sympathetic magic" (373). This same idea of pagan, natural magic is evidenced in Barrie's text. Peter Pan's magic exists both on the "magic shores" of Neverland that the children visit and in a general space of childhood that Mrs. Darling recalls: "after thinking back into her childhood she just remembered a Peter Pan who was said to live with the fairies" (Barrie 9). In *A Little Princess*, magic is sometimes introduced by adults but also comes by itself. When on a particularly hungry evening there is suddenly the promise of a midnight feast, Sara remarks, "[s]omehow, something always happens . . . just before things get to the very worst. It is as if the Magic did it'" (Burnett 220).

Gomme's historicization of games follows typical patterns of anthropological inquiry of her time. Her reading of nature, pagan rituals and belief in "sympathetic magic" (13) is characteristic of Edwardian literature, rather than Victorian literature. Paul March-Russell argues there was a "an emerging dialectic between on the one hand a rational, urban and commercial society, and on the other hand, magical and folkloric beliefs" (25). The 1894 publication of Rudyard Kipling's *The Jungle Book* demonstrates, among other things, ideas of nature coupled with a longing for society. This struggle between the past and the present is represented across children's play anthologies of the time. Anthologies were collections rooted in the experience of real (and recollected) moments of play, yet this play is then analyzed and understood by linking it to ancient pagan rituals and belief in magic.

In Edwardian children's literature, adults are often seen in contest with children's more instinctive and natural understanding of the world. When Wendy decides it is time for her and her brothers to go home, Barrie playfully represents the text's juxtaposition of child and adult values by stating that "[the lost boys] knew in what they called their hearts that one can get on quite well without a mother, and that it is only the mothers who think you can't" (Barrie 130). In *A Little Princess*, Sara's befriending of the mouse, Melchisedec, makes her "the little friend of all things" (Burnett 198) according to the adults who are frightened and disgusted by the animal. In these texts affinity with nature is shown in contrast to adults' bad decision making. Yet in play anthologies, written for adults, adults are the source of trusted knowledge. Children are paradoxically seen as a corrupting force in their own games, and ethnographers look back to earlier, "truer" versions of the game in their "reduced but original form" (Newell 41). When analyzing the origins of *Ring A Ring O' Roses*, Gomme turns to an understanding of the game as linked to pagan origins and states that

> [t]his seems to me to be a very apposite explanation of the game, the rhymes of which are fairly well preserved, though showing in some of the variants that decay towards a practical interpretation which will soon abolish all traces of the mythical origin of game-rhyme. (111)

While the adult ethnographers must go to the children for the games, it is then the adult's responsibility to maintain and store them out of reach, on the shelf, away from sticky, corrupting fingers.

While Gomme was not the first to observe and record children's play, she was the first to conduct such a large, nationwide survey of children's games in the United Kingdom. Gomme and her contemporary folklorists historicize each game and through reference to each other are able to create a sense of validity that removes the children from the picture (Halliwell 1842; Miss Allen 1882; Chamber 1842; Nicholson 1897; Udal 1889). She states regarding the singing game *Queen Anne* that,

> [i]f the Belfast version is the nearest to the original of those at present existing, and there is every probability that this is so, especially as Chambers' version is so similar, an early form of the game might be restored, and from this its origin may be ascertained.
>
> (100)

Gomme and others look to each other to understand game origins and meaning. Udal (1889) demonstrates this approach, stating that, "I verily believe that if it were not for the school-treats . . . school children would soon be the last, instead of the first, to whom one should go for study and information on this interesting subject" (204).

Gomme participates in this trend of observing and recording children's play to paint an image of healthy children enacting old traditions, without inviting the corruptive force of agency into her collection. The innocence of being a cultural vessel is contrasted against the corruptive forces of childhood. Despite Gomme's many Edwardian tendencies, there persists a Victorian and Romantic construction of child and society in her collections. Gubar writes that

> [s]cholars such as Peter Coveney, Hugh Cunningham, and Judith Plotz have ably shown that Victorians committed to this position embraced a strand of Romantic thinking that posits children as a race apart, associating them with 'primitive' people and insisting that their health and happiness depend on remaining detached from and unaffected by contemporary culture.
>
> (4)

While Gubar continues to suggest that Barrie and other Golden Age authors do depict "child characters and child readers as socially saturated beings, profoundly shaped by the culture, manners, and morals of their time, precisely in order to explore the vexed issue of the child's agency" (5), folklorists, with their own agendas of preservation and research, do not appear to do so. Gomme and other contemporary anthologists celebrate children's games and play but not necessarily their agency. As

McGarock argues, "the child's nineteenth century status as a mute image (being 'seen but not heard') prevailed in the twentieth century" (40). Games of children were to be collected and maintained, historicized and rooted in the past. Children are not to be consulted, despite the period's obsession with the cult of the child.

Peter and Iona Opie: Looking At Childhood and Agentive Play

Ethnographers Peter and Iona Opie were also pioneering folklorists in their attitude and method of collecting games. In their 1959 collection of playground activities and games, *Lore and Language*, the Opies embarked on a groundbreaking style of guerilla ethnography. Aware of the many different childhoods experienced in Britain, the Opies attempted a comprehensive survey of the United Kingdom, collecting lore and language from quaint country schools "where squirrels stole from the pockets of children's coats hanging in the porch" to "grim barrack-like [city] buildings" and multilingual, multiclass urban centers. They collected contributions from "some 5,000 children attending, in the 1950s, seventy local authority schools, in different parts of England, Scotland, and Wales, and one school in Dublin" (7).

The legacy of the Opies continues to be celebrated across folklore, childlore and play studies. They recognized that their anthology was made up of "information which would not ordinarily have been written down for another fifty years, for it is made up of what will be the childhood recollections of the older generation after A.D. 2000" (9). The anthologies that followed the Opies' publication saw truth in the wealth of childlore that existed in the 1950s and 1960s and their impressive work is acknowledged as the basis of projects happening today by academic folklorist and play specialists (Roud 2011; Bishop et al.; Burn). The Opies' work has stood the test of time in the way that Gomme's has not. Their methods remain popular today, and their focus on the child as an agentive, active player is still the argument that is being explored, but now the conversation has moved to new spaces of play (for example online), rather than new understandings of children at play. Essentially, the Opies wrote the book on British children's play.

Looking at Childhood

The Opies saw their work as a change in direction regarding the relationship between the player and the adult. They focused on action in contemporary playgrounds, arguing that previous anthologies had not adequately recognized the child of the day. Their playground anthology focuses on the agentive role of children in playing their own games in which they "emphasise the inventiveness and richness of an oral tradition sustained by children alone" (Burn 2). The gaze of the ethnographers is consciously turned toward the child of the day, and their focus was "solely concerned with the contemporary school-child, and wherever possible his story . . . told in his own words" (8). Children are not only seen by the Opies; their voices are actively sought. The Opies clearly thank the students from the schools of their contributors and their own children, "especially when they have been as tolerant of our interests" (16). In the Opies' anthology, children's agency is celebrated and their opinions are valued.

The Opies argued that "the folklorist and anthropologist can, without traveling a mile from his door, examine a thriving unselfconscious culture (the word "culture" is used here deliberately)" (22). The emphasis on culture is a challenge to "most academic and governmental people . . . not aware that English traditional lore exists to be collected" (9). Culture for the Opies is an active and agentive space of play that is being experienced by present day children. It is also a celebrated space that is not necessarily of interest to the adult. As quoted earlier, "[c] hildren's traditional culture is an expression of their own beliefs and values, not isolated from contact with the adult world, but specific to themselves" (Bishop et al. 8). Examples of such folklore include wholesome ideas such as nonsense rhymes, riddles, a children's calendar and singing games. But there is a baser side of childhood, one in which the Opies seem to delight, that involves everything from pranks, "embarrassers," improper rhymes and "spookies" to "tricks of inflicting pain" and "jeers and torments." They are clear in their aims, and in their view of childhood, when they state that the anthology "does not, despite the sections on tortures and pranks after nightfall, set out to include the lore and language of the delinquent. We are concerned here merely with the fun-loving but father-fearing specimen who is typical of the vast majority" (8).

The Opies are therefore painting a picture of a particular childhood in Britain. In their description of that childhood, there is also a focus on class. They accuse Gomme of painting "only a partial picture" that was made up of mostly "country dwellers [who] tended to be well-to-do. The great warren of the city backstreets where the mass of the nation's children are bred and brought up remained *terra incognita*" (6). Thus, they set out to chart that mysterious territory and are clear about their boundaries, stating, "[t]he study does not, however, except incidentally, include the lore current among children in the private, fee-charging establishments" (8). Like Gomme, the Opies are creating an image of play in Britain, and, like Gomme, they are (quite reasonably) setting boundaries around what they want to accomplish. The Opies' focus on the baser nature of childhood; the ordinary lives of the working class and the agency of children is both a turn away from Gomme and an indication of future literary avenues.

Functioning Like Literature

While Gomme's anthology demonstrated many aspects of Edwardian literature, such distinct characterization for the work of the Opies is not evident. However, there are several elements of the *Lore and Language* that can be seen to function like literature published after the Opies' 1959 playground anthology. Roald Dahl's work comprises many "grotesque and taboo" acts that "adults often deplore as tasteless," while "many of the stories, situations, and jokes, children find humorous" (West 115). Dahl's novel *The Twits* (1980) is full of disgusting rather than frightening pranks and "jeers and torments." Mrs. Twit feeds Mr. Twit worm spaghetti, similar to the Opies' collected rhyme "nobody loves me, everybody hates me, going in the garden to eat worms" (195). Dahl's Mr. and Mrs. Twit try to outwit one another by pulling exponentially elaborate pranks. The Opies dedicate seven pages to various door pranks from "kicking doors" to "mechanical knocking," which, according to a 10-year-old from Newcastle, "is how you cause a row between two neighbours" (416). Like Dahl, the Opies appear to enjoy these mischievous activities and happily note that children "with the door-knocker dancing at their command on the end of a thread they can give themselves much cause for merriment" (414). Dahl and Michael Rosen, for example, use themes and humor that correspond closely with the contents of playground anthologies, the texts of childhood, which may be the reason for their popularity with children.

Along with the content similarities there is also the focus on a representation of childhood, which for the Opies was the working-class child both in the country and the city. They were looking at children who were not part of boarding school life or the "private, fee-charging establishments" (Opie 8). These children and their childhood was thus not represented in the school stories of Enid Blyton. Literature was following similar trends, and in 1958 Wallace Hildick produced the novel *Jim Starling*, "set in an ordinary day school rather than the more traditional boarding school" (Pearson 51). The focus was on the ordinary lives of children, especially the working class, however not in the Victorian sense of the suffering, lonely child. There was a push for working-class child readers to be able to see themselves in literature. There was an educational movement in the 1960s to recognize children from around the United Kingdom, and the same ideas may have been present in the folklore society of the Opies. The Opies are clear in their aims of representing "the contemporary school child," though not the public school child, retelling "wherever possible his story . . . in his own words" (8). The Opies focus on recognizing children's agency and ownership of their texts of childhood in order to demonstrate that "children today are storing up for themselves just as lively memories as any of those with which we are now regaled by the old folk" (9).

Conclusion

There is an understanding in folklore that traditions are passed down from generation to generation, and these anthologies demonstrate this custom. How traditions of play are treated by the youngest generation determines how "well" or "correctly" older generations believe they play. Gomme both celebrates children's ability to pass on these customs and criticizes any form of agency in modernizing these texts. The Opies, despite their defense of children's agency in the text, demonstrate this caretaker argument in the summary of their preface, stating that "a generation which cares for the traditions and entertainments which have been passed down to it is not one which is less good than its predecessors" (Opie 9). How such authors construct images of children playing creates a sense of the correct way to play. This construction is imposed by the author's understanding of what play is and what they ought to collect. These anthologies, therefore, function like literature in their representations of childhood and play, which, though rooted in the actions of real (and remembered) children, is in part fictional. Such depictions of play and childhood feed into tensions of understanding play and childhood at a generational level.

New understandings of play are created by each generation of players, and thus they are generationally bound. Each unique experience of childhood founds an understanding of how to interpret play. Adults characterize their own memories of play in nostalgic terms. They construct concepts of play by linking their own experience as produsers and players. Play is felt to be a remembered phenomenon rather than a malleable construct, which creates intergenerational tension in discussions of what play ought to be. This nostalgic characterization of play is clearly evidenced in Gomme's texts, wherein she is critical of child agency as a corruptive force. Although the Opies focus on the child of the day, they also carefully depict childhood as a wholesome and non-delinquent space that celebrates continued forms of play. They are clear in their focus on the child of the day, but even in that characterization there is a sense of a timeless celebration of childhood as ahistorical yet sentimental and nostalgic.

Play anthologies participate in children literature's fictionalization of childhood and play. The ethnographers are writing the child at play, and, in doing so, they are re-imagining and reconstructing the real child they observe into a fictionalized child. They are translating children's actions from oral to text and also from child to adult. The child becomes a representation of themselves through the ethnographer's lens. Thus, although the children they depicted were real and playing, they are also a nostalgic image of past play and recollections of play. These anthologies therefore participate in constructing fictionalized representations of children, play and childhood. These understandings are then read on a generational level. Children read fictionalized representations of how to act like a child and how to play and represent themselves, whereas adults bring their own experiences as produsers of play to texts as both writers and readers of fiction and non-fiction. In writing the child at play, these anthologies participate in promoting nostalgic understandings of play that are generationally bound, further determining how ideas of play and childhood are constructed intergenerationally – or between generations.

Works Cited

Barrie, J. M. *Peter Pan*. 1911. Puffin Classics, 2008.

Bishop, Julia C. "'That's How the Whole Hand-Clap Thing Passes on': Online/Offline Transmission and Multimodal Variation in a Children's Clapping Game." *Children's Games in the New Media Age: Childlore, Media and the Playground*, edited by Chris Richards and Andrew Burn. Routledge, 2014, pp. 53–84.

Bishop, Julia C., et al., editors. *Play Today in the Primary School Playground: Life, Learning and Creativity*. Open UP, 2001.

Boyes, Georgina. "Alice Bertha Gomme (1852–1938): A Reassessment of the Work of a Folklorist." *Folklore*, vol. 101, no. 2, 1990, pp. 198–208.

Burn, Andrew. "Children's Playground Games in the New Media Age." *Children's Games in the New Media Age: Childlore, Media and the Playground*, edited by Chris Richards and Andrew Burn. Routledge, 2014, pp. 1–30.

Burnett, Frances Hodgson. *A Little Princess*. 1905. Puffin Classics, 2008.

Carrington, Victoria, and Jackie Marsh. "Forms of Literacy." *Beyond Current Horizons*, 2008, www.beyondcurrenthorizons. org. uk/evidence/knowledge-creativity-and-communication/. Accessed Dec. 2016.

Cliff, Janet M. "On Relationships Between Folk Music and Folk Games." *Western Folklore*, vol. 51, no. 2, 1992, pp. 129–51, www.jstor.org/stable/1499361. Accessed Dec. 2016.

Dahl, Roald. *The Twits*. Penguin, 2007.

Davis, Robert A. "8.1 Hermeneutics of Linguistic Ethnography: Teachers and Students Losing and Finding Their Voices." *International Handbook of Interpretation in Educational Research*, edited by Paul Smeyers, et al. Springer, 2015, pp. 1415–36.

Gavin, Adrienne E., and Andrew F. Humphries. "Worlds Enough and Time: The Cult of Childhood in Edwardian Fiction." *Childhood in Edwardian Fiction: Worlds Enough and Time*, edited by Adrienne E. Gavin, and Andrew F. Humphries. Palgrave Macmillan, 2009, pp. 1–20.

Gomme, Alice Bertha. *The Traditional Games of England, Scotland, and Ireland: With Tunes, Singing Rhymes, and Methods of Playing According to the Variants Extant and Recorded in Different Parts of the Kingdom*, vol. 2. David Nutt, 1898.

Grenby, Matthew O., and Kimberley Reynolds, editors. *Children's Literature Studies: A Research Handbook*. Palgrave Macmillan, 2011.

Gubar, Marah. *Artful Dodgers: Reconceiving the Golden Age of Children's Literature*. Oxford UP, 2010.

Hardman, Charlotte. "Can There Be an Anthropology of Children?" *JASO: Journal of the Anthropological Society of Oxford*, vol. IV, no. 2, 1973, pp. 85–99. Reprinted in *Childhood*, vol. 8, no. 4, 2001, pp. 501–17 [Online], http://chd.sagepub.com/content/8/4/501.full.pdf. Accessed 26 May 2015.

Kumpulainen, Kristiina. "Literacy in the 21st Century." *Lifelong Learning in Europe*, vol. XVI, no. 3, 2011, p. 127, www.elmmagazine.eu/wp-content/uploads/2017/03/3_2011.pdf. Accessed Feb. 2019.

March-Russell, Paul. "Pagan Papers: History, Mysticism, and Edwardian Childhood." *Childhood in Edwardian Fiction: Worlds Enough and Time*, edited by Adrienne E. Gavin and Andrew F. Humphries. Palgrave Macmillan, 2009, pp. 23–36.

Marsh, Jackie, and Julia Bishop. *Changing Play: Play, Media and Commercial Culture from the 1950s to the Present Day: Play, Media and Commercial Culture from the 1950s to the Present Day*. Open UP, 2013.

McGavock, Karen L. "Cult or Cull? Peter Pan and Childhood in the Edwardian Age." *Childhood in Edwardian Fiction: Worlds Enough and Time*, edited by Adrienne E. Gavin and Andrew F. Humphries. Palgrave Macmillan, 2009, pp. 37–52.

Newell, William Wells. *Games and Songs of American Children*. Harper & Brothers, 1884, https://archive.org/details/gamessongsofamer00newerich. Accessed Nov. 2016.

Opie, Iona, and Peter Opie. *The Lore and Language of Schoolchildren*. Oxford UP Ltd, 1959.

Pearson, Lucy. *The Making of Modern Children's Literature in Britain: Publishing and Criticism in the 1960s and 1970s*. Routledge, 2016.

Roud, Stephen. *The Lore of the Playground: One Hundred Years of Children's Games, Rhymes and Traditions*. Random House, 2011.

Rudd, David, and Anthony Pavlik. "The (Im) Possibility of Children's Fiction: Rose Twenty-Five Years On." *Children's Literature Association Quarterly*, vol. 35, no. 3, 2010, pp. 223–29.

West, Mark I. "The Grotesque and the Taboo in Roald Dahl's Humorous Writings for Children." *Children's Literature Association Quarterly*, vol. 15, no. 3, 1990, pp. 115–16.

10 Representations of Play in Caldecott Medal and Honor Books During 1938–1949 and 2001–2014

Taraneh Matloob Haghanikar and Linda M. Pavonetti

Marla Frazee, author and illustrator of the 2009 Caldecott Honor book, *A Couple of Boys Have the Best Week Ever* (2008), credits her desire to create books for children to her childhood reading:

> I knew I wanted to grow up and make picture books from the time I first saw *Where the Wild Things Are* by Maurice Sendak (1963). I was astonished at those page turns where Max's room magically turns into a forest – page turns that opened onto changing worlds! I had no idea that was possible. I also loved *Blueberries for Sal* by Robert McCloskey (1948). The character of Little Sal was real to me; she was a girl I wished I knew. How did McCloskey do that? (2)

That Frazee was influenced by two Caldecott Medal books with strong, active characters is not surprising. What is interesting *and* surprising is that Max and Sal were both engaged in activities that today's parents and teachers would consider dangerous. During the twentieth century, children's play – and the venues in which they played – seemed to morph from independent activities in the great outdoors to safer and less independent pursuits. This shift in Caldecott books can be viewed as a proxy representing the recent modification in picture storybooks from engaging in explicit physical activities, as in *Blueberries for Sal* (McCloskey 1948), to more intellectually challenging forms of play, i.e. decoding word play, irony, or other types of sophisticated reading. This chapter will clarify for readers our analysis of early and more recent Caldecott Medal books by providing examples from the 103 books we sampled. Furthermore, we propose to accomplish two major objectives: first, to explain our analysis using the data we established as clear indicators of our coding and second, to suggest that this shift from independent outdoor play to more challenging and sophisticated reading requires a shift in pedagogical methods.

One example of a reaction to a book that clearly signaled this shift between current and past concepts of play and what authors and illustrators represent in their books occurred in a children's literature class that we were teaching. We were discussing how illustrators use color to express emotion by examining Molly Bang's Caldecott Honor book, *When Sophie Gets Angry-Really, Really Angry* (1999). The students, all preservice elementary education students, responded instead to the idea that parents would allow a young child (Sophie) to run away without following her to ensure she was safe. They agreed that running is a good outlet for emotions – for adults – but not for children. Their takeaway was that the world is too dangerous for children to play outside.

As a result of the students' attitude, several of us began discussing the representations of play in children's books, in both the text and the illustrations. This study developed from our class discussion. We examined Caldecott Medal and Honor books during the years 1938–1949 and 2001–2014 by exploring the illustrative and textual representations of play in children's picture storybooks. Our purpose in attempting this research was to discover how the portrayal of play in the Caldecott books has evolved over time and if there is any significant change during those decades in their patterns. The other implication of this research was to encourage our students to better understand and interact with metafictional, postmodern, and playful textual and visual narratives. To do that, we examined 103 picture storybooks chosen as Caldecott Medal or Honor books within the first 11 years of the award (56 books) and 11 recent years of the award (47 books). We assumed that these years would provide the most noticeable differences in children's play.

According to the Association for Library Service to Children (ALSC) website, the Caldecott Medal is awarded annually to the artist of the most distinguished American picture book for children published by an American publisher in the United States in English during the preceding year. Within this research we have focused on Caldecott Medal or Honor picture books since award-winning titles will become bestsellers and also "will stay in a library's collection long after popularity of contemporary bestsellers fades" (Moffet 12). It is commonly held that "the shiny sticker appeals equally and brilliantly to a winning picturebook's two primary audiences – children and the adults who nurture them" (Smith 10). Furthermore, "as the longest-running award for children's picture books in the United States, the Caldecott canon is frequently utilized for research examining the culture of children's picture books, including within the broader context of concurrent social issues" (Moffet 7).

Play *In* Books or *Playful* Books: Background and Significance

In a general sense, play refers to any enjoyable and entertaining activity. Play captures and holds participants' interest and makes them happy. In play, children – or adults – participate in solitary or group activities to occupy and entertain themselves. Through play we enhance our understanding of the world, make meaning of other lifestyles, find imaginary or real companions, and expand our ability to communicate with family, friends, and peers. Nespeca contends that "[p]lay encourages healthy brain development while fostering exploration skills, language skills, social skills, physical skills and creativity" (2). Although play can be instructive and productive, the real essence of play is bringing pleasure, joy, and excitement to those who play: "The fun and excitement of playing cannot be calculated in an abstract fashion: it must be experienced" (Salen and Zimmerman 25). Any simple or complex, primitive or advanced form of play, such as board games, crossword puzzles, hide-and-seek, rock-paper-scissors, computer games, video games, and organized sports, offers a simple possibility of pleasure that participants may experience and explore.

A major challenge of defining and describing play is that it has many forms, functions, and users. According to Nespeca, play can be delineated as 1) object play, 2) pretend play, and 3) social play (1). In discussing various types of play, Fromberg and Bergen extend the category to "play with objects, play with others in sociodramatic play, play with rules, play from children's perspectives, and play with humor" (63). Also, as the Dutch anthropologist Johan Huizinga suggested, "play is a free activity standing quite consciously outside 'ordinary' life as being 'not serious' but at the same time absorbing the player intensely and utterly" (qtd. in Salen and Zimmerman 75). While each of these points of view offers a valid way of looking at play, "each person defines games in his own way – the anthropologists and folklorists in terms of historical origins; the military men, businessmen, and educators in terms of usages, the social scientists in terms of psychological and social functions" (Avedon and Sutton-Smith 438).

There are other forms of play, ones that are identified by artists and linguists. Those are the ones we find in museum and picture storybook art, and here we are thinking of well-known works of art by Jean-Michel Basquiat such as "Pez Dispenser, 1984," which appears as the jacket illustration for Maya Angelou's book *Life Doesn't Frighten Me* (1993). In fact, images such as M. C. Escher's surrealistic paintings hold a fascination for children and adults alike with their resemblance to puzzles. Much of Lane Smith's *Grandpa Green* (2011) is implicitly playful like the double-page spread of Grandpa Green's children, grandchildren, and great-grandchildren. The art is reminiscent of surrealist Rene Magritte's painting called "The Blank Check." Other artists have used this type of image – Anthony Browne, for example – to force viewers to look closely for the similarities and differences. Chappell and Cahnmann-Taylor present a review of the research on the value of the arts for children, especially in minoritized communities. Some of the benefits from engaging young people with the arts include imaginative play and interpretative discussions, which can lead to acceptance of ambiguity and others' points of view (247).

Even more pervasive are the linguistic games children as well as adults enjoy, some of which are based on literature. Take for example the lowly "Swifty" descended from the Tom Swift books of the early twentieth century, a series created by the famous Stratemeyer Syndicate. Jon Agee, Fred Gwynne, and Marvin Terban have made writing careers by publishing books of palindromes, homophones, homonyms, and idioms. Frank Viva, a Canadian author and illustrator, recently released a book of oronyms. Authors often implant suggestions about children's nursery rhymes or games in their text. *Where the Wild Things Are* (Sendak 1963) is a good example; Max tames the Wild Things by "staring into all their yellow eyes without blinking once." Max's prize – he became "the most wild thing of all."

However, the vast range of activities that have been identified and described as play by scholars from different disciplines have certain points in common. They occur in a natural way, without being forced. They are planned, directed, and performed mainly by children and include other humans and non-humans. They might be invented, constructed, or selected. To play, participants often make up and negotiate explicit goals, rules, and procedures. Sometimes, the participants embed new meanings in a familiar activity through unstructured and unsystematic dialogue and actions.

Play is often associated with children and childhood. At a certain age, sometime between adolescence and adulthood, people are more likely to view play as a childish behavior and to use their leisure time for non-play activities. However, "studied from the perspectives of many disciplines, play does not end at a particular age but continues to emerge, and occasionally erupt, in shifting forms throughout the life span" (Fromberg and Bergen xvi). For example, regardless of age, when people daydream, their minds move from concrete logical thinking to fantasy and imagination where playful thinking prevails. So, it would be reasonable to say that "play is one of those large ideas that touch [*sic*] a strand of human experience beginning in childhood and, perhaps in different forms, continuing throughout life" (Wiltz and Fein 127). While adults barely show interest in continuing their childhood diversions, they may develop new interests in other forms of play embedded in their social practices.

We found that play falls into two major categories when we reviewed different forms and functions of play: play activities created by external resources and play initiated by children themselves. While the contribution of children to the creation of different types of play has been long recognized as a critical research interest, we turned our attention to play materials provided by adults for children to use and from which they could augment their understanding of the world. In particular, among the materials that seem influential in – and a reflection of – children's play are picture books. There are several potential expressions of play in picture books including text, pictures, and the interaction of text and pictures.

Exploring the representations of play in Caldecott Medal or Honor books during the 11 years between 1938–1949 and 2001–2014 shows that the picture storybooks chosen as Medal or Honor recipients within the first 11 years of the award have more illustrations of characters playing (68%) compared to the books within 2001–2014 period (53%). In contrast, the more recent books tend to include playful pictures instead of explicit pictures about play. According to our findings, this tendency has significantly changed from 7% in 1938–1949 to 47% in 2001–2014. So, what appears to be an emerging trend in creating picture storybooks is a shift from what had been conventional to more unconventional modes. In other words, today's authors and illustrators are more likely to promote the primacy of play through playing with the reader. (See Table 10.1.)

While there is definitely less portrayal of explicit play in contemporary Caldecott books, their fast-growing implied playfulness will continue to engage readers emotionally and intellectually, "a playfulness that invite [*sic*] the reader or viewer into a co-construction of meaning" (Pantaleo 49). In an overwhelming majority of older Caldecott books, written text and visual imagery have been stable, linear, and less playful. The emergence and growth of irony and playfulness in contemporary picture books challenge the conventional expectations and redefine or subvert the picture book norms. Although artfully constructed early Caldecott books might be as appealing as the more recent books, these early award-winners do not demand the same type of aesthetic appreciation as the more recent books.

Metafictional Picture Storybooks and the Meaning of Play

Unlike earlier picture storybooks, the illustrations of the most recent books do not tend to mirror or enhance the text; instead, they prompt the reader to think, to feel uneasy, to discover, to move "back and forth between the trivial and the profound" (Salen and Zimmerman xi), to revisit and to rediscover. In metafictional picture storybooks, as Nikolajeva (2010) calls them, there are visible signs of an invisible play, the means by which the author or illustrator has chosen not to shape any meaning but to foster the skill of meaning-making. The cover of Marla Frazee's 2008 *A Couple of Boys Have the Best Week Ever* is an excellent example of this concept. The ironic tenor of the book's contents is signaled by the replica of a comic book price tag with a wry parenthetical "*you wish*" and the boys' speech bubbles asking how long they have to smile.

In order for a picture storybook be considered metafictional, authors and illustrators draw the reader's attention to the book's fictionality. The complex verbal and mainly "visual figurative language" (Nikolajeva 37) of metafictional picture storybooks creates a high-tension reading, which by no means guarantees a mutual agreement between the author's or illustrator's ideas and what the reader perceives. Metafictional picture storybooks with verbal as well as visual allusions and illusions enhance the primacy of curiosity, imagination, and therefore play. Part of the playing lies in the reader's personal perception of textual-pictorial codes. In this sense, what Iser (1974) states about all books can be applied to a greater extent to metafictional picture storybooks:

> The reader acts as co-creator of the work by supplying that portion of it that is not written but only implied. Each reader fills in the unwritten work or the 'gaps' in his or her own way, thereby acknowledging the inexhaustibility of the text.
>
> (qtd. in Sipe 99)

As Iser further indicates, when we read "we look forward, we look back, we decide, we change our decisions, we form expectations, we are shocked by their nonfulfillment, we question, we muse, we accept, we reject; this is the dynamic process of recreation" (Sipe 223). Yet, meaning-making in metafictional picture storybooks requires a playful and persistent mindset to pursue and understand the multiple levels of story. Reading metafictional books is not a casual reading, and therefore it needs to be ruled by readers' intellects as well as feelings. "Unsophisticated readers" oftentimes are not prepared for this kind of a complex challenge (Nikolajeva 39). While "puzzling through multiple layers of meaning and ambiguity" (Sipe and Pantaleo 4) might be pleasurable and exciting for some readers, it might be intolerable for others.

Postmodernism and Play in Picture Storybooks

McCallum, Sipe, and Pantaleo note that several of the features associated with postmodernism are also applicable to the concept of metafictional picture storybooks. For example, some common features of both postmodernism and metafiction are "narrative fragmentation and discontinuity, disorder and chaos, code mixing and absurdity as well as openness, playfulness and parody" (3). In particular, Sipe and McGuire identify playfulness as a technique "in which readers are invited to treat the text as a semiotic playground" (qtd. in Sipe and Pantaleo 3). Readers can revisit a book with the fresh excitement of reading and playing, and each time they are challenged to *re*-play both the familiar and unfamiliar in different contexts.

To explore the essence of picture storybooks more deeply and bring the discussion of play and picture storybooks into full view, the rest of the chapter reviews the study of play in Caldecott Medal and Honor books during 1938–1949 and 2001–2014, focusing on how play has been represented in text and in illustration. Additionally, one of the sidelights of the study produced insights into how metafictional picture storybooks evoke emotional as well as intellectual responses in readers/players.

Context of the Study and Methodology

Rather that reviewing the thousands of picture storybooks published every year, we sampled the first 11 years and 11 recent years during which children's book experts (librarians, educators and other professionals) selected Caldecott Medal and Honor books. According to the Association for Library Service to Children (ALSC) website, the Caldecott Medal has been a sign of excellence in "artistic technique" and "pictorial interpretation" in children's picture storybooks. On the one hand, our research sample could provide insight into what outstanding American authors and illustrators offer and, on the other hand, could "maximize the likelihood of examining books that young children are most likely to encounter" (Williams 150). In reviewing the award books, we were particularly interested in comparing the old and the new. The purpose of our study was to examine the way and the extent to which play has been portrayed in children's picture storybooks and to explore whether the representation of play has changed over time. In order to do that, we examined the content of all 103 picture storybooks that received the Caldecott Medal or Honor during the periods 1938–1949 and 2001–2014. According to Krippendorff, "[c]ontent analysis is a research technique for making replicable and valid inferences from texts (or other meaningful matter) to the contexts of their use" (18). Content analysis is a method of analyzing content to find patterns, to examine what the patterns are, and to determine to what category these patterns belong. The presence or absence of patterns of play in our research sample shows the extent and nature of change in Caldecott books during the 22 years we examined. To conduct a content analysis, we assigned codes to our books based on four specific variables: 1) representation of play in text, 2) representation of play in pictures, 3) representation of playfulness in text, and 4) representation of playfulness in pictures. For the purposes of this study, we defined explicit play as any direct reference to play in text or images of picture books and also implicit play when there is no direct or obvious reference to play in text or images but an implied reference. Furthermore, we defined playfulness as the highest embodiment of representing play in the form or content of picture books, that is, when we see the author or the illustrator playing with the reader. Playfulness is a continuum of representing the conventional and the unconventional. The extent the attributes move along the continuum shows the playfulness or un-playfulness of text and art. With these four coding frames in mind, first we explored the text for *any* representation of play, including the existence of any play-related words or any direct or indirect references to play. Then we examined the text for playful plots and playful language. We also examined the illustrations to identify any representation of explicit or implicit play within visual information; we looked closely at visual elements such as color, shape, placement of objects, line, texture, and amount of light in the pictures and examined every book for the presence of play within the visual plot.

For this discussion of the essence of play in Caldecott Medal and Honor books, we have focused on four books from our sample: two titles from the earlier period (1938–1949) and two from the more recent period (2001–2014). As described in detail later, these four books are significant examples of our coding frames, and therefore they best represent the sample.

Discussion

The four books selected for more in-depth discussion are *Blueberries for Sal* (1948) by Robert McCloskey, which was awarded a 1949 Caldecott Honor award; *Mei Li* (1938) by Thomas Handforth, which received the 1939 Caldecott Medal; *Blackout* (2011) by John Rocco, which received the 2012 Caldecott Honor award; and *Grandpa Green* (2011) by Lane Smith, which also received a 2012 Caldecott Honor award.

Blueberries for Sal, written and illustrated by Robert McCloskey, is a fictional picture storybook published in 1948 that received a Caldecott Honor in 1949. The protagonist is Sal, a young girl who, with her mother, goes to Blueberry Hill to pick blueberries and preserve them for the winter. At the same time, at the other side of the same hill, a bear cub and his mother are eating and gathering blueberries, too. The parallel stories that first echo – then intersect – each other represent the playfulness of the textual and visual plot. For example, as Sal goes higher and higher, she becomes so involved in her blueberry picking that she does not notice she is following the mother bear; the same scenario plays out as the bear cub follows the human mother. Interestingly, each mother is unaware that a wrong child is following her. Also, the front endpapers of the book show Sal playing with the canning rings and trying to pass a spoon through the rings. This illustration is an example of implicit play since the picture shows no direct reference to toys or games but the mischievous look on Sal's face and in her posture suggests her playful nature. One example of explicit play in the text is the counterpoint created by phrases like "Little bear and little Sal's mother and little Sal and little bear's mother." Another example of explicit language play is McCloskey's use of sound imagery as Sal drops blueberries into her pail, "ku-plink, ku-plank, ku-plunk." *Blueberries for Sal* is an excellent example of a classic picture storybook with all of the codes used for this study: 1) representation of play in text, 2) representation of play in pictures, 3) representation of playfulness in text, and 4) representation of playfulness in pictures.

While *Blueberries for Sal* presents one or more instances of all of four codes used for this study, the representations of playfulness in text and pictures are insignificant and not more than just the literal text. In other words, as readers move between text and illustrations, there are not many gaps they need to fill to comprehend the story.

Mei Li, written and illustrated by Thomas Handforth, is a fictional picture storybook published in 1938. It won the 1939 Caldecott Medal. The setting is a Chinese New Year's festival, and Mei Li is a Chinese girl who sneaks out – contrary to the customs of her society – to attend the New Year's Fair in the city with her brother, San Yu. Mei Li proves that girls can compete equally with boys and enjoy a full day of adventure. There are many examples of explicit references to play and playthings in the text such as "firecracker," "the circus," "dressed himself up as a wise old man with a silly long beard," "kite," and "toy shop." Also, there are explicit references to play in the illustrations that reveal the circus, kite,

Figure 10.1 Robert McCloskey, *Blueberries for Sal.* Viking, 1948. Written and illustrated by Robert McCloskey

Source: Courtesy Viking

and children dressed up and playing. Given this view, *Mei Li* is an example of a classic picture storybook with only explicit references to play in text and pictures.

Blackout, written and illustrated by John Rocco, is a fictional picture storybook published in 2011. It received a Caldecott Honor award in

Figure 10.2 Thomas Handforth, *Mei Li*. Doubleday, 1938. Written and illustrated by Thomas Handforth

Source: Courtesy Doubleday

2012. One hot summer night in Brooklyn, the unnamed little character (probably a girl) tries to play with other family members, but everyone is too busy to play with her until the power goes off. That is when the busy family goes to the roof and then to the street to renew their familial connections and also to enjoy the bright starry night with many of their neighbors. When the power is restored, the family does not want to return to normal, and so the unnamed character turns off the lights and the family plays a board game. There are explicit references to play in the illustrations, such as the board game's label, "2 or more players," making shadows on the wall, and playing a video game. In addition to the explicit references to play, there are instances of implicit play in illustrations. For example, the pre-title page illustration represents a little girl with a TV screen behind her. This opening conveys the story of a frustrated child who has no interest in watching TV. Another example is the portrait of Thomas Edison framed on the wall. Edison's expression looks dour, foreshadowing that soon there will be a power outage. Another brilliant example of implicit play is the scared cat running from a hand shadow of a dog on the wall. Also, as the story unfolds and when the electricity is restored, the delighted little girl switches off the lights, and all family members choose to play the board game together. *Blackout* is one example of a modern picture storybook with a balance of both implicit and explicit references to play and playfulness in text and pictures. The implicit examples of play in *Blackout* engage readers, arouse their excitement as well as their curiosity, and incite them to think about the visual and verbal narrative codes and surprises.

Grandpa Green written and illustrated by Lane Smith is a fictional picture storybook published in 2011 that won a Caldecott Honor in 2012. The story opens with a picture of a topiary baby with the text "He was born a really long time ago." Narrated from the point of view of a little boy, the story is a lifetime retrospective of the old man – Grandpa Green – portrayed through topiary sculptures. *Grandpa Green* includes numerous layers of play and playfulness both in text and pictures. Playing in the garden, chasing a rabbit, swinging on a tree, and engaging in pretend sword fights are explicit examples in the illustrations, while references to classic tales such as *The Wonderful Wizard of Oz* (Baum) and *The Little Engine that Could* (Piper) in the illustrations represent the playfulness of the story. Also, the surprises in the visual and textual narration make the book more playful and in some cases more challenging than books with cognitively undemanding text and illustrations. For instance, the narrator in *Grandpa Green* reveals his identity when he says, "They had kids, way more grandkids, and a great-grandkid, me" near the picture in which only one child stares at the reader. Another visual surprise is on the final page, when the boy creates a topiary of Grandpa Green. Hence *Grandpa Green* is an excellent example of a modern picture storybook with both implicit and explicit references to play in the illustrations and playfulness in textual language.

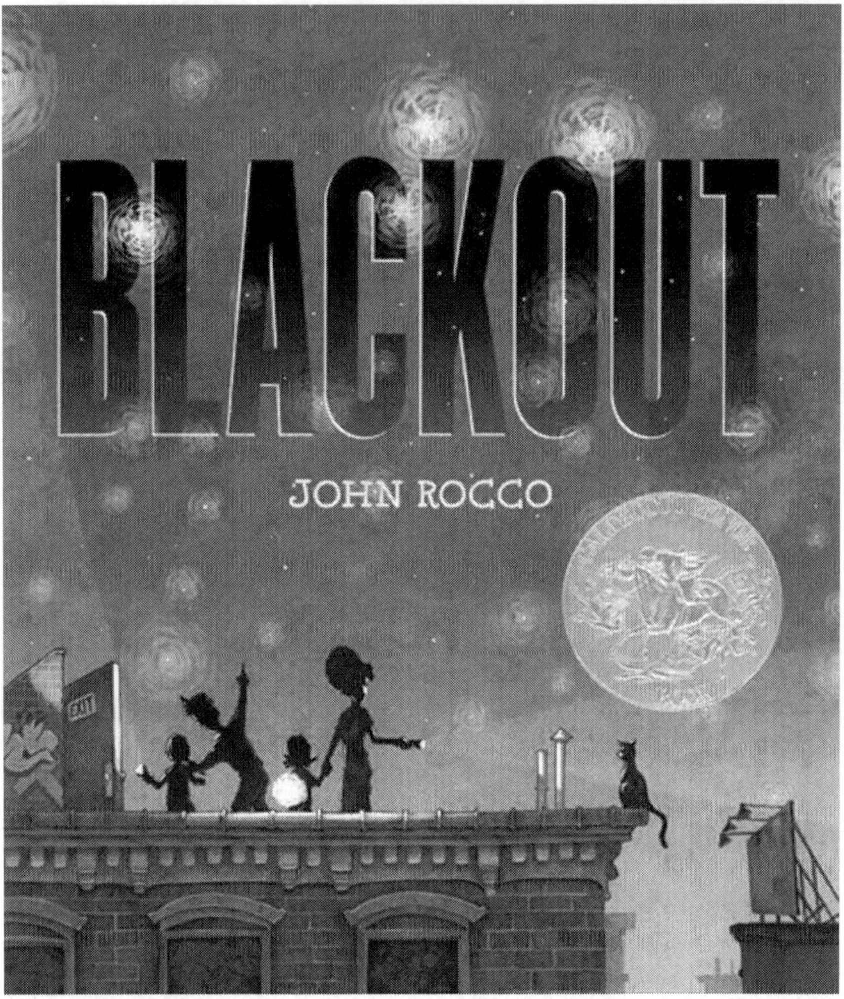

Figure 10.3 John Rocco, *Blackout*. Hyperion Books, 2011. Written and illustrated by John Rocco

Source: Courtesy Disney Hyperion Books, an imprint of Disney Book Group

Implications for Sharing Caldecott Books

By using Caldecott books as proxies for all picture storybooks, readers can observe that there has been a modification in children's picture storybooks from engaging in explicit physical activities, as in *Blueberries for Sal* (McCloskey), to more intellectually challenging forms of play, i.e. decoding word play, irony, or other types of sophisticated reading.

Figure 10.4 Lane Smith, *Grandpa Green*. Roaring Brook Press, 2011. Written and illustrated by Lane Smith

Source: Courtesy Roaring Brook Press, a division of Holtzbrinck Publishing Holdings Limited Partnership

How do these changes affect adult interactions with young people? As parents, teachers, and librarians, how do we encourage young people to interact with metafictional and postmodern books? How do we engage with recent Caldecott books on an intellectually playful plane as opposed to a physically playful level?

Whereas past wisdom suggested a quick picture walk as an effective way to introduce a picture storybook before reading aloud with children, some recent books might be spoiled if the child views the illustrations before actually engaging with the text. *This Is Not My Hat*, the 2013 Caldecott Medal winner by Jon Klassen (2012), is a good example of the irony established by the tension between text and illustrations. To guide a group of children on a picture walk through this book would prematurely disclose the "got 'cha" ending. *This Is Not My Hat* is a book that benefits from thoughtful discussion that enables even older children to grasp that there are inconsistencies between the small fish's assumptions and the large fish's determination.

Figure 10.5 Jon Klassen, *This Is Not My Hat*, Candlewick Press, 2012. Written and illustrated by Jon Klassen

Source: Courtesy Candlewick Press

There are numerous techniques in place of a picture walk that will encourage young people to make predictions both before and during a read aloud. Just as in a picture walk, we need to elicit children's predictions based on the cover art, but then what happens if we turn to the back cover instead of proceding through each page? When we read Klassen's book to a kindergarten class shortly after it was released and before it won any awards, the children examined the cover and predicted what was going to happen after each page. The children were unerring in their interpretations of the bubbles indicating directionality and the results of crab's decision to tattletale on the little fish. No one was upset at the end of the story because, "the little fish was bad and he deserved to be eaten!" Ending with a discussion of the back cover provided a wonderful chance for the children to end the story according to their interpretation: does the big fish loose his hat? Does a bigger fish eat him? Does the little fish decide he doesn't like his hat any more? Does the big fish feel sorry for what he did to the little fish? What did the big fish do to the little fish? All of these are legitimate discussion prompts for this book.

A Caldecott Medal book published after the conclusion of our study, *The Adventures of Beekle: The Unimaginary Friend* by Dan Santat (2014), presents an idea that is common to many children – an imaginary friend. And yet, there is an overwhelming lonliness that permeates most of the story. To read this book – before revealing the happy ending through a picture walk – enables children to talk about how sad Beekle appears. Even the two-year-old daughter of an acquaintance told her dad that she could always tell Beekle because he was the sad one. As adults, we want to ignore the forlorn and abandoned feeling that all children experience from time to time, no matter how well-adjusted they may be. We have shared this as a read aloud with young children, starting with the title and then analyzing the word "unimaginary." Then we focused on Beekle's expression and discussed how he might feel standing at the bus stop with no one to talk to. With older children, it is possible for them to compare they way they feel if they are not chosen for playground games. The art in this book allows for great imagining – what friend would you choose? Or for creativity by writing and illustrating pictures and stories about an imaginary friend. It also encourages a sense of empathy for Beekle and, by transferral, to other children who are sad or lonely. The artist's role in generating meaning can be examined with questions such as why is Beekle white? Is he scary like a ghost?

Marla Frazee's book *A Couple of Boys Have the Best Week Ever* (2008) is another Caldecott Honor book that is better allowed to unfold naturally. The title suggest that the entire week is fantastic, but as the story unfolds, James and Eamon deny that they are enjoying their week at a nature camp. By closely examining the illustrations, readers see that all of the planned activities fall flat, and it is not until their final night, when they are free of adult supervision to create their own (imaginary) Antartica, that James and Eamon admit they want to return next year for another nature camp. From the cover illustrations to the jacket flaps and end papers, there are contradictions between what the text says and what the illustrations depict. Readers are free to draw their own conclusions about whether the boys really do have the best week ever.

Before reading any book aloud, it is important to spend time with the illustrations and the text. However, by comparing more recent Caldecott Medal and Honor books to the earliest award-winners, we believe that librarians, teachers, and parents should consider skipping or paring down the picture walk so that the story can unfold naturally through *both* the words and the pictures. New and more challenging picture storybooks require adults to change their approach to picture storybook read alouds. The presence of ironic elements, emotional triggers, and contradictions between words and pictures demands that adults slow down their reading to enable children to express their understandings, predictions, and befuddlement at the story. As authors and illustrators continue to push

Figure 10.6 Dan Santat, *The Adventures of Beekle: The Unimaginary Friend*. Little, Brown, 2014. Written and illustrated by Dan Santat

Source: Courtesy Little, Brown and Company, a division of Hachette Book Group, Inc.

the envelope by challenging their readers' imaginations, award committees will also search for – and select – more unique books. The practical conclusion, we believe, is that we who select and read books to children should be open to all of the changes in picture storybooks and allow children to show they understand concepts far beyond our imagining.

Figure 10.7 Marla Frazee, *A Couple of Boys Have the Best Week Ever*. Harcourt, 2008. Written and illustrated by Marla Frazee

Source: Courtesy Harcourt, Inc.

Conclusion

We analyzed 103 picture storybooks receiving Caldecott Medals or Honor awards during 1938–1949 and 2001–2014. The content changes during these two time periods suggest that explicit representations of play within text and pictures in 1938–1949 books are significantly more than in the 2001–2014 books. However, in 2001–2014 books, playful illustrations are substantially more frequent than in the 1938–1949 award books. The more recent Caldecott books suggest that there is a growing interest in creating playful text and pictures instead of explicit representations of characters playing. Furthermore, there is a significant increase in nonlinear storylines in text and pictures that demand more sophisticated readers who can follow a playful visual plot. Our study indicates that today's children are exposed to relatively few *images* of characters engaged in play and even fewer *images* of players interacting with each other. In contrast, there is a significant increase in "multimodal" (Nikolajeva 27) books with nonlinear, playful, and more complex storylines both in text and pictures. The "metafictional" (35) content of contemporary Caldecott books demands more sophisticated readers and suggests that reading is not always a straightforward process. Modern Caldecott Medal and Honor books demand creative reading not only by child readers but also by teachers, librarians, and caregivers who will find themselves engaged in exploring dynamic activities and discovering new environments.

Works Cited

Angelou, Maya. *Life Doesn't Frighten Me*, illustrated by Jean-Michel Basquiat. Stewart, Tabori and Chang, 1993.

Association for Library Service to Children (ALSC). "Caldecott Medal – Terms and Criteria." 2015, www.ala.org/alsc/awardsgrants/bookmedia/caldecottmedal/caldecottterms/caldecottterms. Accessed 21 Mar. 2019.

Avedon, Elliott M., and Brian Sutton-Smith. *The Study of Games*. Ishi Press, 2015.

Bang, Molly. *When Sophie Gets Angry . . . Really, Really Angry*. Blue Sky Press, an imprint of Scholastic, 1999.

Baum, L. Frank. *The Wonderful Wizard of Oz*, illustrated by W. W. Denslow. George M. Hill, 1899.

Chappell, Sharon Verner, and Melisa Cahnmann-Taylor. "No Child Left with Crayons: The Imperative of Arts-Based Education and Research with Language 'Minority' and Other Minoritized Communities." *Review of Research in Education*, vol. 37, no. 1, 2013, pp. 243–68. JSTOR, www.jstor.org/stable/24641963. Accessed 21 Mar. 2019.

Frazee, Marla. *A Couple of Boys Have the Best Week Ever*. Harcourt, 2008.

———. *Marla Frazee: Author, Illustrator*. Children's Books, www.marlafrazee.com/. Accessed 21 Mar. 2009.

Fromberg, Doris Pronin, and Doris Bergen. *Play from Birth to Twelve: Contexts, Perspectives, and Meanings*. Taylor and Francis, 2006.

Genette, Gérard. "Introduction to the Paratext." Translated by Marie MacLean. *New Literary History*, vol. 22, no. 2, 1991, pp. 261–72.

Haghanikar, Taraneh Matloob, and Linda M. Pavonetti. "Is It Safe to Play? Representations of Play and Playfulness in Caldecott Medal and Honor Books 1938–1949 and 2001–2012." Children's Literature Association (ChLA) Conference, 15 June 2013. U of Southern Mississippi, Biloxi.

Handforth, Thomas. *Mei Li*. Doubleday, 1938.

Iser, Wolfgang. *The Act of Reading: A Theory of Aesthetic Response*. Johns Hopkins UP, 1974.

Klassen, Jon. *This Is Not My Hat*. Candlewick Press, 2012.

Krippendorff, Klaus. *Content Analysis: An Introduction to Its Methodology*. Sage Publications, 2004.

Magritte, René. *The Blank Signature*. Washington, DC: National Gallery of Art, 1965. Image, www.artexpertswebsite.com/pages/artists/magritte.php. Accessed 21 Mar. 2019.

McCloskey, Robert. *Blueberries for Sal*. Viking, 1948.

Moffett, Angela Christine. *Exploring Racial Diversity in Caldecott Medal-Winning and Honor Books*. San Jose State UP, Master's Theses, 2016. doi://doi.org/10.31979/etd.8khk-78uy.

Nespeca, Sue McCleaf. "The Importance of Play, Particularly Constructive Play, in Public Library Programming." A White Paper Written for the Association for Library Service to Children and Adopted by ALSC's Board of Directors, 10 Sept. 2012, www.ala.org/alsc/importance_of_play. Accessed 4 Feb. 2013.

Nikolajeva, Maria. *Children's Literature and Culture: New Directions in Picturebook Research*. Routledge, 2010.

Pantaleo, Sylvia J. "Everything Comes from Seeing Things': Narrative and Illustrative Play in Black and White." *Children's Literature in Education*, vol. 38, 2007, pp. 45–58. doi:10.1007/s10583-006-9029-x.

Piper, Watty. *The Little Engine That Could*, illustrated by Lois Lenski. Platt and Munk, 1930.

Rocco, John. *Blackout*. Hyperion Books, 2011.

Salen, Katie, and Eric Zimmerman. *Rules of Play: Game Design Fundamentals*. MIT Press, 2004.

Santat, Dan. *The Adventures of Beekle: The Unimaginary Friend*. Little, Brown, 2014.

Sendak, M. *Where the Wild Things Are*. Harper and Row, 1963.

Sipe, Lawrence R. "How Picture Books Work: A Semiotically Framed Theory of Text-Picture Relationships." *Children's Literature in Education*, vol. 29, no. 2, 1998, pp. 97–108.

Sipe, Lawrence R., and Sylvia Pantaleo. *Postmodern Picturebooks: Play, Parody, and Self-Referentiality*. Taylor and Francis, 2008.

Smith, Lane. *Grandpa Green*. Roaring Brook Press, 2011.

Smith, Vicky. "The Powerful Impact of Those Shiny Stickers." *Children Libraries the Journal of the Association for Library Service to Children*, vol. 11, no. 1, 2013, pp. 9–13.

Williams, J. Allen, et al. "The Human-Environment Dialog in Award-Winning Children's Picture Books." *Sociological Inquiry*, vol. 82, no. 1, 2012. pp. 145–59.

Wiltz, Nancy W., and Greta G. Fein. "Play as Children See It." *Play from Birth to Twelve: Contexts, Perspectives, and Meanings*, edited by Doris Pronin Fromberg and Doris Bergen, Taylor and Francis, 2006, pp. 43–54.

Appendix: Tables

Table 10.1 Representations of Play in Caldecott Medal and Honor books

	1938–1949	*2001–2012*
Explicit pictures about play	68%	53%
Playful pictures	7%	47%

Table 10.2 Caldecott Medal and Honor Books, 2001–2013 (47 Awards)

Award	*Title*	*Illustrator*	*Author*	*Publisher*
2013 Medal	***This Is Not My Hat***	Jon Klassen	same	Candlewick Press
2013 Honor	***Creepy Carrots!***	Peter Brown	Aaron Reynolds	Simon & Schuster
2013 Honor	***Extra Yarn***	Jon Klassen	Mac Barnett	HarperCollins/ Balzer + Bray
2013 Honor	***Green***	Laura Vaccaro Seeger	same	Roaring Brook Press/Neal Porter
2013 Honor	***One Cool Friend***	David Small	Toni Buzzeo	Penguin/Dial
2013 Honor	***Sleep Like a Tiger***	Pamela Zagarenski	Mary Logue	Houghton Mifflin
2012 Medal	***A Ball for Daisy***	Chris Raschka	same	Random House/ Schwartz & Wade
2012 Honor	***Blackout***	John Rocco	same	Disney/Hyperion
2012 Honor	***Grandpa Green***	Lane Smith	same	Holtzbrinck/ Roaring Brook Press
2012 Honor	***Me . . . Jane***	Patrick McDonnell	same	Hachette/Little, Brown

Award	*Title*	*Illustrator*	*Author*	*Publisher*
2011 Medal	***A Sick Day for Amos McGee***	Erin E. Stead	Philip C. Stead	Holtzbrinck/ Roaring Brook Press/Neal Porter
2011 Honor	***Dave the Potter: Artist, Poet, Slave***	Bryan Collier	Laban Carrick Hill	Hachette/Little, Brown
2011 Honor	***Interrupting Chicken***	David Ezra Stein	same	Candlewick Press
2010 Medal	***The Lion & the Mouse***	Jerry Pinkney	same	Little, Brown
2010 Honor	***All the World***	Marla Frazee	Liz Garton Scanlon	Beach Lane
2010 Honor	***Red Sings from Treetops: A Year in Colors***	Pamela Zagarenski	Joyce Sidman	Houghton Mifflin Harcourt
2009 Medal	***The House in the Night***	Beth Krommes	Susan Marie Swanson	Houghton Mifflin
2009 Honor	***A Couple of Boys Have the Best Week Ever***	Marla Frazee,	same	Harcourt
2009 Honor	***How I Learned Geography***	Uri Shulevitz	same	Farrar Straus Giroux
2009 Honor	***A River of Words: The Story of William Carlos Williams***	Melissa Sweet	Jen Bryant	Eerdmans for Young Readers
2008 Medal	***The Invention of Hugo Cabret***	Brian Selznick	same	Scholastic Press
2008 Honor	***Henry's Freedom Box: A True Story from the Underground Railroad***	Kadir Nelson	Ellen Levine	Scholastic Press
2008 Honor	***First the Egg***	Laura Vaccaro Seeger	same	Roaring Brook/ Neal Porter
2008 Honor	***The Wall: Growing Up Behind the Iron Curtain***	Peter Sís	same	Farrar Straus Giroux/ Frances Foster

(*Continued*)

Table 10.2 (Continued)

Award	*Title*	*Illustrator*	*Author*	*Publisher*
2008 Honor	***Knuffle Bunny Too: A Case of Mistaken Identity***	Mo Willems	same	Hyperion
2007 Medal	***Flotsam***	David Wiesner	same	Clarion
2007 Honor	***Gone Wild: An Endangered Animal Alphabet***	David McLimans	same	Walker
2007 Honor	***Moses: When Harriet Tubman Led Her People to Freedom***	Kadir Nelson	Carole Boston Weatherford	Hyperion/Jump at the Sun
2006 Medal	***The Hello, Goodbye Window***	Chris Raschka	Norton Juster	Hyperion/ Michael di Capua
2006 Honor	***Rosa***	Bryan Collier	Nikki Giovanni	Henry Holt
2006 Honor	***Zen Shorts***	Jon J. Muth	same	Scholastic Press
2006 Honor	***Hot Air: The (Mostly) True Story of the First Hot-Air Balloon Ride***	Marjorie Priceman	same	Simon & Schuster/Anne Schwartz/ Atheneum
2006 Honor	***Song of the Water Boatman and Other Pond Poems***	Beckie Prange	Joyce Sidman	Houghton Mifflin
2005 Medal	***Kitten's First Full Moon***	Kevin Henkes	same	HarperCollins/ Greenwillow
2005 Honor	***The Red Book***	Barbara Lehman	same	Houghton Mifflin
2005 Honor	***Coming on Home Soon***	E. B. Lewis	Jacqueline Woodson	Penguin/G.P. Putnam's Son's
2005 Honor	***Knuffle Bunny: A Cautionary Tale***	Mo Willems	same	Hyperion
2004 Medal	***The Man Who Walked Between the Towers***	Mordicai Gerstein	same	Millbrook / Roaring Brook Press
2004 Honor	***Ella Sarah Gets Dressed***	Margaret Chodos-Irvine	same	Harcourt

Award	Title	Illustrator	Author	Publisher
2004 Honor	***What Do You Do with a Tail Like This?***	Steve Jenkins and Robin Page	same	Houghton Mifflin
2004 Honor	***Don't Let the Pigeon Drive the Bus***	Mo Willems	same	Hyperion
2003 Medal	***My Friend Rabbit***	Eric Rohmann	same	Millbrook/ Roaring Brook Press
2003 Honor	***The Spider and the Fly***	Tony DiTerlizzi	Mary Howitt	Simon & Schuster
2003 Honor	***Hondo & Fabian***	Peter McCarty	same	Henry Holt
2003 Honor	***Noah's Ark***	Jerry Pinkney	same	North-South/ SeaStar
2002 Medal	***The Three Pigs***	David Wiesner	same	Houghton Mifflin/Clarion
2002 Honor	***The Dinosaurs of Waterhouse Hawkins***	Brian Selznick	Barbara Kerley	Scholastic
2002 Honor	***Martin's Big Words: the Life of Dr. Martin Luther King, Jr.***	Bryan Collier	Doreen Rappaport	Hyperion/Jump at the Sun
2002 Honor	***The Stray Dog***	Marc Simont	same	HarperCollins
2001 Medal	***So You Want to Be President?***	David Small	Judith St. George	Penguin/ Philomel
2001 Honor	***Casey at the Bat***	Christopher Bing	Ernest Thayer	Handprint
2001 Honor	***Click, Clack, Moo: Cows that Type***	Betsy Lewin	Doreen Cronin	Simon & Schuster
2001 Honor	***Olivia***	Ian Falconer	same	Simon & Schuster/ Atheneum

Caldecott Medal & Honor Books, 1938–1949 (56 Awards)

Award	Title	Illustrator	Author	Publisher
1949 Medal	***The Big Snow***	Berta and Elmer Hader	same	Macmillan
1949 Honor	***Blueberries for Sal***	Robert McCloskey	same	Viking

(*Continued*)

Table 10.2 (Continued)

Award	*Title*	*Illustrator*	*Author*	*Publisher*
1949 Honor	***All Around the Town***	Helen Stone	Phyllis McGinley	Lippincott
1949 Honor	***Juanita***	Leo Politi	same	Scribner
1949 Honor	***Fish in the Air***	Kurt Wiese	same	Viking
1948 Medal	***White Snow, Bright Snow***	Roger Duvoisin	Alvin Tresselt	Lothrop
1948 Honor	***McElligot's Pool***	Dr. Seuss, [pseud. Theodor Seuss Geisel]		Random House
1948 Honor	***Stone Soup***	Marcia Brown	same	Scribner
1948 Honor	***Bambino the Clown***	Georges Schreiber	same	Viking
1948 Honor	***Roger and the Fox***	Hildegard Woodward	Lavinia R. Davis	Doubleday
1948 Honor	***Song of Robin Hood***	Virginia Lee Burton	*Anne Malcolmson	Houghton
1947 Medal	***The Little Island***	Leonard Weisgard	**Golden MacDonald,	Doubleday
1947 Honor	***Rain Drop Splash***	Leonard Weisgard	Alvin Tresselt	Lothrop
1947 Honor	***Boats on the River***	Jay Hyde Barnum	Marjorie Flack	Viking
1947 Honor	***Timothy Turtle***	Tony Palazzo	Al Graham	Welch
1947 Honor	***Pedro, the Angel of Olvera Street***	Leo Politi	same	Scribner
1947 Honor	***Sing in Praise: A Collection of the Best Loved Hymns***	Marjorie Torrey	***Opal Wheeler	Dutton
1946 Medal	***The Rooster Crows***	Maud & Miska Petersham		Macmillan
1946 Honor	***Little Lost Lamb***	Leonard Weisgard	**Golden MacDonald,	Doubleday
1946 Honor	***Sing Mother Goose***	Marjorie Torrey	****Opal Wheeler	Dutton
1946 Honor	***My Mother is the Most Beautiful Woman in the World***	Ruth Gannett	Becky Reyher	Lothrop
1946 Honor	***You Can Write Chinese***	Kurt Wiese	same	Viking
1945 Medal	***Prayer for a Child***	Elizabeth Orton Jones	Rachel Field	Macmillan

Award	Title	Illustrator	Author	Publisher
1945 Honor	***Mother Goose***	Tasha Tudor	same	Oxford U.P.
1945 Honor	***In the Forest***	Marie Hall Ets	same	Viking
1945 Honor	***Yonie Wondernose***	Marguerite de Angeli	same	Doubleday
1945 Honor	***The Christmas Anna Angel***	Kate Seredy	Ruth Sawyer	Viking
1944 Medal	***Many Moons***	Louis Slobodkin	James Thurber	Harcourt
1944 Honor	***Small Rain: Verses From The Bible***	Elizabeth Orton Jones	***Jessie Orton Jones	Viking
1944 Honor	***Pierre Pidgeon***	Arnold E. Bare	Lee Kingman	Houghton
1944 Honor	***The Mighty Hunter***	Berta and Elmer Hader	same	Macmillan
1944 Honor	***A Child's Good Night***	Jean Charlot	Margaret Wise Brown	W. R. Scott
1944 Honor	***Good-Luck Horse***	Plato Chan	Chih-Yi Chan	Whittlesey
1943 Medal	***The Little House***	Virginia Lee Burton	same	Houghton
1943 Honor	***Dash and Dart***	Mary and Conrad Buff	same	Viking
1943 Honor	***Marshmallow***	Clare Turlay Newberry	same	Harper
1942 Medal	***Make Way for Ducklings***	Robert McCloskey	same	Viking
1942 Honor	***An American ABC***	Maud and Miska Petersham	same	Macmillan
1942 Honor	***In My Mother's House***	Velino Herrera	Ann Nolan Clark	Viking
1942 Honor	***Paddle-To-The-Sea***	Holling C. Holling	same	Houghton
1942 Honor	***Nothing At All***	Wanda Gág	same	Coward
1941 Medal	***They Were Strong and Good***	Robert Lawson	same	Viking
1941 Honor	***April's Kittens***	Clare Turlay Newberry	same	Harper
1940 Medal	***Abraham Lincoln***	Ingri and Edgar Parin d'Aulaire		Doubleday
1940 Honor	***Cock-a-Doodle Doo***	Berta and Elmer Hader	same	Macmillan

(*Continued*)

Table 10.2 (Continued)

Award	*Title*	*Illustrator*	*Author*	*Publisher*
1940 Honor	***Madeline***	Ludwig Bemelmans	same	Simon & Schuster
1940 Honor	***The Ageless Story***	Lauren Ford	same	Dodd
1939 Medal	***Mei Li***	Thomas Handforth	same	Doubleday
1939 Honor	***Andy and the Lion***	James Daugherty	same	Viking
1939 Honor	***Barkis***	Clare Turlay Newberry	same	Harper
1939 Honor	***The Forest Pool***	Laura Adams Armer	same	Longmans
1939 Honor	***Snow White and the Seven Dwarfs***	Wanda Gág	same	Coward
1939 Honor	***Wee Gillis***	Robert Lawson	Munro Leaf	Viking
1938 Medal	***Animals of the Bible, A Picture Book***	Dorothy P. Lathrop	***Helen Dean Fish	Lippincott
1938 Honor	***Four and Twenty Blackbirds***	Robert Lawson	*****Helen Dean Fish	Stokes
1938 Honor	***Seven Simeons: A Russian Tale***	Boris Artzybasheff	same	Viking

* Editor
**Golden MacDonald is a pseudonym for Margaret Wise Brown.
*** Selected by
**** Music composed by
*****Compiled by

Part 3

Materialities of Play

11 Encounters with Metafiction

Playing with Ideas of What Counts When It Comes to Reading

Jennifer Farrar

The Changing Face of Literacy

As readers in a rapidly changing 21st century, we are now bombarded by a bewildering array of text types, many of which appear to deviate from conventional forms and formats (Anstey 445) and challenge normative definitions of what constitutes a text. According to Rowsell and Pahl, the field of literacy can be envisaged as "in transit" (14), a phrase that suggests the evolving, shifting nature of understandings in this area. No longer bound by taken-for-granted, "autonomous" conventions of schooled literacy (Street 19), current theoretical perspectives depict literacies as a fluid and wide-ranging "ensemble of communicative practices" (Rowsell and Pahl 14).

Research[1] involving children's literature has responded positively to the challenges posed by such change within the broader literacy landscape. In particular, work within the vibrant and multi-faceted sub-field of picturebook studies has revealed how these multimodal texts can act as "bridges" between the print-based approaches used in traditional reading instruction and the multiliteracies demanded by contemporary society (Serafini 26). Classroom-based picturebook studies have demonstrated that engaging with picturebooks can enhance children's multimodal understandings and promote language skills and creativity (Arizpe and McAdam 227), while also providing young readers with access to a broad range of texts and modalities that can help to advance "understanding[s] of the nature of stories and the multiple ways that narratives can be written, represented and told" (Pantaleo 61). Reading picturebooks can teach valuable, transferable lessons about narrative structure, discourse (Meek 19) and visual grammar, while supporting the development of alert, flexible and potentially more critical readers who are more likely to respond positively to the demands of complex texts (McClay 94).

Given the predominantly school-based and child-focused nature of such research, a central premise of this chapter is that it is not only the younger readers in classrooms who need access to new, transforming understandings about literacy. Older readers – parents and carers – who often read alongside their children at home also require support and guidance about what these new literacies are, why they are significant and how they are shaping conceptions of "what counts" when it comes to reading.[2] As Bearne and Kress have noted, the increasing prominence of the "logic of display" in new and emerging text types may seem "utterly unremarkable" to those born *into* such a world (89), possibly because it is what has always been known, making it seem everyday (91) and rendering it largely invisible. In other words, young children seem not to be troubled by the increasingly visual and postmodern nature of contemporary forms of communication perhaps because it is all they have known (McClay 91). Yet, for older readers, those born into a world that was dominated by the linear "logic of narrative, of structures, of events sequenced in time," the task of reconfiguring "Literacy" from a monolith into multiple multiliteracies (New London Group 60) may prove rather less straightforward.

The case for exploring *what counts* about reading – a phrase used here to suggest the normative assumptions that shape how reading occurs, what is privileged and what is ignored – with *both* parents and children has been strengthened by theoretical agreement about the importance of the literacies practiced within families. A crucial site for learning, the home has also been acknowledged as a powerful social environment (Tizard and Hughes 249) that both consciously and unconsciously teaches individuals "how life is lived" (Pahl 48) within a particular context, at a particular time. According to Bourdieu, the dispositions that are cultivated and acquired within the family provide the basis of any subsequent experiences, schooled or otherwise, an idea that acknowledges the "durable and transposable, structuring and structured" (72) force of familial knowledge. *What counts* as literacy at home – "who has the right to speak, when, [and] about what" (Luke 24) – is therefore a crucial part of an individual's literate identity or *literate habitus* (Carrington and Luke 100) that is continually reconfigured throughout life.

Why Picturebooks and Parents?

A review of picturebook scholarship reveals why these multimodal texts make such ideal vehicles for inquiring into adult readers' taken-for-granted assumptions about reading. At the heart of the picturebook – a compound term used to emphasize the "synergy" that exists between the different modes (Sipe 98) – is an inseparable process of "mutual interanimation" (Lewis, *Reading Contemporary Picturebooks* 36) between words and pictures. By challenging readers to extract and assemble meaning from *across* the different modes (rather than from one or the other), the picturebook's "intrinsically plural nature" (Lewis, "The Constructedness of Texts" 141) can come as something of an intellectual surprise to older readers who may have been taught to "skip and scan" over pictures and may consequently perceive them as less significant or valuable in meaning-making terms (Meek 19). The potential of these texts also stems from the fact that they tend to be read aloud between readers across a generational divide who bring different and, as described earlier, sometimes contesting sets of understandings to the shared reading experience. While I agree with Meek (40) and Nodelman (79) that picturebooks contain important lessons for readers of all ages, in the next section I suggest that certain types of picturebook are particularly well-suited to this task.

Metafictive Picturebooks

According to Mackey, a metafictive text "is to stories what the Pompidou Centre in Paris is to architecture: all the pipes and fixtures are displayed on the outside" (184). As this excellent image suggests, an effect of metafiction is to draw attention to how fictional texts function by making all of the editorial or authorial "workings" visible: boundaries are broken by narrators who directly address the reader or interrupt other characters; plot-lines become multiple and subject to fragmentation or frequent dispute and any sense of "narrative logic and consistency" is surrendered to playfully carnivalesque displays that can be characterized by excess, inversion and indeterminacy (Lewis, "The Constructedness of Texts" 144). In fact, the presence of metafiction is said to transform a picturebook into a "semiotic playground" (Sipe and McGuire 283); a place where rules or conventions are flaunted, boundaries are broken, words toyed with and narratives fractured.

By playing with the illusion of fiction, metafiction can undermine and challenge readers' pre-existing expectations of how texts *should* work and how they *ought* to be read by interrupting the "usual" flow of the reading experience. It is also likely that such challenges may register all the more acutely when encountered between the pages of a picturebook, a form and format that feels familiar, comfortable and predictable to many and one that is therefore ripe for disruption. By interrupting such expectations and by refusing to permit readers access to a vicarious or lived-through story experience (Sipe and McGuire 284), metafiction can create a sense of distance between a reader and a text. As Mackey has suggested, the effect of such a gap can be to foster readers with a "reflective and detached awareness of how the processes of fiction are operating as they read. They are simultaneously caught up in the story and standing back from it, watching it work" (179). By extension, the effect of such distancing can also support the development of more critically literate stance by creating room for the consideration of a text as a deliberate construct while gesturing toward the ideological decisions made by publishers, authors and illustrators (Farrar 50).

Given that much of the literature in this area has focused on how children respond to metafiction in picturebooks, the aim of this chapter is to broaden the focus by including the perspectives of their parents, a set of readers who are often positioned "off the landscape" in broader educational research (Pushor and Murphy 224) but particularly in terms of picturebook studies, where they tend to be given instrumental roles. Grounded in the understandings outlined previously, the research question under consideration here is whether the playfully disruptive characteristics of metafictive picturebooks can make adult readers more aware of the "force of the habitus" (Fowler 1) by drawing attention to the literacy practices they employ while reading with young children.

The Project: Rationale and Participants

The overarching project referred to here took place over several months in a western suburb of Edinburgh, Scotland and involved a group of parents, their eight primary school-aged children (aged between 4.5 and 6 years) and four metafictive picturebooks. The texts used in this project, which were selected on the basis of their metafictive characteristics, were sent home in an order that reflected my understanding of their increasing complexity. The texts (and the order) were as follows: *The Bravest Ever Bear* by Allan Ahlberg and Paul Howard, *No Bears* by Meg McKinlay and Leila Rudge, *The Three Pigs* by David Wiesner and *Black and White* by David Macaulay. While this chapter is particularly focused on and around the parents' responses to the metafictive devices at work in *Black and White*, the fact that it was the fourth (and final) book in the series prompted some to return to the earlier texts, a move that enabled the adults to make connections and comparisons across the selection. Therefore, the comments included here are intended to reflect a sense of the parents' accumulating understandings, something I hope also conveys the transformative potential of metafiction.

Broadly speaking, the study fell into two methodologically distinct yet intertwined parts. In the first, I discussed the books with the children inside their school building but outside of their usual classroom contexts; in the second, I met with the children's parents across a range of settings outside of the classroom walls. The family units were recruited voluntarily via letters distributed to two separate classes. Participants were not provided with any information or guidance about metafiction or picturebooks beforehand, and the texts were sent home on a fortnightly basis in the children's schoolbags. Although the primary school was used as a site from which to recruit families onto the project and also offered a safe and convenient space for my conversations with the children, the class teachers were not involved in administering the project in any way. Nor did they discuss the picturebooks or the project with either the children or their parents. In school, the picturebooks were explored within literature circles: small groups comprised of a maximum of four child readers – plus myself – that promote dialogue, pupil-led interruptions and digressions above the teacher-led talk that can often dominate reading in school (Short 321). As Souto-Manning has shown (59), reading and discussing literature in small groups can enable children to generate themes and ideas in a spirit akin to Freire's culture circles.

Discussions with parents took place out-of-school. As with the children, our conversations started with "tell me what you thought of the book" and spiraled off from there. Inspired by Moles' positive description of using walking as method – also known as bimbling – I aimed to offer parents a less restricted, more fluid way of talking with me about the books (4.3). During the project, I bimbled on the way to school pick-up with one mother and met other parents in the local play park or at the school gates. Regular chats about the books took place amid the turbulence of the playground, after school had finished for the day. With several parents, conversations took place in the evening, by telephone, when the children were in bed and more time was available.

After transcription, conversations were analyzed using a theoretical framework that was informed by Freebody and Luke's Four Resources Model (8–14), Serafini's expanded version of the Four Resources (152) and key understandings about critical literacy drawn from the writings of Barbara Comber and Anne Simpson. In addition, when reading and re-reading the transcripts, I focused on whether the participants had responded to the metafictive aspects of the text, and if so, I considered what they had decided to tell me about them and broadly categorized the sorts of responses that emerged through a Bourdieusian-infused lens. In the next section, after briefly summarizing *Black and White*, I present some of the parents' responses to the book as well as the project in general.

Black and White

Macaulay's award-winning picturebook begins with a warning: readers are advised that it may (or may not) contain more than one story, and a "close inspection" of both words and pictures is recommended (1). The double-page spreads are divided into quadrants, each carrying a narrative thread that varies in subject matter, visual style or grammar, font and narrative perspective. The aforementioned warning to readers on the title page suggests that it is up to individuals to decide how to read the text (all four boxes at once, left to right, or should it be one box at a time?) and to determine whether the stories are separate entities or all part of a singular story. By constructing the text as a playful challenge or a puzzle for readers to work through, Macaulay positions his audience as co-authors while also challenging their perceptions about how books are normally read. The multiple ways of reading this book presented readers with a level of ambiguity not found in the other project picturebooks.

How the Parents Responded

In the years since its publication, Macaulay's *Black and White* has been described as "boundary-breaking" (McClay 91), "infinitely varied" (Nikola-Lisa 37), and a "prototype of literature for a young person of the electronic age" (Dresang and McClelland 704), given its multilayered structure and interactive approach. More recently, it has been reviewed as "weird – but enjoyable" (Michelle); "challenging in the sense that it didn't conform" (Diana) and "more rewarding" (Helena) – a series of responses from the parents in this study that support McClay's suggestion that a key part of this text's appeal is the sense of *intrigue* that can be sparked by its highly transgressive nature (94).

For the parents in this study, much of this intrigue stemmed from the text's unusual demands. "It was weird," remarked Michelle. "But it was enjoyable. It really made me really think. You really had to think, hold on, there's four different stories and do you read across the way or down the way – what do you do? Does it matter?" As suggested by her repeated emphasis of "*really think*," Michelle drew attention to the decision-making processes she had engaged in while puzzling her way through *Black and White*. This was a book that "*engaged her brain*," partly because of its difference to the books she usually read at home with her sons. In fact, this heightened contrast forced Michelle to deliberately alter her usual approach to reading at home with Matthew, her son. Earlier in the project, Michelle had informed me that her preferred approach was *always* to privilege the written text when reading:

MICHELLE: "What we always do is that I will read the book first and then when he is reading the book he always starts talking. He'll start [she mimes pointing as if at illustrations on the page] and I'll say no, no! Wait until after and we'll discuss it."

JENNIFER: "Do you stop him?"

MICHELLE: "Yes, so I stop him! But he carries on anyway!" (Michelle on *No Bears*)

Her reasons for equating reading with the process of decoding printed text were quite specific:

MICHELLE: "It's not always going to be picturebooks so [I say] let's concentrate on the story first and then we can go back and look at them. Because when they get older, there's not going to be pictures anymore."

JENNIFER: "What about movies and the telly and adverts? They are pictures and we need to read them."

MICHELLE: "Yeah, but when you are reading a book. . . . What I try to say is that the pictures are sort of secondary, so read the words and

> understand what they mean. And then go back to the pictures if you don't understand, you can maybe get a little bit more. But to me, reading is reading." (Michelle, on *No Bears*)

As indicated previously, Michelle tried to adhere to her approach throughout the project yet found it increasingly difficult. When faced with the narrative complexities of *Black and White*, she found that pausing, mid-page, to talk about the words *and* pictures was both unavoidable and necessary: "I *had* to explain a lot of things to him. . . . If I had just read it through and not talked about the pictures at all there is no way he would have got anything."

By forcing Michelle to extend her reading focus to both images and words, the disruptive effects of the metafictive devices at work in *Black and White* became visible although it was not clear to me how deeply the shift had registered. A change in emphasis was also clear from her recount of one of the most confusing spreads in the picturebook, when fragments of torn-up mail mix with drifting pages from the passengers' newspapers and fall together as the snowflakes that envelop the boys' trains:

> "Like for instance the snow. We were like, 'oh, it's snowing' and turned the page and then I was thinking, 'is that snow?' and then we turned another page and then I said, 'no, I think that's newspaper.' So it was like you were getting it just before [it happened]. It was like a page turner."
>
> (Michelle, on *Black and White*)

Spurred onwards by the "drama of the turning page" (Bader 1), Michelle's comment revealed how the unusual interplay of images and words in this text had influenced what she chose to look at and discuss, while also highlighting the iterative, highly active nature of her own thought processes in response to this text.

Similar patterns were visible in the comments made by Niamh's mum, Diana, a primary school teacher, who became involved in the project together with her husband, Niall. On *Black and White*, she noted:

> "I mean, [Niamh] was thinking, she was really thinking. She was looking back, going back, [asking] 'Is that the boy's? Is he having a dream?' And then you are picking up clues from the pictures, picking up clues from the text. . . . She was really thinking about her reading and thinking about the text."
>
> (Diana, on *Black and White*)

Like Michelle, Diana's emphasis on Niamh's "thinking" highlighted the active reading and metacognitive processes that had been made visible in connection with the text's multiple narrative strands and contesting discourses. Recognizing their presence seemed to come as something of a pleasant surprise to Diana, causing her to reconfigure what she knew about her daughter's capabilities as a reader:

JENNIFER: "One of the first things Niall said was that he didn't know if Niamh would be able to . . . he thought the first book was too sophisticated."

DIANA: "Yes, I would certainly back him up on that, I mean, in terms of was she quite ready for that sort of thing, and yet she was. She would see things in them [the books] that we didn't necessarily think. . . . As a teacher, children always surprise you. This was really surprising – that she was getting so much from it." (Diana, on *Black and White*)

Speaking separately from his wife, Niall described how his own understandings had also been altered as a result of such "feedback." Like Diana, he was surprised by Niamh's dexterous handling of these sophisticated texts, a recognition that caused him to adjust his own practices as a co-reader:

> I think I was quite surprised at the first [book] because I thought that maybe it was too sophisticated, because all we had read were fairly simple books. But I think now, having read all four books, she is now appreciating the books in different ways than I would have thought. I think she enjoys these books – she just enjoys the stories – and now when I am reading, I am reading different stories to her. More chapter books and also more books with slightly different types of approaches to the writing and to the pictures.
>
> (Niall)

Another parent to have made conscious changes in response to the study was Brendan, father of Eve. Like several other adult readers, Brendan had reacted with a mixture of surprise and frustration to the disruptive effects of the metafictive devices found in the first couple of books. When responding to *No Bears*, a text in which the words and pictures carry contradictory narratives,[3] he admitted, "I'll be honest, the first time I read *No Bears*, I didn't even notice the bear was in the story." After reading *The Three Pigs*,[4] a book he described as being a "completely new concept, not just in reading but in all things," he began to consider how the book had prevented him from assuming his usual role in the shared reading process: "You want to try to explain, but I'm opening up page two, the pigs have already been blown out of the page and the story doesn't match what's going on. It's not quite knowing what I need to say. . . . I just cannot work out how I can explain it to my daughter."

Having reflected privately on these frustrations, Brendan decided to adopt a different reading style when discussing *Black and White* at home with Eve:

BRENDAN: "After the chat we had last time, I took a step back, just to sort of see how Eve reacted to it really."

JENNIFER: "Oh that's interesting. Why did you do that?"

BRENDAN: "It was just from talking to you. I was thinking, 'how much am I steering?' I thought I would try to . . . leave pauses and see what happens. Just be a little less guiding . . . rather than putting my ideas on her, just trying to give her the opportunity. . . . I was consciously not putting ideas in her head. It was more of a pull than a push, if you see what I mean? I was trying to extract information from her, rather than impact my views." (Brendan on *Black and White*)

By acknowledging the directional differences between "pulling" or "extracting" and "pushing" or "impacting," Brendan also seemed to recognize the ideological impact of his own role during shared reading, thereby showing some critical awareness of reading as a social process of epistemological sculpting and development. Consequently, it seemed he had been able to "grasp" at the habitus, this time maintaining his grip long enough to make some deliberate adjustments to his practice (Fowler 1).

Conclusion

According to Nikola-Lisa, the power of inherently playful texts such as these metafictive picturebooks lies in their ability to provoke surprise by unsettling past ideas and suggesting the direction of "new beginnings" (38). But as Nikola-Lisa also makes clear, simply experiencing the surprise is not sufficient: it is what happens next that is critical: "It is not enough to be merely amused by surprise/ we must be transformed by it" (38).

As the responses included here illustrate, encountering the surprising effects of metafiction in picturebooks enabled some parents to *play around* with their normative understandings about reading with children, leading to moments of transformation, however small. For Michelle, who was initially resistant, this involved her tacit acknowledgement that reading *could* be about more than decoding the printed word. For Brendan, Niall and Diana, the transformation was more conscious, tangible and linked to a consideration of *what else* could be read or done when reading at home. By inspiring such change, it is clear that the playful aspects of metafiction did more than "merely amuse" the readers in this study (38): they also frustrated, irritated and provoked the parents into positions of increased uncertainty, which then, eventually, reconfigured into more settled, adjusted understandings. As this last sentence suggests, not all of the parents enjoyed these unruly books and found engaging with them both discomfiting and discombobulating. Yet, the experience of resistance as a reading response helped to open up new and exciting spaces for conversations with a more critical edge, in which some of the adult readers started to inspect – more consciously and deliberately – both *how* they read and what *normally* took place when they shared a book at home.

For several parents in this study, engaging with metafiction led to new insights about reading, suggesting that there may be scope for larger, more wide-ranging enquiries along similar lines. Given that *what mattered* about reading to the majority of the adult readers tended to be largely tethered to the print-centered "basics" of years gone by, it is clear that there is a need to share research-led insights about what literacy looks like now, for both child and adult readers in a multiliterate age. While the parents' lack of conceptual awareness about visual literacy can be attributed to generational shifts in literacy theory and the relative infancy of visual and critical literacies within emerging curricular frameworks, it is clear that there is also room for schools and other organizations to work alongside parents and carers to help "fill in the blanks" while also extending the conversations in inspiring new directions. Indeed, with some additional and well-placed support, it is possible to imagine how the discussions initiated by metafiction in this study could be encouraged even further in order to stimulate deeper and more widely held understandings about how words are read – and could also be read differently – across the generational gap.

Notes

1. The study was funded by a scholarship from the UK's Economic and Social Research Council.
2. The word "parent" is used here to indicate the relationships between the children and adult pairings within this study although it is recognized that other family configurations are possible.
3. In *No Bears*, Ruby the (rather unkind) narrator's attempt to tell a totally bear-free story is surreptitiously interrupted by a parallel visual narrative, in which a benevolent-looking bear manages to save the day – and Ruby.
4. In *The Three Pigs*, Wiesner's protagonists escape from the wolf's clutches by deconstructing their traditional narrative and by creating a new one in the safe space of the white space that surrounds the story frames.

Works Cited

Anstey, Michelle. "'It's Not All Black and White': Postmodern Picture Books and New Literacies." *Journal of Adolescent and Adult Literacy*, vol. 45, no. 6, 2002, pp. 444–57.

Arizpe, Evelyn, and Julie E. McAdam. "Crossing Visual Borders and Connecting Cultures: Children's Responses to the Photographic Theme in David Wiesner's

Flotsam." *New Review of Children's Literature and Librarianship*, vol. 17, no. 2, 2011, 227–43.

Bader, Barbara. *American Picture Books: From Noah's Ark to the Beast Within*. Palgrave Macmillan, 1976.

Bearne, Eve, and Gunther Kress. "Editorial." *Reading*, vol. 35, no. 3, 2001, 89–93.

Bourdieu, Pierre. *Outline of a Theory of Practice*. Cambridge UP, 1997.

Carrington, Vicki, and Allan Luke. "Literacy and Bourdieu's Sociological Theory: A Reframing." *Language and Education*, vol. 11, no. 2, 1997, pp. 96–112.

Comber, Barbara. "Critical Literacy: What Does It Look Like in the Early Years?" *Handbook of Early Childhood Literacy*, edited by Nigel Hall, Joanne Larson, and Jackie Marsh. Sage Publications, 2003, pp. 355–68.

Dresang, Eliza, and Kate McClelland. "Black and White: A Journey." *The Horn Book*, vol. 71, no. 6, 1995, pp. 704–11.

Farrar, Jennifer. "I Didn't Know They Did Books Like This! An Inquiry into the Literacy Practices of Young Children and Their Parents, Using Metafictive Picturebooks." PhD Thesis, U of Glasgow P, 2017, http://theses.gla.ac.uk/8017/. Accessed 27 Feb. 2017.

Fowler, Bridget. *Reading Bourdieu on Society and Culture*. Blackwell Publishing, The Sociological Review, 2000.

Freebody, Peter, and Allan Luke. "Literacies Programs: Debates and Demands in Cultural Context." *Prospect: An Australian Journal of TESOL*, vol. 5, no. 3, 1990, pp. 7–16.

Freire, Pierre. "Reading the World and Reading the Word: An Interview with Paulo Freire." *Language Arts*, vol. 62, no. 1, 1985, pp. 15–21.

Lewis, David. "The Constructedness of Texts: Picture Books and the Metafictive." *Signal*, vol. 62, 1990, pp. 31–146.

———. *Reading Contemporary Picturebooks*. London: Routledge Farmer, 2001.

Luke, Allan. *The Social Construction of Literacy in the Primary School*. Palgrave Macmillan, 1994.

Mackey, Margaret. "Metafiction for Beginners: Allan Ahlberg's *Ten in a Bed*." *Children's Literature in Education*, vol. 21, no. 3, 1990, pp. 179–87.

McClay, Jill K. "'Wait a Second . . .': Negotiating Complex Narratives in Black and White." *Children's Literature in Education*, vol. 31, no. 2, 2000, pp. 91–106.

Meek, Margaret. *How Texts Teach What Readers Learn*. Thimble Press, 1988.

Moles, Kate. "A Walk in Thirdspace: Place, Methods and Walking." *Sociological Research Online*, vol. 13, no. 4, 2008, www.socresonline.org.uk/13/4/2.html. Accessed 27 Feb. 2017.

New London Group. "A Pedagogy of Multiliteracies: Designing Social Futures." *Harvard Educational Review*, vol. 66, no. 1, 1996, pp. 60–92.

Nikola-Lisa, W. "Play, Panache, Pastiche: Postmodern Impulses in Contemporary Picture Books." *Children's Literature Association Quarterly*, vol. 19, no. 1, 2004, pp. 35–40.

Nodelman, Perry. "Decoding the Images: Illustration and Picture Books." *Understanding Children's Literature*, edited by Peter Hunt. Routledge, 1999, pp. 128–39.

Pahl, Kate. "Habitus in the Home: Texts and Practices in Families." *Ways of Knowing Journal*, vol. 2, no. 1, 2002, pp. 45–53.

Pantaleo, Sylvia. "Warning: A Grade 7 Student Disrupts Narrative Boundaries." *Journal of Literacy Research*, vol. 43, no. 1, 2011, pp. 39–67.

Pushor, Debbie, and Bill Murphy. "Parent Marginalisation, Marginalised Parents: Creating a Place for Parents on the School Landscape." *The Alberta Journal of Educational Research*, vol. 50, no. 3, 2004, pp. 221–35.

Rowsell, Jennifer, and Kate Pahl. "Introduction." *The Routledge Handbook of Literacy Studies*, edited by Jennifer Rowsell and Kate Pahl. Routledge, 2015, pp. 1–14.

Serafini, Frank. "The Pedagogical Possibilities of Postmodern Picturebooks." *Journal of Reading, Writing and Literacy*, vol. 2, no. 3, 2008, pp. 23–41.

———. "Expanding the Four Resources Model: Reading Visual and Multi-Modal Texts." *Pedagogies: An International Journal*, vol. 7, no. 2, 2012, pp. 150–64.

Short, Kathy. "Researching Intertextuality Within Collaborative Classroom Learning Environments." *Linguistics and Education*, vol. 4, no. 3–4, 1992, pp. 313–33.

Simpson, Anne. "Critical Questions: Whose Questions?" *The Reading Teacher*, vol. 50, no. 2, 1996, pp. 118–27.

Sipe, Lawrence. "How Picture Books Work: A Semiotically Framed Theory of Text-Picture Relationships." *Children's Literature in Education*, vol. 29, no. 2, 1998, pp. 97–108.

Sipe, Lawrence, and Caroline McGuire. "The Stinky Cheese Man and Other Fairly Postmodern Picture Books for Children." *Shattering the Looking Glass: Challenge, Risk and Controversy in Children's Literature,* edited by Susan Lehr. Christopher-Gordon Publishers, 1996, pp. 273–88.

Souto-Manning, Mariana. "Negotiating Culturally Responsive Pedagogy Through Multicultural Children's Literature: Towards Critical Democratic Literacy Practices in a First Grade Classroom." *Journal of Early Childhood Literacy*, vol. 9, no. 1, 2009, pp. 50–74.

Street, Brian V. *Literacy in Theory and Practice*. Cambridge UP, 1986.

Tizard, Barbara, and Martin Hughes. *Young Children Learning: Talking and Thinking at Home and at School*. Fontana Press.

Picturebooks

Ahlberg, Allan, and Paul Howard. *The Bravest Ever Bear*. Walker Books, 1999.

Macaulay, David. *Black and White*. Houghton Mifflin, 1990.

McKinley, Meg, and Leila Rudge. *No Bears*. Walker Books, 2013.

Wiesner, David. *The Three Pigs*. Andersen Press, 2001.

12 Playing and Reading Together

The Beginnings of Literary Socialization

Zofia Zasacka

Reading is a process of constructing meaning from a written text. My approach defines reading as an element of literacy and focuses on the circumstances of reading practices, accounting for their situational and functional variability (Barton and Hamilton 7–15). Embedding reading into the socio-cultural context, my argument is therefore based on social and cultural theories of reception that frame reading as an effect of transactions between the text and the reader. In this model, the reader relies on his/her own life experience, knowledge of literary codes and conventions, and reading experiences, all of which shape his/her expectations toward the text and facilitate understanding of its meanings (Martin 156–72). In other words, the reader has an active attitude to the text. As viewed by cultural anthropology and sociology, reading as part of literacy is also a factor in the habitus (Bourdieu 466–67), an internalized universe of cultural experiences bound up with literacy skills.

Empirical research on reading practices in Poland reveals a clear trend; namely, the young adult reading population is shrinking (Zasacka and Bulkowski 85–97). A growing percentage of young people give up reading as soon as they complete their school education, and the number of those who read for pleasure is falling (Michalak et al. 12–16). A recent national survey on reading indicates reasons why students read or do not read (Zasacka, *Czytelnictwo* 73–84). The following dimensions of reading motivations were assessed in the study: self-efficacy, defined as self-belief that one can be successful at reading (individuals' efficacy expectations for reading achievement tasks; willingness to exert effort to persist in the reading challenge; or, alternately, inclination to avoid difficult reading activities); intrinsic motivation designating the choice to read for the sake of reading (inclusive of reading curiosity, desire to learn about a particular topic and reading involvement, which refers to the pleasure from reading a well-written book or article on a topic of interest and the relevance of reading to the reader's life); extrinsic motivation, representing the decision to read for a variety of gains (e.g., the competitive drive to outperform others in reading and to garner recognition for reading, including tangible gratifications and/or grades for reading success); and social reasons behind reading (e.g., sharing the meanings gained from reading with friends and family and compliance, i.e., engagement in reading to meet others' expectations) (Wigfield and Guthrie 422; Dunston and Gambrell 270–75). As children become older, they read less in leisure time, and their reading motivation – particularly its extrinsic variety of reading for grades – decreases. The findings imply that such motivation decline coincides with the lower secondary school period (children aged 12 to 15 years of age). Girls' advantage over boys in terms of reading motivation grows, primarily because boys' intrinsic motivation falters faster. The survey has also found a strong correlation between reading motivation, Polish grades at school, and reading activity for academic or recreational purposes.

Research suggests that to be a life-long reader, one needs to be an engaged reader (Marinak et al. 1–5). Engagement in reading occurs when reading is closely, transparently even, interwoven in the texture of the person's everyday life, that is, when it is part of what Swidler calls one's cultural toolkit. This takes place when reading is one of the strategies of action (Swidler 273–86) and is prompted by intrinsic motivation, that is, the willingness to read because the activity itself is regarded as satisfying and rewarding. Engaged readers are intrinsically motivated to read by a variety of personal goals; they are strategic in their reading behaviors and experienced in constructing new understandings from the texts they read. Engaged readers' eagerness to read is fueled by the perceived pleasure and gratification from reading and by possibilities of social interaction afforded by their reading activity (Guthrie and Wigfield 420–24; Guthrie and Wigfield 403–20; Dunston and Gambrell 269–86). This idea of engagement correlates with some criteria of play as defined by Burghardt (9–18). Burghardt proposes five groups of general characteristics of play: play occurs when behavior is autotelic rather than functional; when it is spontaneous, voluntary, and rewarding; when it is structural and performed repeatedly but with improvisation; and when it takes place instinctively and in relaxed circumstances.

This chapter explores the role of play in the development of reading habits in young children and, potentially, in raising life-long readers. It discusses ways in which engagement in reading associated with involvement in literary texts in early childhood fosters adult interest in fiction and representational arts (Walton 11–16). I argue that play based on a literary text is a useful tool in developing reading motivation. Such motivation can be strengthened through literary socialization, for example by reading together with caregivers, browsing through and talking about books with them at home or at kindergarten, playing pretend or make-believe games based on the text that has been read, etc. This also contributes to nurturing engagement in reading, which is crucial to my argument because, as Kendall L. Walton insists, involvement in literary texts in early childhood fosters adult interest in fiction and representational arts (11–16).

Engagement in reading can be seen as a factor in literary reading (Miall 189–202). When reading a novel, readers become immersed in the world depicted in the narrative (Nell 243–55); they are transported to new places with new people (Gerrig 157–95). In these narrative worlds, readers experience a simulated reality and feel real emotions in response to the conflicts and relationships of the protagonists (Oatley 53–74). Narratives thus seem to offer readers a deeply felt simulation of social experience that may produce real consequences for their real-life social worlds (Mar et al. 407–28). Specifically, engaging with narrative fiction and mentally simulating social experiences represented therein may improve or consolidate social skills, especially the skills of empathy and social understanding (Andringa and Shreier 161–69). Engagement is also described in terms of emotions toward literary characters aroused in the reading process (Oatley 53–70). Such emotions trigger cognitive processes, self-reference memory, anticipation (e.g., figuring personality traits of a literary character), and empathic responses (e.g., wanting to befriend a literary protagonist). Readers follow the narrator into a fictional world, which enables them to experiment with their own states of mind, develop their empathy, and identify with the characters (Koopman and Hakemudler 79–111).

Method

This chapter focuses on primary literary socialization in preschool childhood. It is based on the qualitative stage of a study of reading habits and attitudes of children and adolescents conducted in Poland in 2013. The study used 48 individual in-depth interviews (IDI): 24 with primary school students aged 12–13 years old and 24 with lower secondary school students aged 15–16 years old (Zasacka, *Czytelnictwo* 9–11). Out of the 48 interviews, 16 were conducted with book-reading students of small rural schools, 8 with students of schools in small towns up to 20,000 inhabitants, and 24 with students of schools in various socio-economic communities of a city of over 500,000 inhabitants. Half of the sample were girls and half were boys at every school level. The aim of the study was to trace reading biographies of girls and boys in various social environments (regarding, in particular, the social circumstances of the literary initiation and the patterns of reading acquired at home, in the peer community, and transmitted by other socializing institutions), to establish their association with the practiced reading strategies, to identify teenage readers' expectations and their book-reading needs, and to determine the differences in spontaneous and school reading as well as the related emotions and motivations. This chapter uses the qualitative analysis of the interview data concerning the preschool period and the beginnings of the respondents' reading biographies. The data were analyzed for the presence of selected themes and patterns describing early book reading experiences, their proximity to attributes ascribed to (Burghardt 9–8), and their significant differences by sociodemographic factors.

The Rituals and Cultural Patterns of Reading in Early Childhood: The Children's Perspective

Significant others in primary literary socialization

The interview script focused on reading biographies of the respondents and their first contacts with books. The surveyed teenagers' earliest memories of reading practices at their homes go back to childhood, when they were a few years old and could not read themselves yet. The reading initiation took place most often in the family home while kindergarten reading was mentioned only exceptionally.

The students' responses suggest that, in early childhood, reading books aloud – irrespective of the type of the respondents' social and family background – was common and most often ritualized. It was done at home, daily (or almost daily), in the form of evening reading to children at bedtime or in kindergartens during rest time. The following student's response is generally representative of the entire sample: "Yes, my mother and grandmother read to me. Very often at bedtime. Perhaps not every day, but often. When mother had time, if she didn't read a book, there would be a song or something else for goodnight, to make me sleep better" (G02–3B20–0).[1]

Only few respondents, predominantly rural area residents, reported that book reading had been sporadic and taken place mainly in autumn and winter (when their parents had fewer daily farming chores) or in special situations (e.g., when the child was sick). As the participants' memories reveal, the situations involving reading aloud were usually of a ritual nature and became a familiar and frequently repeated practice occurring in pleasant circumstances.

The children's contact with books was initiated mainly by parents, especially by mothers. According to the respondents, fathers often did not have time to read books to them. One father was apparently an exception to that rule as he took over the reading instruction of his children, first reading aloud to them and, then, taking them to the library, but, as his daughter described it, "he was himself a bit of a bookworm." Other family members, especially grandmothers, played a role in the children's first reading experiences, too. Grandfathers, aunts, older and younger siblings often helped or substituted for parents in reading aloud. The respondents' recollections sometimes included scenes of the family reading together; they looked at such occasions as important moments in family life, when siblings of different ages had an opportunity to bond. In rural families, especially multigenerational ones, members of the household, as well as younger and older siblings, would gather for collective evening book reading around grandfather or grandmother: "When we all got together, Grandpa would start reading a book aloud. He would sit down on the bed and all of us – me, my three siblings, my older siblings – we would sit by his side. We would sit by his side, and he would tell us stories and read" (P31–6B15–1).

Though crucial, adults' support was not always necessary as, besides reading aloud, another form of engaging with books in early childhood was when the child was left alone with picturebooks, invited to look at the pictures, and encouraged to imagine the stories described in them. A respondent says: "I preferred looking at the illustrations on my own, and figure out on my own what they could possibly mean" (P11–6B18–1). These are the first examples of the child playing alone with a book. They exemplify solitary active play, which involves engagement in pretense, e.g., playing make-believe and, perhaps, even dramatizing (Coplan 185–97). In this case, the pretender plays an unsocial game as the child performs it all alone. This is an example of a moment when a child's reading and browsing books independently becomes its individual play involving spontaneous selections of texts at random moments. This kind of play can be characterized in Burghardt's terms as spontaneous, autotelic, satisfying, and relaxing. However, according to the respondents, the process through which reading becomes a rewarding and pleasant activity takes a long time. Later I discuss factors shaping this process and outline its subsequent stages.

The first books and stories as stepping stones to engagement in reading

Interestingly, children from different backgrounds, homes with varying collections of books, different levels of parental education, and different frequency of book-reading by household members mentioned the same literary works. They were first of all nursery rhymes by popular Polish poets Julian Tuwim and Jan Brzechwa and fairy tales by the Brothers Grimm and Hans Christian Andersen: "I liked 'Zosia Samosia,' 'Pan Pomidor' and other nursery rhymes about vegetables, also 'Cuda i Dziwy.' There was also 'Lokomotywa' and 'Słoń Trąbalski' " (P14–6A16–1).

The students' narratives point to two social status-related models of book circulation that accompany the primary literary socialization and determine which books are selected. One model is found in homes with large book collections, often amassed by several generations; the other model is characteristic of homes with a small number of books, where they are rarely bought or received as gifts. In the former, children and parents select their readings together from the multitude of the titles available on the shelves. Teenagers in such homes have their own libraries, tend to select books with their parents, and often receive them as gifts. In the latter model, prevalent in small towns and rural areas, books that are read together by the family usually come from the local public library. In such circumstances, the family readings are selected by the parents, usually the mother. The respondents describe the two models:

> Both my parents would choose what we had on the shelves . . . there was a lot of Andersen, sometimes also Kasdepke, I liked *Bon czy Ton* a lot. And there were other ones, too, some British authors, Dickens, they were interesting, I liked them, legends and what not.
>
> (P23–6C04–0)

> My mother would take books from the public library. She would read to me and to my brother . . . So we would sit down, and Mom would read us various fairy tales, and so on. Andersen's fairy tales . . . "The Ugly Duckling," a short story . . . There was also a story about a little soldier. Also Andersen's, I think.
>
> (G01–3B23–1)

At that early stage of developing reading habits, some of the interviewed students had an influence on what books would be read to them; their parents let them choose, and sometimes the children would take the initiative and pick the books they wanted: "I was always, really always, asked what I wanted to have read to me. I mean, my mother would ask me what I wanted her to read to me, and I would then say *Harry Potter* or some nursery rhymes, or something like that" (G38–3A02–0). In such circumstances, reading is similar to play in that it becomes a practice in which the child's spontaneous choice is of utmost importance. Sometimes, at their children's request, parents would read them the same book over and over again. The surveyed students knew the books they chose perfectly well. They derived satisfaction from rereading them and anticipated the well-known pleasure. The repetitiveness of the expected award in the form of the child's contact with a book constitutes an important factor shaping its reading expectations. This is an example of reading as one's own "domesticated" activity that, just as everyday play, is friendly and worth taking up.

Three Functions of Emergent Literacy

The students' interviews point to three important functions of joint reading in early childhood. They are social, emotional, and cognitive functions. The social function appears in all interviews, regardless of the respondents' socio-cultural background and the circumstances in which their literary socialization took place. For all the surveyed teenagers, joint reading was conducive to building a relationship with the caregiver who read books to them and gave them a sense of security and belonging. Almost all the subjects reported having fond memories of the occasions in their childhood when they listened to books being read aloud. It was evident in respondents' answers that they found the emotional bond that had formed between the readers and the listening children supremely important. This relationship evoked positive feelings: love, pleasure, closeness, and a sense of security fostered by the special atmosphere of evening readings, including peace, quiet, and focus. Such feelings are commonly associated with play as well. Just as play, reading involves relaxation and pleasant interactions with others.

The emotional function observable in early literary experiences is crucial also to play. In having books read to them, the respondents developed the ability to derive pleasure from listening to and imagining the events and scenes from the story or the poem. These experiences were triggered by joint reading and by the child's text-triggered thoughts before falling asleep. This function of reading works on two levels: one of them is the reception of a particular text, involving feelings associated with its content; the other is the overall situation of reading together, involving emotions which arise from the "mood" that envelops it. The respondents mentioned both aspects of the emotional function:

First of all, it made falling asleep much easier. I remember that the rest of my evening would be much nicer as I could imagine everything that I'd heard in that fairy tale" (G05–3B18–1).

> I was still at an age where I either couldn't read or I wasn't very good at reading, and, if I'd had to read on my own, I'd never have read so many pages in such a short time, and it surely felt good that I could imagine all that without looking into the book. I would simply close my eyes and imagine it all – it was certainly very satisfying. What else? Well, my mother's voice, of course. For me, a six-year-old, the sound of my mother's voice as she read books to me was very pleasant. Besides this, I don't know what else could make me happy because my mother was reading to me.
>
> (G38–3B19–0)

The passages exemplify the autotelic satisfaction of imagining stories and literary works. Experiencing a story through replaying situations and images in one's mind can be seen as a training through which one becomes an independent reader belonging to a literary audience. At the same time, such play with the text provides very important training of skills employed in literary reading. Promoting engagement in text reception, such situations enhance internal motivation, that is, the conviction that reading certain texts brings satisfaction. For example, stories that were read to the children stimulated pleasant dreams and nice thoughts before falling asleep. They were early exercises in involvement in and imagining the described situations and the world depicted in literature. They also fostered the children's inclination to identify with the characters and to invent sequels and/or endings to the stories. Children relive stories read to them just as they engage in pretend play and impersonate various characters. The students clearly emphasized that by listening to stories being read to them they learned to imagine the world described in them:

> I would lie in bed and my mother would be sitting next to me; sometimes when the reading ended because she had grown too tired, I would spend the whole following day imagining how the story would continue, how it was going to end.
>
> (G39–3F26–0)

> As I was easily able to imagine that world, I would lie in bed and, because of that, I would fall asleep in a good mood, feeling happy. It's definitely what appealed to me in reading aloud. After my mother read to me, I would fall asleep easier; I imagined, I had positive thoughts, I would fall asleep with a smile on my face.
>
> (P28–6B16–0)

A girl from a rural family with poor socio-cultural capital, but with effective and comprehensive primary literary socialization, reported:

> My mother would read lots of books to me, I liked it very much. . . . I imagined being one of the main characters, I knew "Pimpuś Sadełko" by heart . . . my first fairy tales were "Snow White" and "Puss in Boots."
>
> (P31–6A1–31)

The other emotional effect of reading together involves the impact of the reception setting and circumstances. The respondents reported that the atmosphere accompanying reading aloud was the most important characteristic of the activity for them. The memory of pleasure experienced while listening is brought to the fore in the interviews:

> It was so pleasant, peaceful, no disturbance at all, particularly as we lived in a quiet neighborhood. . . . The TV set was in another room so we could hardly hear it and. . . . Also Dad has a voice that was so nice to listen to.
>
> (P23–6C14–1)

The good atmosphere while reading was also supported by the works that were read to the children: they rhymed or they narrated cheerful, funny, and interesting adventures. Such absorbing stories fostered interest in and curiosity about the books and encouraged the children to explore them further and also to find out about other stories: "I was always curious about how the story would end and, well, I liked it very much" (P28–6C18–0). Such "ambiance" is one of conditions for play to come about. It functions as a sensitive barometer of the individual's psychological and physical well-being. Play happens more often when the individual is relaxed and feels comfortable in her/his surroundings (Burghardt 14–16). In the students' recollection, such relaxing circumstances conducive to play accompanied reading aloud. The cognitive function of reading aloud concerned increased reading competence and knowledge acquired from reading. In retrospect, the surveyed students also perceived cognitive values in the books they came across in childhood; they cherished the discovery and enrichment of knowledge about the world and human attitudes: "They would show another person's viewpoint and a fate that wasn't mine. (G39–3D16–1) I think that [I liked] adventure stories most; when someone in the story went to the seaside, I would try to imagine that sea" (P11–6B18–1). Reading means experiencing the character's adventures and in effect becomes the reader's or listener's own adventure or play. This is one more way in which reading is remembered as close to play: it is a pleasant and spontaneous activity enabling a transition into a different reality than the one known from one's everyday life.

Teenage readers are conscious of the impact of those earliest literary experiences on their later reading preferences. Some state directly that evening reading-aloud sessions formed their views on literature and their expectations toward their favorite stories. A respondent recounts characteristically:

> My favorite in preschool reading aloud was . . . I don't know, also *Harry Potter*. The first part of *Harry Potter*. The rest I read on my own. But my parents read to me the first part. And that's it, I can say that it's one of my favorite book series, which I came to know thanks to my parents, who read the beginning to me.
>
> (G38–3A25–1)

The Transition to Independent Reading

The surveyed students began to read independently at different ages; their early reading abilities varied, and some learned to read under strong parental pressure. As reported by them, they learned to read simple texts even as early as at the age of 4 or 5. Most of the teenagers remember the first book they read on their own in the preschool period; it is often still important to them, and if they still have that book, they would not like to give it away. Some of them return to it time and again. It reminds them of pleasure, play, and freedom that accompanied their early reading. One pupil comments, expressing this attitude:

> I wouldn't like to get rid of any of these books. After all, simply by reading them again I can go back to the past. . . . It's because they always remind me of some moments in the past, that I had more freedom then, that there was no pressure to do well in school, and when I read them, I can reminisce about those times.
>
> (P28–6B13–1)

Quite often, the first books read by the children on their own were books that had been read aloud to them before. Here is an example: "*Franklin* – I read it over and over again" (P14–6A13–0).

The children's memory of their first independent readings is more vivid especially when they chose them on their own. The active choosers also went quicker through the transition from having books read to them by their parents to becoming independent readers:

> The first book in the *Harry Potter* series. Later I would prefer to read by myself. But my parents read the first book in the series to me. Exactly, it was one of my favorite book series, thanks to my parents, who began reading it to me.
>
> (G38–3B19–0)

The surveyed students highlighted the fact that reading the first book in their lives on their own had been associated with great difficulty as a rule, but the effort had given them a lot of satisfaction. A respondent commented on this experience in the following way: "My first 'real' book – not just a nursery rhyme – was, I think, *Miasto Nocą*. That's what it was, I think, just a thin, little book, but I remember that it gave me so much joy that I read it on my own from cover to cover" (P11–6B13–1).

For most of the surveyed students the period of joint family reading extended over several years. When the children finally mastered reading skills, they searched for reading material on topics that interested them. A respondent says: "That was the title: *Egypt*. Because I have a lot of books about ancient Egypt . . . and so do my mother and father. . . . Yes, I read it at least five times" (P28–6B13–1).

The ability to read accelerated independent selection of readings, reading settings, and reading times. This in turn could have a significant impact on the relatively early development of new, more mature reading attitudes, e.g., the individualization of reading. It was precisely this need for independent reading that often motivated the children to learn to read. This a new stage: reading becomes a thoroughly spontaneous practice dependent only on the child's preferences and choice. It is its own way of playing with texts.

Playing Games with Literary Texts and Becoming an Engaged Reader

Stories and characters may inhabit the imagination of a child reader only through training. Children need to learn to accept situations in which they encounter their literary friends and share their adventures. This necessitates numerous repetitive experiences of certain kinds of stories so that these texts become close to children and bring expected rewards. Such a process could be seen as the shaping of readers' expectations. The surveyed students often regarded their favorite stories and readings from early childhood as similar to play and adventure:

I: What books did you like to read most as a child?
B: Those that were about adventures, and I could imagine that, for example, I was the protagonist . . . that, for example, I was having various adventures. (P28–6B13–1)

Some works were read to the surveyed children repeatedly. In such cases, when they could read them themselves, they would do it multiple times. Such repeated reading was fun for them. The favorite texts often inspired play, for example, dress-ups or, on most occasions, musings about the fate of the protagonists and possible sequels to the story: "I liked to invent what would happen next and how all this would pan out; I would develop subsequent threads of the story. I would make fun of myself for doing it – it was a fairy tale after all" (P11–6B18–1). When a literary text and its protagonists become so familiar or even close to the child reader that they seem almost like friends, there emerges a new stage of reading engagement: a fictional text enters the reality, and so the play with a text becomes real. This shows how literary reading involvement, which constitutes the basis of reading engagement, continues as a real experience. Some of the students mentioned organizing their play under the influence of the fairy tales they read:

> [Fairy tales read first]. . . . They were certainly very magical, but overall I think that I liked this type of fairy tales, like those with princesses. I've always liked dressing up as a princess, so it was such a favorite, with a prince in it and always a happy ending. I really liked that.
>
> (G38–3A25–1)

However, literary reading, like play, has different rules than the reality. Identifying with the protagonist, imagining the situation, and experiencing it together with the characters is not transferred to the here and now. Some of the surveyed teenagers admit that now, as teenage readers, they neither bring the attitudes of literary characters into their everyday lives nor try to imitate them anymore. They also point out that the world of fiction and actual life are separate. They have grown up as readers and as people as well. At such moments, playing with a literary text is not total and does not overwhelm the reader's imagination. It does not enter everyday play either as it is limited to the reading situation.

Conclusion

The findings from the students' interviews about the earliest stages of their reading biographies imply the important role of caregivers, especially parents, in children's first contact with literature. Collective reading aloud of fairy tales, nursery rhymes, and other literary works at home is recalled by the surveyed students as a ritual invaluable to their subsequent reading practices. The students' statements indicate that the atmosphere accompanying such reading-aloud sessions was crucially relevant to the development of their early text-reception skills. Just as play, reading becomes a repetitive activity that is relaxing and spontaneous. It is also associated with the lack of pressure and satisfaction. The calm, focus, and emotional intimacy gave reading a particular significance, turning it into a precious and eagerly anticipated ritual. Having books read aloud to them in such circumstances served as an initial practice promoting the participants' later independent and engaged reading. It afforded them opportunities to learn how to derive satisfaction from the reception of literature. Emphatically, as reported by the subjects, their first literary experiences took place in the circumstances that encouraged play and, as such, effectively shaped their intrinsic reading motivation, a crucial factor in engaged reading. Children's literature-informed play fosters skills that underpin emotional involvement in reading literary text, such as the imagination, the experience of being transported while reading, an ability to identify and empathize with fictional characters, etc. Regrettably, a growing group of young adult school graduates, especially boys in families with weak literary socialization, lack the experience of reading engagement. This deficit can be redressed if literary reading and play based on literary texts are given more time and emphasis in preschool education facilities.

Note

1. Parenthetical citations accompanying quotes from the interviews contain the respondents' identification numbers and IDIs. P stands for primary school, G for lower secondary school, while the following digits and letters are school and respondent codes. 0 and 1 at the end represent the respondent's gender, with 1 standing for the female and 0 for the male.

Works Cited

Andringa, Els, and Margrit Shreier. "How Literature Enters Life: An Introduction." *Poetics Today*, vol. 25, no. 2, 2004, pp. 161–69.

Barton, David, and Mary Hamilton. *Local Literacies: Reading and Writing in One Community*. Routledge, 1998.

Bourdieu, Pierre. *Distinction: A Social Critique of the Judgement of Taste*, translated by Richard Nice. Harvard UP, 1984.

Burghardt, Gordon M. "Defining and Recognizing Play." *The Oxford Handbook of the Development of Play*, edited by Anthony D. Pellegrini. Oxford UP, 2011, pp. 9–18.

Coplan, Robert J. "Not Just 'Playing Alone': Exploring Multiple Forms of Nonsocial Play in Childhood." *The Oxford Handbook of the Development of Play*, edited by Anthony D. Pellegrini. Oxford UP, 2011, pp. 185–97.

Dunston, Pamela J., and Linda B Gambrell. "Motivating Adolescents Learners to Read." *Literacy Instruction for Adolescents: Research Based Practice*, edited by Karen D. Wood and William E. Danton. Guilford Press, 2009, pp. 269–86.

Gerrig, Richard J. *Experiencing Narrative Worlds: On the Psychological Activities of Reading*. Westview Press, 1998.

Guthrie, John T., and Allan Wigfield. "Engagement and Motivation in Reading." *Handbook of Reading Research. Volume III*, edited by Michael L. Kamil, et al. Lawrence Erlbaum Associates, 2000, pp. 403–22.

Koopman, Eva M., and Frank Hakemulder. "Effects of Literature on Empathy and Self-Reflection: A Theoretical-Empirical Framework." *Journal of Literary Theory*, vol. 9, no. 1, 2015, pp. 79–111.

Mar, Raymond A., et al. "Exploring the Link Between Reading Fiction and Empathy: Ruling Out Individual Differences and Examining Outcomes." *Communications*, vol. 34, no. 4, 2009, pp. 407–28.

Martin, Wallace. *Recent Theories of Narrative*. Cornell UP, 1986.

Miall, David S. *Literary Reading: Empirical and Theoretical Studies*. Peter Lang, 2006.

Michalak, Dominika, et al. *Stan Czytelnictwa w Polsce w 2015 Roku: Wstępne Wyniki*. Biblioteka Narodowa, 2015, http://ksiegarnia.bn.org.pl/pdf/Stan%20czytelnictwa%20w%20Polsce%20w%202015%20r..pdf. Accessed 23 Jan. 2017.

Nell, Victor. *Lost in a Book: The Psychology of Reading for Pleasure*. Yale UP, 1988.

Oatley, Keith. "A Taxonomy of the Emotions of Literary Response and a Theory of Identification in Fictional Narrative." *Poetics*, vol. 23, 1994, pp. 53–74.

Swidler, Anne. "Culture in Action: Symbols and Strategies." *American Sociological Review*, vol. 51, no. 2, 1986, pp. 273–86.

Walton, Kendall L. *Mimesis as Make-Believe: On the Foundations of the Representational Arts*. Harvard UP, 1990.

Wigfield, Allan, and John T Guthrie. "Relations of Children's Motivation for Reading to the Amount and Breadth of Their Reading." *Journal of Educational Psychology*, vol. 89, no. 1, 1997, pp. 420–32, www.cori.umd.edu/research-publications/1997-wigfield-guthrie.pdf. Accessed 13 Feb. 2018.

Zasacka, Zofia. *Czytelnictwo dzieci i młodzieży*. Instytut Badań Edukacyjnych, 2014, file:///C:/Users/user/Downloads/ibe-raport-czytelnictwo-dzieci-i-mlodziezy%20(3).pdf. Accessed 20 Jan. 2016.

———. "Reading Satisfaction: Implications of Research on Adolescents' Reading Habits and Attitudes." *Polish Libraries*, vol. 4, 2016, pp. 40–64.

Zasacka, Zofia, and Krzysztof Bulkowski. "Reading Engagement and School Achievements of Lower Secondary Students." *Edukacja*, vol. 2, 2017, pp. 78–99.

13 Crossing Boundaries in Children's Books

The Role of Authors, Illustrators, and Publishers in Creating Playful and Play-inducing Books for Young Readers

Elżbieta Jamróz-Stolarska

The history of children's books is relatively short. In Poland, first writings intentionally and specifically dedicated to young children only appeared in the first half of the nineteenth century. According to the literature, the first specimens of the genre included *Wiązanie Helenki* [*Helen's Book*] by Klementyna Hoffman nee Tańska (1823) and *Bajki i powieści* [*Fables and Stories*] by Stanisław Jachowicz (1824), which, though published in a very modest form, conquered the readers' hearts and powerfully fueled the further development of writing for a young readership (Dunin 34; Lebecka 100). Nevertheless, for nearly a century, Polish children's books remained in large measure visually unappealing, had small print runs, and included illustrations purchased from Western (mainly German) publishers. Refreshing exceptions to this dismal rule were the publishing houses of Gebethner and Wolff, Jakub Mortkowicz, and Michał Arct, who were committed to high artistic quality and careful editorial designs of their releases at the turn of the nineteenth century. Book publishing for a young readership was given a powerful boost in Poland when the country regained independence in 1918 and the publishing company Nasza Księgarnia [Our Bookstore] was founded in 1921 to promote educational and children's literature.[1] Yet the industry genuinely started to thrive in the aftermath of the Second World War. Over a mere few decades, a real revolution surged across the field, transfiguring the children's book to adapt it to the changing needs of its target readers.

Books for young readers stand out against the backdrop of overall book production. A single glance at a bookshelf in a bookstore or a library suffices to unmistakably recognize the publications for children, as they differ from adult books not only in the content tailored to young minds and sensibilities but also, emphatically so, in their custom-made, often highly original graphic design. Authors, illustrators, and editors spare no effort to outbid each other in ingenious ideas devised in order to attract the prospective readers' attention, while their inventiveness often pushes the codified boundaries of the canonical book form. Admittedly, this is no novelty in and by itself. As Jacqueline Reid-Walsh observes, as early as in the seventeenth century, attempts were made to increase children's reading pleasure and engagement by including movable elements in books and embellishing them with spread-out plates. Movable books resembled games and jigsaw puzzles, which allowed more than just one configuration and required the readers' active involvement. Besides, children's books were given interesting shapes and unusual formats, were printed on other materials than paper, and sometimes had card- or board-games attached to them. The verbal message was also enhanced by augmenting books with sound, first by furnishing them with built-in music boxes and then by appending records or tapes to them.

With the rise of mass media and new media, apprehensive questions about the future of the book were asked and have been reiterated ever since. The major recurrent anxiety has been that books will be ousted by more attractive and less demanding media. While books have always had to fend off one or another form of competition, we know today that new media complement rather than pose a hazard to books.

The Book in Digital Culture

As the technological capacities of computing advanced and the Internet spread, it became increasingly clear that the vision of new digital literature would not only be limited to hypertext. In response to the needs of new generations of readers, enhanced e-books, multibooks, hybrid books, and convergent books appeared on the publishing market side by side with electronic books. With touch-screen devices, in particular Apple iPads, which became available in 2010, new editorial opportunities proliferated, and publishers were quick to seize them. Soon, first book applications appeared in which word was combined with sound, moving image, animation, and game, providing a wealth of simultaneous visual, tactile, and aural stimuli for children and thus promoting a polysensory engagement with the work.

The new genre has stirred considerable interest across academic disciplines, as evinced by the growing number of research studies on picturebook apps (Yokota and Teale; Schwebs; Stichnothe; Turrión; Al-Yagout and Nikolajeva, "Re-Conceptualising Picturebook", "Digital Picturebooks"; Sargeant). Regrettably, this intellectual ferment has not reached Poland yet, where digital picturebooks have barely attracted any scholarly attention. So far, the topic has been addressed only in a handful of articles (Cackowska; Cackowska and Zając; Zając, "Aplikacje książkowe dla dzieci młodszych," "Książka edukacyjna dla dzieci i młodzieży," "Cyfrowe książki obrazkowe"), which may be explained by the scarcity of Polish book apps.

Highlighting the significance of picturebook apps, Junko Yokota and William Teale insist that "the typical e-book read on a dedicated e-reader has not hit the children's literature world in a particularly big way" and add that the feat has instead been accomplished by "e-books and apps that incorporate text, illustration, and interactive features and that are often thought of as the e-equivalent to picturebooks" (577). Ghada Al-Yagout and Maria Nikolajeva point out that "picturebook apps differ from e-books because they include modes such as written and oral language, sound, music, still images, moving images and haptic elements" (271). Bettina Kümmerling-Meibauer observes that

> e-books usually follow the print version of the books and do not have any playful or informational elements. Enhanced e-books can be equipped with audio and video elements, while picturebook apps can be anything that can be programmed, from a movie to a game and beyond.
>
> (260)

She also claims that today the first picturebooks that children get in their hands are often electronic ones, mediated by interactive platforms accessed through mobile apps (260). Yokota and Teale, admittedly, believe that picturebooks are "the most exciting innovation in literature for children in a long time," yet they emphasize that, "in early childhood literacy education, both kinds of books – print and digital – should play central roles" (577–78). They also explain that the literary and artistic quality of publications should be regarded as a priority, irrespective of their format.

Authors, artists, and publishers of digital books and of printed books alike are eager to use any available tools to produce children's books of literary value. Given this, it is indeed puzzling that although mobile touch-screen devices are very popular in Poland, the interest in children's book apps is so meager, while the printed book market is robustly burgeoning year by year. Are the approaches and features used in the former indeed innovative? In my chapter, I discuss selected older and recent – predominantly Polish – children's books in which authors, illustrators, and publishers have used interactive, play-promoting modalities and, thereby, crossed the boundaries demarcated for printed books. Subsequently, I address Polish picturebook apps, their literary and aesthetic properties, and the interactive opportunities they offer, at the same time arguing that book apps have only helped implement ideas and solutions that children's book makers have forged over decades in order to enhance the appeal of printed books. In doing this, I also examine major challenges that may affect the Polish market of children's book apps.

Crossing the Boundaries in Printed Children's Books

To a greater degree than any other types of publications, children's books have traditionally been a site of vibrant experimentation and invention, in which the boundaries set for the printed book have been pushed and re-drawn. Time and again, book makers have sought to give children's books attractive graphic designs capable of affecting all the senses of their young readers. However, Polish studies on changes in editorial practices associated with children's books are few and far between. Researchers tend to focus on the development and relevance of illustrations (Szuman; Słońska; Wiercińska; Wincencjusz-Patyna), while other editorial properties are mainly tackled in the literature on toy books (Zając, "Książki-zabawki"; Maroń) and popular-science or educational books (Zając, "Książka edukacyjna dla dzieci i młodzieży"; Wandel). Research into the formal evolution and transformations of children's books is both conducted in the historical framework (Dunin; Jamróz-Stolarska) and focused on the recent books, which are currently available on the Polish market (Biernacka-Licznar et al.).

As shown by Janusz Dunin, children's books in Poland also functioned as toys already in the late nineteenth century. This role was sometimes suggested by their revealing titles, such as *Zabawka dla młodszej dziatwy w obrazkach i wierszykach* [*A Toy for Young Children in Pictures and Verse*] (1884). Occasionally, thin books were carved into shapes resembling a dog, a cat, or a doll. Some books were printed as stiff cardboard *leporellos*, which could be not only looked at and read but also manipulated in various ways and folded into eye-catching structures. Besides, some books had movable elements that could be used to create a kind of theater (Dunin 103). As the readers' needs changed and multiple technical possibilities developed, the form and structural elements of books continued to evolve, also impacted by newly emerging mass media, e.g., radio, television, and cinema. In the wake of each new invention, the prophesy of the death of the printed book was reiterated with an even greater fervor than before. Yet authors, illustrators, designers, and publishers had other ideas and used their capacities to create interactive books in which various media were combined.

Despite the challenges that the Polish publishing industry faced, especially when struggling to make up for the losses incurred in the Second World War, first original editorial projects involving children's books were launched soon after the war. In 1947, the "Czytelnik" [Reader] Publishing Cooperative started the *Kino Książka* [*Cinema Book*] series, whose volumes gave young readers an opportunity to screen a film. The authors of *Bibliografia literatury dla dzieci 1945–1960* [Bibliography of Children's Literature, 1945–1960] describe the physical form of the Cinema Book publications as "book-shaped glass boxes containing a strip of paper wound to and fro on a reel" (Neubert et al. 191). Among the texts published in this way was Julian Tuwim's highly popular poem "Pan Maluśkiewicz i wieloryb" ["Mr Miniscule and the Whale"], illustrated by the renowned Polish artist Jerzy Srokowski. This suggests that the compelling form was just an accessory to a good literary text, rather than an aim in itself.

Children's book makers as a rule eagerly strive to vivify illustrations. Polish editors were no different in this respect. One of their interesting projects was the *Książeczki z Misiowej Półeczki* [*Teddy Bear's Bookshelf*] initiated by Nasza Księgarnia in 1960, a series in which short prose or verse texts were framed in uncommon editorial formats and embellished with colorful illustrations produced by recognized artists. An excellent case in point is Helena Bechler's *Miś na huśtawce* [*Teddy Bear on a Swing*] illustrated by Janusz Jurjewicz. The episodes of the protagonist's story were described on split pages that looked like a stop-motion animation when flipped in a fast sequence. The information on the title page specifies that the writer herself came up with the idea of this book design. Other picturebooks in the series included added boards or cut-out elements in inserts placed at the end of the book (Czesław Janczarski's *Przedszkole Krysi i Jurka* [*Kiki and Georgie's Kindergarten*] illustrated by Hanna Czajkowska); split illustrations, flaps and windows (Helena Bechler's *Otwórz okienko* [*Open the Window*] illustrated by Hanna Czajkowska); or unfinished drawings to be completed by the reader (Czesław Janczarski's *Czy wiesz która godzina?* [*Do you know What Time It Is?*] illustrated by Juliusz Makowski).

Some book makers pursue a bolder goal of, so to speak, "drawing" young readers into the world conjured up in the text and kindling their imaginations by transgressing the canonical conventions. Such attempts were successfully undertaken as early as in the nineteenth century, when German publishers Ernest Nister and Lothar Meggendorfer released pop-up and movable books. In their publications, children could explore three-dimensional illustrations and additionally use special in-built mechanisms to move them in various directions (Montanaro Staples 182–83). Although the invention has been popular ever since, the Polish market, dominated by foreign productions as it is, is still waiting for a native master of the genre. Recent valuable Polish works of the kind include *Archi. TEKTURKI. Powojenne budynki warszawskie* [*Cardboard Architecture: Warsaw's Postwar Buildings*] by Marlena Happach (published by the Warsaw Rising Museum in 2015) and *Książka o strachach* [*A Book of Fears*] by Dorota Wątkowska (her 2009 graduation project at the University of Arts in Poznań), which has not been published and is available only on request.

The illusion of direct participation in the depicted events and places can also be achieved by employing 3D techniques in books, an approach pioneered in Poland by Bohdan Butenko. Counted among the Polish school of illustration artists, Butenko is called a book architect. He was one of the first Polish authors to create both the text and illustrations for his picturebooks, making sure that all their elements should constitute a coherent project. The innovativeness of his books defied the technical and financial constraints of the day. In his *Przygoda zajączka* [*Bunny's Adventures*] of 1975, Butenko illustrated the fortunes and misfortunes of the eponymous protagonists with partly overlapping drawings sketched in red and blue lines, respectively. The book included stereoscopic glasses with one lens red and the other blue, looking through which the reader had an impression of depth and could read two alternative narratives of the protagonist's escapades. Butenko relied on a varied array of devices to transcend the conventional boundaries of children's books. Importantly, he belongs to path-breakers who first encouraged children to co-author books by, for example, inviting them to contribute to the narrative. In *Pierwszy! Drugi!! Trzeci!!!* [*First! Second! Third!*], a picturebook of his own design, he left empty asterisked speech bubbles. The explanation at the bottom of the page said that they were to be filled in by the readers as they found fit. In this way, Butenko's book provided children with a space of creative play and unfettered game of the imagination (Maroń 306).

As Kümmerling-Meibauer emphasizes, the tendency to draw the reader's attention to the book's material aspects and to encourage active engagement by including interactive features is by no means exclusive to picturebooks for the youngest children (252). In another appealing variation, the idea also informs gamebooks for older children, in which the reader's involvement is reinforced by an opportunity to decide about the protagonists' fate. In such publications, the main text contains links to various other parts of the book (resembling hyperlinks to a degree), and the readers are free to follow whichever of them they wish, their choice determining how the story develops and what happens with and to the protagonists. Such an arrangement inclines the readers to read the narrative several times and to playfully produce new, alternative versions of the plot. The genre is represented in Poland by Dorota Sidor's *Gdzie jest wydra? – czyli śledztwo w Wilanowie* [*Where is the Otter? Or an Investigation in Wilanów*], published in 2012. An additional merit of the book lies in its graphic design, which was developed by the world-famous illustrators Aleksandra and Daniel Mizieliński.

Importantly, cross-breeding books and games is by no means a novelty. As early as in 1829, Klementyna Hoffman's *Assarmot. Gra historyczna* [*Assarmot: A Historical Game*] was published in Warsaw. It consisted of a booklet describing Poland's history contained and a gameboard with two dice. The product was very popular, as attested by its multiple re-editions (Dunin 48). Board games have had their renaissance in recent years; however, book makers know young readers' tastes and also employ new media to attract and retain their attention for a longer time. This approach is perfectly exemplified in Aleksandra and Daniel Mizieliński's work. For example, their 2011 Bologna Ragazzi Award-winning book *Co z ciebie wyrośnie?* [*What Will Become of You?*] is accompanied by a dedicated website, where the users can read excerpts of the text and play amusing games related to the book's content.

Adding sound modalities has also been widely used to increase the appeal of books. First attempts of this kind were made in Germany in the nineteenth century, when Ernest Nister published celebrated books with in-built music boxes. As Dunin observes, there is no conclusive evidence as to whether or not such publications also appeared in the Polish version at that time (104). What we certainly know is that in the 1970s books with attached cardboard records appeared in Poland. (By the way, cardboard records enjoyed an enormous popularity in the People's Republic of Poland era.) In this period, Krajowa Agencja Wydawnicza [National Publishers] released the *Książeczki z Wkładką Dźwiękową* [*Little Books with Sound Inserts*], a series in which poems and/or stories by recognized authors were accompanied by vinyl mini-records placed in envelops attached to the back cover. Notable volumes in the series included Wanda Chotomska's *Gdyby tygrysy jadły irysy* [*If Tigers Ate Toffees*] and Adam Bahdaj's *Najpiękniejsza fotografia* [*The Most Beautiful Photograph*] (Maroń 305). Since the 1970s, recording literary texts on sound carriers (vinyl records, tapes, CDs, and digital devices) has become a widespread practice. Some of the recordings have presented individual narrators' interpretations of the texts, while others have been produced as radio plays.

Today, sound effects are a common feature in children's books. Toy books and educational books with buttons imitating various sounds and noises, with mini-keyboards and/or music boxes (e.g., the *Music Box Series* released by Olesiejuk Publishing) are offered by many publishers. Attention-worthy is the work of the Akademia Rozwoju Wyobraźni Buka [Buka Academy of Imaginative Development], founded in 2004 and dedicated to projects that bring together music and literature. Records with literary texts read by professional actors and accompanied by original music and acoustic effects are published in jackets designed by recognized illustrators, sometimes with an attached booklet, which is graphically chiseled as well. Instead of calling them audiobooks, as the convention has it, the publisher refers to the projects as books (Zabawa 33). In fact, most audiobooks for children do not boast such a refined form, though they also tend to be equipped with the printed text and other features, such as games, jigsaw puzzles, riddles, and coloring sheets.

Book makers persist in looking for new editorial approaches to attract a young readership. However, going beyond the conventional format, traditional writing materials, or entrenched modes of content preservation has been an integral part of book culture practically since its beginnings (Góralska 99). Crucially, literary texts that come enveloped in image, sound, and/or film are an influential factor in fostering the autonomy of young readers, particularly those who have not mastered the art of reading yet, as they become independent of adults in the reading process. Several barriers to engaging with, appreciating, and understanding books are dismantled when children's various senses are stimulated, their curiosity and imaginations are aroused, and their eagerness to play is fueled.

Polish Children's Book Apps

The Polish publishing market was quick to respond to the affordances offered by new technologies. As early as in 2011, first book apps appeared in Poland, and their number grew steadily year by year for some time. However, the market is currently dominated by publications with pedestrian narratives and hackneyed graphic designs, many of them representing franchises of big companies, such as Lego, Disney, and Egmont. Original Polish digital picturebooks are relatively scarce. Their major producer, the Fundacja Festina Lente [Festina Lente Foundation], has fifteen titles on offer at the moment, while other developers (e.g., Big Rabbit, Suqoon Project, Crocolabel, OhNoo Studio, Ładne Halo) have limited themselves to releasing just one or a handful of items. Importantly, the unimpressive quantity is somewhat recompensed by the remarkable quality of their apps, which abundantly use the interactive potential of respective devices and boast original and finely honed graphic designs.

A considerable proportion of Polish book apps are digital versions of books that first appeared in the printed format. Many of them are revered classics, now presented to the users in new visual iterations. To my knowledge, only four Polish picturebook apps were digitally born, including *Halo, Rozalia! Wieczorne rozmowy owcy i krowy* [*Hello, Rosalie! Evening Conversations between a Sheep and a Cow*] released by Crocolabel and the OhNoo Studio's apps, e.g., *Amelia i Postrach Nocy* [*Amelia and Terror of the Night*]. Apps based on Polish and foreign classics are signature products of the Fundacja Festina Lente, which calls its products hybrid books, because each app is paired with the paper version of the work. So far, the foundation has released, for example, beloved nineteenth-century classics: Józef Ignacy Kraszewski's *Dziad i baba* [*The Old Man and His Wife*], Stanisław Jachowicz's *Chory kotek* [*The Sick Kitten*], and Lewis Carroll's *Alice in Wonderland*. Other interesting works on offer are apps based on the books by Franciszka and Stefan Themerson, avantgarde artists of the interwar period. Both *Kolory – niezwykłe przygody* [*Colours: Extraordinary Adventures*] and *O stole, który uciekł do lasu* [*The Table that Ran Away to the Woods*] prove that good illustrations defy time and are equally effective, irrespective of the medium, the device, or the carrier.

What features and advantages that are unavailable in printed books can be found in digital picturebooks? For one, apps can overcome age barriers by including two versions – an easier and a more challenging one – of the same story or game. For example, *Halo, Rozalia!* contains two variants of the text, adapted to children older than 1.5 and 4 years of age, respectively. In each of them, the content is deliberately tailored to suit the target readers' different cognitive capacities. Another advantage is that digital books can help surmount linguistic and cultural barriers by offering the text in several languages. In the OhNoo Studio's latest apps, the users can choose from among the English, Spanish, Polish, Russian, and even Chinese versions (e.g. *Lisie opowieści* [*Fox Tales*]). First and foremost, however, book apps promote interaction, which, if properly utilized, can encourage children to engage with the text by affording opportunities of pleasurable play.

Young readers – or, rather, users – can approach the text in many different fashions (or, rather, modes). Basically, children can read all digital books on their own or rely on the narrator, which makes the app closer to an audiobook. In some of them, the role of the narrator can be taken by the children themselves or by their family, which is an option offered by the *Halobajki* [*Hellofables*] series published by Ładne Halo (*Sklepy* [*Shops*] and *Kiedy będę duży, to zostanę dzieckiem* [*When I Grow up, I'll Be a Child*]). Well-known actors often serve as narrators. *Halo, Rozalia!* makes it possible to read the text alongside the narrator; additionally, children are supposed not only to follow the text (which is highlighted in different colors) but also to complete sentences with suitable onomatopoeic expressions.

Some apps, e.g., *Młynek do kawy* [*The Coffee Grinder*] and *Kto zabił Robcia Kogucika* [*Who Killed Cock Robin*], include animated films and make it possible to watch shortened versions of the stories, whose impact is intensified by background music suggestive of their atmosphere and meanings. In *Lokomotywa* [*The Locomotive*], produced by Big Rabbit, the work's second part is presented as an animated film. When the eponymous train gets going, the illustrations come into life without the child's intervention. *Lokomotywa*, which is without doubt one of the best Polish book apps, combines Julian Tuwim's brilliant classic text, Maciej Szymanowicz's superb illustrations, and the expressive voice of the popular Polish actor Piotr Fronczewski (who can also be heard in some other Festina Lente apps). Absorbing and rewarding as this combination is in and by itself, it is additionally complemented by a song written especially for the app. Attention to technical detail is also remarkable in the product.

At the core of book apps lies the possibility of active involvement in reading, impacting the course of the story, and becoming immersed in it. Readers can directly interact with book protagonists. For example, in *Lokomotywa* and *Słoniątko* [*Baby Elephant*] (graphically embellished by Józef Wilkoń, a co-founder of the Polish school of illustration), the child can make the protagonists perform various activities, move, or produce sounds by touching the screen. In *Halo, Rozalia!*, the user goes through the pages collecting "stickers," which can be stored and displayed in a multimedia album. *Amelia i Postrach Nocy* offers an option of collecting stars, for which the user must look throughout the story in order to unblock a secret screen at the end. Such features do not divert the reader's attention from the plot but make interaction part of the narrative. At the same time, they require focus and engagement, as the child must carefully scrutinize successive screen images to find the interactive elements.

Apps are frequently equipped with educational games, which are as a rule associated with the book's content. In integrating such tools (memory cards, coloring sheets, jigsaw puzzles, quizzes, etc.), the producers rely on a variety of approaches. Sometimes the game features are placed in a separate menu tab, which is the case, for example, in *O stole, który uciekł do lasu* and *Kolory – niezwykłe przygody*. Occasionally, however, they are built into the book's successive screens and, consequently, inscribed into the work's narrative structure. This option is used, for instance, in *Kto zabił Robcia Kogucika*, where some screens contain simple games, such as spotting differences, doing jigsaw puzzles, shooting bows and arrows, and learning the piano. Sporadically, the games included in apps are only tangentially associated with the book itself, which is what happens in the *Dziad i baba* app, where children can chart their family tree using pictures of relatives they take themselves. This activity helps connect the user's world to the app world and even bridge the gap between the two.

Yet book apps are not only amusing and serene stories replete with interactive modalities that induce play. How the opportunities offered by contemporary technologies can be used in children's books is powerfully demonstrated in *Asiunia*, published by the Warsaw Rising Museum. A highly ambitious project based on the autobiography of Joanna Papuzińska, an eminent Polish author for children and children's literature scholar, *Asiunia* tells the story of her wartime experiences as seen by a young child. The book carries a profoundly emotional load, with animated illustrations and sounds that accompany them additionally enhancing the verbal message.

In what ways reading is made more captivating and enjoyable depends largely on the inventiveness of app developers. For example, the image accompanying the text can be foregrounded and enlarged (*Asiunia*), or an impression of 3D depth can be achieved by tilting the screen (*Amelia i Postrach Nocy*). Also, the protagonists can be made to move by manipulating the device (*Halobajki*). The modes and possibilities of interacting with apps are so numerous and diversified that describing them all is a sheer impossibility in this chapter. An important observation is that they are not necessarily all very successful. In some apps, interactive features, even though relevant to the narrative, are so multiple that they thwart the reception of the text and divert the reader's attention from the plot. Other apps are found deficient in that they have too few interactive features (*O stole, który uciekł do lasu*). Still other apps seem to suffer from ill-advised designs; for example, animations make portions of the text disappear (*Asiunia*), or the text covers a sizeable part of illustrations (*Halo, Rozalia!*). For this reason, it seems recommendable to follow experts and researchers (e.g., Yokota and Teale) when assessing and choosing book apps.

The Polish Book Apps Market

The Polish book apps market offers products whose quality equals the world's best and most popular titles. One of the most successful Polish book apps is the *Halobajki* series, which has already garnered international acclaim and won prestigious awards, including the Red Dot Design Award (referred to as the "Design Oscar") in 2014 and the iF Design Award in 2015. Importantly, the apps are very cheap, costing a mere few Polish zloty (i.e., about €1–2, while the standard price of printed books is about €7–10), and many of them can be downloaded for free (e.g., most apps developed by the Festina Lente, which received funding from the National Audiovisual Institute). Small publishers, such as Crocolabel, often limit themselves to developing only one app. Considerable production costs make further production impossible. The Crocolabel owner states that to be in the black, apps would have to contain advertisements, which contravenes the company's mission.[2]

A serious obstacle is that not all apps are compatible with different operating systems. *Asiunia*, though available for free, only works on the Android. Developed in collaboration with Microsoft Polska, *Halobajki* can exclusively be used on one phone model with the Windows system. Such arrangements automatically exclude owners of other devices.

Another obstruction to the development of this segment of the market is the still steep price of the equipment (in particular, Apple devices), which makes companies abandon book app projects, even if based on foreign licenses (e.g., Media Service Zawada). The market of e-books is grappling with similar problems. Nearly 90% of their users insist, however, that the prices of electronic books are too high as compared with their printed counterparts. Although the value of e-book sales increased from nine million zloty in 2010 to seventy-five million zloty in 2016, its share in the overall book market in Poland does not exceed 3%. For several years now, there has been a clear stagnation in this segment. As in the case of apps, the reasons for this situation cannot be clearly identified, as the availability of e-book readers and mobile devices in Poland is growing year by year ("Rynek książki w Polsce 2017: Wydawnictwa" 91–104).

The ignorance and unawareness of adult mediators of reading – parents in most cases – are likely another hindrance to the development of the book app market in Poland. Many adults simply do not even realize that such products are available, because reliable sources of information (catalogues, databases, and app reviews) are scarce, like in other countries, which is indicated, for example, by Al-Yagout and Nikolajeva ("Digital Picturebooks" 272). Parents and caregivers tend to be afraid that mobile devices will have an adverse effect on the children's health. Still, research suggests that over fifty percent of Polish children under six years of age often use mobile devices, and most of them use educational and creativity-boosting apps (Bąk).

As the publishers themselves emphasize, children's involvement with the tablet is stereotypically associated with playing games that do not offer intellectual entertainment, rather than with reading. The Fundacja Festina Lente launched a concerted action to challenge the stereotype by disseminating information and knowledge about digital picturebooks. The campaign included, for example, arts workshops taught by Józef Wilkoń, where children and artist collaboratively created multimedia paintings, meetings with parents and bloggers, and lectures for librarians. Another fresh initiative was a series of multimedia spectacles for children at Warsaw's Teatr Lalka [Puppet Theatre], in which elements of the graphic design of the apps developed by the Foundation were used. Apparently, all these efforts have produced only little effect, judging by the fact that the Festina Lente has not put any new titles on the market over the last two years.

Conclusion

Although Polish publishers have shown they are capable of developing picturebook apps whose literary and artistic quality equals that of the international production, the book app segment of the Polish publishing market still seems to be in its nascent state. The few initial years of the industry's booming development, which saw the most successful Polish picturebook apps hit the market, have been followed by a decrease in the public's interest in the genre and the publishers' gradual abandonment of it. The situation is caused by an interplay of various factors, the chief of them in all likelihood being the lack of reliable, professional information for parents and caregivers coupled with the strong resemblance of apps to games.

Book apps can stimulate readers' (users') various senses and promote an active engagement in the reception of the text. Such outcomes have been sought in children's books ever since the seventeenth century. The pursuits of authors, illustrators, or publishers to make the reading more attractive by moving illustrations, sound, unusual forms, and/or original narrative strategies have become real. Books can now cross preestablished boundaries, combine various media, and turn reading into an engrossing adventure. Owing to the creativity of app developers and technological inventions, books can really come to life.

Al-Yagout and Nikolajeva point out that "for the current generation in the Western world at least, apps are likely to be the first kind of multimedial text they encounter, and possibly the first kind of any text" and emphasize that, just as there are good and bad printed picturebooks, there are also good and bad picturebook apps ("Digital Picturebooks" 277). While the Polish publishing market abounds in good picturebook apps, the researchers' prognosis is not likely to come true in Poland any time soon.

Notes

1. However, children's books continued to be expensive and poorly accessible, especially during the crisis at the turn of the 1920s (Lebecka 102).
2. Information from the publisher's email, Nov. 2015.

Works Cited

Al-Yaqout, Ghada, and Maria Nikolajeva. "Re-Conceptualising Picturebook Theory in the Digital Age." *Nordic Journal of ChildLit Aesthetics*, vol. 6, 2015, pp. 1–7.

———. "Digital Picturebooks." *The Routledge Companion to Picturebooks*, edited by Bettina Kümmerling-Meibauer. Routledge, 2018, pp. 270–78.

Amelia i Postrach Nocy. Version 1.2.0. OhNoo Studio, 2013.

Bąk, Agnieszka. *Korzystanie z urządzeń mobilnych przez małe dzieci w Polsce: Wyniki badania ilościowego*. Fundacja Dzieci Niczyje, 2015.

Bechlerowa, Helena. *Miś na huśtawce*. Nasza Księgarnia, 1960.

———. *Otwórz okienko*. Nasza Księgarnia, 1969.

Biernacka-Licznar, Katarzyna, et al. *Lilipucia rewolucja. Awangardowe wydawnictwa dla dzieci i młodzieży w Polsce w latach 2000–2015. Analiza produkcji wydawniczej wraz z bibliografią*. Wydawnictwo Stowarzyszenia Bibliotekarzy Polskich, 2018.

Blaźniak, Maciej. *Kiedy będę duży, to zostanę dzieckiem*. Ładne Halo, 2013.

Butenko, Bohdan. *Pierwszy! Drugi!! Trzeci!!!* Nasza Księgarnia, 1975.

———. *Przygoda zajączka*. Nasza Księgarnia, 1975.

Cackowska, Małgorzata. "Co ma książka obrazkowa do interaktywnej aplikacji książkowej." *Ryms*, no. 20, 2013, pp. 2–4.

Cackowska, Małgorzata, and Michał Zając. "Social Issues in Children Picturebook Apps and Their Reception by the Parents of Children in Early Education." *Problemy Wczesnej Edukacji/Issues in Early Education*, vol. 34, no. 3, 2016, pp. 132–42.

Dunin, Janusz. *Książeczki dla grzecznych i niegrzecznych dzieci. Z dziejów polskich publikacji dla najmłodszych*. Wydawnictwo Zakładu Narodowego im. Ossolińskich, 1991.

Gałczyński, Konstanty Ildefons. *Młynek do kawy*. Fundacja Festina Lente, 2014.

Góralska, Małgorzata. *Książki, nowe media i ich czasoprzestrzenie*. Wydawnictwo Stowarzyszenia Bibliotekarzy Polskich, 2009.

Halo, Rozalia! Wieczorne rozmowy owcy i krowy. Crocolabel, 2013.

Happach, Marlena. *Archi.TEKTURKI. Powojenne budynki warszawskie*. Muzeum Powstania Warszawskiego, 2014.

Hoffmanowa, Klementyna. *Assarmot. Gra historyczna*. Warszawa, 1829.

Jachowicz, Stanisław. *Chory kotek*. Version 2.0. Fundacja Festina Lente, 2013.

Jamróz-Stolarska, Elżbieta. *Serie literackie dla dzieci i młodzieży w Polsce w latach 1945–1989. Produkcja wydawnicza i ukształtowanie edytorskie*. Wydawnictwo Stowarzyszenia Bibliotekarzy Polskich, 2014.

Janczarski, Czesław. *Przedszkole Krysi i Jurka*. Nasza Księgarnia, 1967.

———. *Czy wiesz która godzina?* Nasza Księgarnia, 1970.

———. *Kto zabił Robcia Kogucika*. Fundacja Festina Lente, 2013.

Kraszewski, Józef Ignacy. *Dziad i baba*. Fundacja Festina Lente, 2013.

Kümmerling-Meibauer, Bettina. "From Baby Books to Picturebooks for Adults: European Picturebooks in the New Millennium." *Word & Image: A Journal of Verbal/Visual Enquiry*, vol. 31, no. 3, 2015, pp. 249–64.

Lebecka, Hanna. "Edytorstwo książek dla dzieci." *Słownik literatury dziecięcej i młodzieżowej*, edited by Barbara Tylicka and Grzegorz Leszczyński. Wydawnictwo Zakładu Narodowego im. Ossolińskich, 2003, pp. 99–106.

Lisie opowieści. Version 1.0. OhNoo Studio, 2016.

Maroń, Agnieszka. "Książka zabawka na polskim rynku wydawniczo-księgarskim w PRL-u." *Literatura dla dzieci i młodzieży*, edited by Krystyna Heska-Kwaśniewicz and Katarzyna Tałuć, vol. 4. Wydawnictwo Uniwersytetu Śląskiego, 2014, pp. 295–309.

Mizielińska, Aleksandra, and Daniel Mizieliński. *Co z Ciebie wyrośnie?* Dwie Siostry, 2010.

Montanaro Staples, Ann. "Pop-up and Movable Books." *The Routledge Companion to Picturebooks*, edited by Bettina Kummerling-Meibauer. Routledge, 2018, pp. 180–90.

Neubert, Felicja, et al. *Bibliografia literatury dla dzieci i młodzieży 1945–1960*. Wydawnictwo Stowarzyszenia Bibliotekarzy Polskich, 1963.

Papuzińska, Joanna. *Asiunia*. Muzeum Powstania Warszawskiego, 2013.

Reid-Walsh, Jacqueline. *Interactive Children's Texts and Movable Books: Playful Media Before Pop-Ups*. Routledge, 2017.

Sargeant, Betty. "What Is an Ebook? What Is a Book App? And Why Should We Care? An Analysis of Contemporary Digital Picture Books." *Children's Literature in Education*, vol. 46, no. 4, 2015, pp. 454–66.

Schwebbs, Ture. "Affordances of an App – A Reading of the Fantastic Flying Books of Mr. Morris Lessmore." *Nordic Journal of ChildLit Aesthetics*, vol. 5, 2014, http://dx.doi.org/10.3402/blft.v5.24169.

Sidor, Dorota. *Gdzie jest wydra? – czyli śledztwo w Wilanowie*. Dwie Siostry, 2012.

Słońska, Irena. *Psychologiczne problemy ilustracji dla dzieci*. Państwowe Wydawnictwo Naukowe, 1969.

Stichnothe, Hadassah. "Engineering Stories? A Narratological Approach to Children's Book Apps." *Nordic Journal of ChildLit Aesthetics*, vol. 5, 2014, https://doi.org/10.3402/blft.v5.23602.

Szuman, Stefan. *Ilustracja w książkach dla dzieci i młodzieży: Zagadnienia estetyczno-wychowawcze*. Wiedza-Zawód-Kultura, 1951.

Themerson, Stefan. *Kolory – niezwykłe przygody*. Fundacja Festina Lente, 2013.

Turrión, Celia. "Multimedia Book Apps in a Contemporary Culture: Commerce and Innovation, Continuity and Rupture." *Nordic Journal of ChildLit Aesthetics*, vol. 5, 2014, https://doi.org/10.3402/blft.v5.24426.

Tuwim, Julian. *Pan Maluśkiewicz i wieloryb*. Czytelnik, 1947.

———. *Lokomotywa*. Big Rabbit, 2013.

Wandel, Agnieszka. "Zarys dziejów encyklopedii dla dzieci i młodzieży w Polsce do 1989 roku." *Acta Universitatis Lodziensis. Folia Librorum*, no. 24, 2017, pp. 29–45.

Waszczyk, Paweł, editor. *Rynek książki w Polsce 2017: Wydawnictwa*. Biblioteka Analiz, 2017.

Wiercińska, Janina. *Sztuka i książka*. Państwowe Wydawnictwo Naukowe, 1986.

Wincencjusz-Patyna, Anita. *Stacja ilustracja. Polska ilustracja książkowa 1950–1980. Artystyczne kreacje i realizacje*. Akademia Sztuk Pięknych im. Eugeniusza Gepperta, 2008.

Yokota, Junko, and William H. Teale. "Picture Book and the Digital World: Educators Making Informed Choices." *The Reading Teacher*, vol. 67, 2014, pp. 577–85.

Zabawa, Krystyna. *Rozpoczęta opowieść. Polska literatura dziecięca po 1989 roku wobec kultury współczesnej*. Wydawnictwo WAM, 2013.

Zając, Michał. "Aplikacje książkowe dla dzieci młodszych: między książką a grą komputerową." *Ars Educandi*, vol. X, 2013, pp. 63–70.

———. "Książka edukacyjna dla dzieci i młodzieży: wczoraj, dziś i jutro." *Książka i młody czytelnik: zbliżenia, oddalenia, dialogi. Studia i szkice*, edited by Grzegorz Leszczyński and Michał Zając. Wydawnictwo Stowarzyszenia Bibliotekarzy Polskich, 2013, pp. 259–65.

———. "Książki-zabawki: długa historia i dzień dzisiejszy." *Książka i młody czytelnik: zbliżenia, oddalenia, dialogi. Studia i szkice*, edited by Grzegorz Leszczyński and Michał Zając. Wydawnictwo Stowarzyszenia Bibliotekarzy Polskich, 2013, pp. 251–57.

———. "Cyfrowe książki obrazkowe – Picturebook Apps." *Ksiażka obrazkowa. Wprowadzenie*, edited by Małgorzata Cackowska, et al. Instytut Kultury Popularnej, 2017, pp. 107–16.

Coda

14 Reflections on Playing and Puzzling with Alice and Tom

Jean Webb

As an academic and a literary critic working in the field of children's literature from a social and historical perspective, I usually consider the text in an inter-relationship with the contemporary contexts both literary and social and also, where relevant, the author's biographical history and views. However, for this discussion, my subject is a reflexive consideration of the significance of play and puzzlement in reading as a child and also how such reading history has an effect on thinking in adult life. The following discussion is not a piece of reader-response research but a reflection on the development of processes of thinking through the interaction between text and play combined with the added effect of intergenerational social interaction. An inspiration for this approach is taken from Margaret Mackey's ground-breaking *One Child Reading: My Auto-Bibliography*, which is a study of her own reading practices and experiences as a child in Novia Scotia in the 1950s and 1960s. This extensive and detailed work raises the subject of the child reader in interaction with the text and how personal experiences place the reader in relation to a text in terms of the creation of identity and subjectivity. Mackey considers the influences of place, her family, experiences of school, the politics of Novia Scotia, Canada and the British Empire in relation to her reading and a formation of identity. Whilst these outer circumstances influenced her reading, her reading also shaped her inner world of the imagination. Reflecting on the ways in which her reading was absorbed into and became part of her imaginary play, Mackey refers to Eve Bearne's observation that "[r]eading is a transformative act, having power not only to transform the here-are-now into what-might-be, but also transforming us as we develop as readers" (186).

For me Lewis Carroll's *Alice's Adventures in Wonderland* and *Through the Looking Glass* were texts that both transformed the "here-are-now into what-might-be" and also had a transformative effect as I developed as a reader. They were two of the central texts in my reading as a child. From the age of six I had two copies of the *Alice* books: one for everyday use with black and white illustrations by Tenniel and another, a school prize which I kept for "Sunday best" as it had colored pictures in addition to the black and white line illustrations. The text as a material object was also important as I often carried round the everyday copy. The "Sunday best" was kept as a special treat, for I could then become deeply engaged with the richly colored illustrations and in particular the line drawing of Alice and the Unicorn reflecting on the quotation: "If you'll believe in me, I'll believe in you" (*Looking-Glass* 175). This seems to me to be a pertinent thought to keep in mind as professionals, for as an academic community we posit ideas and theories that require, as it were, belief and trust.

In addition to engagement with the illustrations I also spent time memorizing the poems for the challenge and playfulness. "You Are Old Father William" was the challenge of remembering all the verses. "The Jabberwocky" carried the fascination of the complexity of language and thinking of translations from the quasi-Medieval English for:

> 'Twas brillig, and the slithy toves
> Did gyre and gimble in the wabe:
> All mimsy were the borogoves,
> And the mome raths outgrabe.
>
> (*Alice* 37)

The sense of danger and adventure was also attractive as one imagined these mythical creatures and a sense of energetic adventure that was generally missing in books for girls published in the UK in the 1950s. The following lines conjure danger, potential heroism and mythical creatures:

> Beware the Jabberwock, my son!
> The jaws that bite, the claws that catch!
> Beware the Jubjub bird, and shun
> The frumious Bandersnatch!
>
> (*Looking-Glass* 117)

The specificity of gender was immaterial as my imagined scenes stimulated by the poem were vivid and energetic with no connotations of gender to exclude my sense of involvement.

The language was also a challenge as to meaning, for then it was impossible to find out about the origins of Carroll's portmanteau "frumious" by searching for it on the internet. One had to think hard through the possibilities, trying out meanings through linking with other words. Now one is able to track the explanation of the construction of "rumious" given by Carroll in the Preface to the *Hunting of the Snark*, where he guides the reader into this kind of exploratory thinking to be employed in the pursuit of meaning:

> For instance, take the two words "fuming" and "furious." Make up your mind that you will say both words, but leave it unsettled which

> you will first. Now open your mouth and speak. If your thoughts incline ever so little towards "fuming," you will say "fuming-furious;" if they turn, by even a hair's breadth, towards "furious," you will say "furious-fuming;" but if you have the rarest of gifts, a perfectly balanced mind, you will say "frumious."
>
> (*Snark*)

Part of being an academic is to play with words and ideas, which to me is intellectual engagement at the highest level. Carroll invites the reader into such playfulness and to engage with language. The experience of my childhood reading of *Alice* was to enter into this intellectual game, creating images, emotions and action from the possibilities Carroll opens up. It was also a kind of training ground where one could practice and play, being limited only by one's own imagination and linguistic curiosity.

The *Alice* texts were not a solitary preoccupation as my mother and my sister, my elder by sixteen years, also participated in these games. Snippets from the poem about "Tweedledum and Tweedledee" or the scene in the Duchesses' kitchen from the chapter "Pig and Pepper" would enter our everyday conversations. The most remarkable memory I have of *Alice* in our lives was when my mother, who was not always the most playful of women with the stresses of bringing up a family in the working class area of London's East End in the 1950s, would dance across the kitchen singing:

> *"Will you walk a little faster?" said a whiting to a snail.*
> *"There's a porpoise close behind us, and he's treading on my tail.*
>
> *See how eagerly the lobsters and the turtles all advance!*
> *They are waiting on the shingle – will you come and join the dance?*
>
> *Will you, won't you, will you, won't you, will you join the dance?*
> *Will you, won't you, will you, won't you, won't you join the dance?"*
>
> (*Alice* 79 italics in the original)

The kitchen floor would bounce to the rhythm of the "Mock Turtle's Song," for the Victorian house in in the East End of London in which we lived had suffered damage during the Blitz in World War Two. It was as though the very fabric of the property joined in. These were memorable moments of free playfulness and an exuberance across generations in the comically ridiculous, which was given an authenticity by the narrative.

In addition to the communal possibilities offered by the poems, I also learned about the more sophisticated elements of language through Carroll's affinity with puns. The Mock Turtle was an expert guide at the beginning of a career where one is endeavoring to understand the slippery nature of language, for Carroll's Mock Turtle took the reader into his very own schoolroom as he recounted his experiences as a youngster, enabling Alice to compare it with her own:

> "We had the best of educations – in fact, we went to school every day – "
>
> "*I've* been to a day-school, too," said Alice; "you needn't be so proud as all that."
>
> "With extras?" asked the Mock Turtle a little anxiously.
>
> "Yes," said Alice, "we learned French and music."
>
> "And washing?" said the Mock Turtle.
>
> "Certainly not!" said Alice indignantly.
>
> "Ah! then yours wasn't a really good school," said the Mock Turtle in a tone of great relief. "Now at *ours* they had at the end of the bill, "French, music, *and washing* – extra."
>
> (*Alice* 76)

Washing is not plausible for Alice as an academic subject, and, logically, it would not have been necessary as they lived at the bottom of the sea, where one would surmise that the act of laundering clothes was redundant. Carroll's joke here is the incongruity of the optional extra subject of washing punning on the fact that hotels or boarding houses offered laundry with an additional payment. The question of money opens up an implied inequality on educational opportunity in the Victorian era, which could well be applied to the situation of university students in the UK, for whom fees are very high: " 'I couldn't afford to learn it.' said the Mock Turtle with a sigh. 'I only took the regular course.' " (*Alice* 76). The Mock Turtle and the Gryphon's explanation of their curriculum is a brilliant exhibition of punning on the school curriculum of middle class children at that time, which consisted of reading, writing, mathematics, history, geography, drawing, sketching and painting in oils. He expounds on the course he undertook in the following manner:

> "Reeling and Writhing, of course, to begin with," the Mock Turtle replied; "and then the different branches of Arithmetic – Ambition, Distraction, Uglification, and Derision."
>
> "I never heard of 'Uglification,' " Alice ventured to say. "What is it?"
>
> The Gryphon lifted up both its paws in surprise. "What! Never heard of uglifying!" it exclaimed. "You know what to beautify is, I suppose?"
>
> "Yes," said Alice doubtfully: "it means – to – make – anything – prettier."
>
> "Well, then," the Gryphon went on, "if you don't know what to uglify is, you *are* a simpleton."

> Alice did not feel encouraged to ask any more questions about it, so she turned to the Mock Turtle, and said 'What else had you to learn?'
>
> "Well, there was Mystery," the Mock Turtle replied, counting off the subjects on his flappers," – Mystery, ancient and modern, with Seaography: then Drawling – the Drawling-master was an old conger-eel, that used to come once a week: *he* taught us Drawling, Stretching, and Fainting in Coils."
>
> (*Alice* 76)

Puns make you connect with language and put you on the inside of the writer's mind, for you are thinking through the joke with them and working out the linguistic puzzle: it is a perfect part of training for being a literary scholar who interrogates literature. Furthermore, the episodic structure of *Alice* presents a different way of thinking: one has to be prepared to meet the unexpected and to make connections, all of which form a necessary preparation not only for the unexpectedness of academic career but also for contemporary life.

The relationship between imaginative play, creativity, and analytical thinking has been a debated area in psychology, with recent studies affirming the positive relationship between pretend play and the "creative thought process" (Silverman 136). Reading is an extension of play. For me, reading texts such as Carroll's *Alice* and Charles Kingsley's *The Water Babies* in my childhood has been a strong contributory factor in developing creative, divergent and analytical thinking. Whereas *Alice*, as I have evidenced, influenced my linguistic awareness and confidence, *The Water Babies* opened up my thinking in terms of puzzle solving. I was very familiar with the framing story of Tom the chimney sweep's misadventure in Hartover Castle as this was a story we were told regularly at Infant's School, which was, in the 1950s, for children aged five to six. We children were seated on the floor in the school hall while the headmistress recounted her version of Tom unfortunately coming down the wrong chimney and landing in little Ellie's white bedroom. The pristine middle class girl was confronted by a confused and very dirty chimney sweep's boy covered in soot. Tom then escaped, chased by the members of the household. He ran until he could run no further; exhausted, he lay by the river and awoke transformed into a Water Baby. This part of Kingsley's text works in a fairy tale mode. Here the headmistress finished her version. In my home Kingsley's characters of Mrs Doasyouwouldbedoneby and Mrs Bedonebyasyoudid were part of my behavioral education. Kingsley's fairytale matriarchs were called upon by my mother and sister to point out any misdemeanors I may have committed. In addition, as a slightly older child, I was given a copy of Kingsley's *Water Babies* that had belonged to my sister. She had written her name on its flypaper.

Being sixteen years older than myself, she had left home when I was aged four. The books that I inherited from her, *The Water Babies* and Kenneth Grahame's *The Wind in the Willows*, were precious to me especially since they were both fine hard backed copies. As said, I was familiar with the opening sections of Tom's adventures and could easily read these building on the experience of the storytelling at school. I remember reading my sister's copy of *The Water Babies* on a long train journey to visit her when I was nine years old. A gentleman seated in the same railway carriage asked my mother what I was reading. She replied that it was Kingsley's *Water Babies*, to which he retorted that it was far too difficult for a child of my age and that I could not be really reading it, whereon my mother firmly asserted that I was. This is still a strong and vivid memory for me six decades later. What I knew was that I was reading but not fully understanding what happened, for the chapters following Tom's emergence as a Water Baby are a combination of divergences into natural history, Greek mythology, Tom's moral education and Kingsley's literary outbursts against political and educational attitudes and ideas of his time. That I know now. Then it was a whole series of puzzles. Part of my intent from childhood has been to try to solve the puzzles that arose from my early reading experience of reading *The Water Babies*. I could not, even years after my mother's death, have let her down by admitting that although I was reading, I was not understanding. Neither could I have betrayed my sister's confidence in me to read her book, which I had inherited. Consequently, a good deal of my research efforts as a professional resulting in academic publications have been on this personal project to understand Kingsley's text. The practice of writing for publication entails, as said, preparatory research. It also means that one has to understand the subject matter sufficiently to express the analysis, thoughts and ideas in a clear and communicative manner. The puzzles have to be fully solved or explored as far as possible so that others might find a position of understanding. My interaction with the text of *The Water Babies*, the text embedded in family interactions and emblematic of relationships, my very early school experiences and a chance encounter on a train have all rolled together to produce an academic drive and approach. The early experience of puzzlement is fundamental to analytical thinking to gain a sense of control and understanding and fulfil a familial responsibility, albeit unspoken: again a kind of high-level intellectual play.

I also use the *Alice's Adventures in Wonderland* as a reference point for reflecting upon the puzzles of contemporary life, albeit in a somewhat playful way associated with the processes of lateral thinking stimulated by Carroll's writing. The embeddedness in my childhood and family life gives it an unspoken authority to be used as an intellectual compass to navigate the complexities of the twenty-first century. One hundred and fifty years after the publication of *Alice's Adventures in Wonderland*, which can be read as a satire on Victorian society, episodes from the text can be applied in the same mode to life in Britain in the twenty-first century. For example, the 1897 edition begins with a poem epitomizing the peace of a leisurely afternoon as Charles Dodgson/Lewis Carroll rowed the Liddell children along the river, yet the peace is interrupted by the three children calling for a story. Voices intrude upon the rural idyll in very similar ways to which the ever present mobile phone cuts into the peace of the present day. There are further contemporary resonances with the beginning of Alice's journey, starting with her questioning "the use of a book" "without pictures or conversations?" (Carroll "Alice" 7), which prefigures the ongoing debate of our time about the book versus digital media. Alice allies with the modern child in this respect, by abandoning the book and heading off into a series of episodic encounters that are controlled by unpredictable, confrontational, bizarre characters using language as their primary weapon and a source of power. Such use of language is a mode of behavior typical of politicians especially within the current atmosphere in British and world politics concerning attitudes toward immigration. Alice herself can be regarded as an immigrant, for she is a stranger in the world of Wonderland. She is unsure of her identity as she asks herself: "Who in the world am I?" (*Alice* 15). On emerging from The Pool of Tears, a quasi-rebirth, Alice begins her education into understanding this new world. The primary factors governing her situation are that what she knows is alien to the world of Wonderland, for instance, facts she has learned at school become muddled whilst references to her cat Dinah are seen as a threat to the Wonderland animals; the consequences are that neither her knowledge nor her history are valid as a means of understanding or socially navigating this new world. One can draw parallels with the experiences of immigrants endeavoring to enter the UK, as they have to pass a test for citizenship where knowledge of Britain becomes essential for acceptance, overriding knowledge of their birth country and, by implication, their personal history. In like manner, Alice is given an equivalent education by the Mouse, who says: " 'Let us get to the shore, and then I'll tell you my history, and you'll understand why it is I hate cats and dogs' " (*Alice* 19).

Alice's history is given very little recognition as the Mouse overlays it with the history that is important to him, that is British history since the time of William the Conqueror. He never explains why cats and dogs are hated by mice: what is clear is that they are perceived by him as life-threatening, which is the opposite of Alice's view. Reminiscent of Alice's encounter with the Mouse is the "Life in the UK" test for those immigrants who wish to have "Indefinite Leave to Remain' in the UK or to take British citizenship" ("Life in the UK" practice test 5). For contemporary immigrants there are twenty four questions in the test. In a brief survey of the numerous sample tests provided by the government border agency, I found that between three and six questions in each set of twenty four were on "British" history, although oddly Scotland and Wales did not seem to feature, whilst there was one question about Ireland (now Eire). The history the Mouse recounts is equally idiosyncratic for he highlights obscure details such as those who submitted to the rule of William the Conqueror, that is, "Edwin and Morcar, the earls of Mercia and Northumbria" (*Alice* 22). In like vein it is thought essential that those taking the "Life in the UK" test, of which 75% needs to be right to pass, should know the answer to so called essential questions relevant to contemporary British life such as whether Bouddica built Hadrian's Wall or Stonehenge or whether she fought the Romans (Life in the UK practice test 5). The effect of the Mouse's dominant assertion of ancient British history as the "essential" knowledge is to blank out Alice's knowledge in similar ways to how contemporaneously the history of immigrants is erased by being silenced by British history. Immigrants have to learn the rules of the dominant order, and Alice, the immigrant in Wonderland, has to try to do so as well. However, for immigrants applying for entry into the UK, this will be their chance to make a new life, a new reality, whereas for Alice this is part of her adventure, her journey through this world of fantasy. Alice is only a temporary migrant, for this is a dream from which she will awake.

Following Alice's history lesson from the Mouse, the solution to solving the problem of getting dry after the mass immersion in The Pool of Tears is proposed by the Dodo, a species that has been extinct since 1662. This outmoded figure suggests that they have a Caucus Race. A Caucus Race is the competitive process by which a political party select their candidate. However, the Dodo's race is somewhat less organized and is a subtle satirical comment on political practices. This episode seems to me rather like the aftermath of an election or referendum in current politics, as will become evident. Sensibly, Alice asks: " 'What *is* a Caucus-race?' 'Why,' said the Dodo, " 'the best way to explain it is to do it' " (*Alice* 23). Traditional British pragmatism is being satirized. The Dodo is, in common British parlance, a term for someone who is not up to date with practice or new ideas; his being in charge of the race is therefore ironic. He organizes the ensuing race in a bizarre manner as follows with the race-course:

> "in a sort of circle." ("the exact shape doesn't matter," it said,) and then all the party were placed along the course, here and there. There was no "One, two, three, and away," but they began running when they liked, and left off when they liked, so that it was not easy to know when the race was over. However, when they had been running half an hour or so, and were quite dry again, the Dodo suddenly called out "The race is over!"
>
> (*Alice* 23)

There is a potential comic prefiguring here of the situation in the UK following the Brexit referendum on membership of the European Union, 2016, where the heavily defeated major political parties had to hastily reformulate their previously stated positions and work out strategies for UK removal from the EU with metaphorical "tears" being shed since the political desire to remain had been outvoted by the populist desire to leave.

On a more personal level, there are parallels to be drawn between Carroll's Caucus Race and contemporary corporate working life. The stimulation for this connection began with a conversation with my husband very early one morning. He was not sleeping because of his frustrations with a major utility company for which he was working. The company is comprised of a conglomerate of smaller companies, each with their individual identities, like the different animals and birds in Carroll's Caucus Race, equally as disorganized. My husband was particularly vexed by the ongoing chaos in which he had to work, typified by an executive management decision to have hot-desking in an open-plan office. Without consultation, the assigned desks were removed, the room re-designed and new office furniture put in place. Unfortunately, there had not been any consultation as to how many people worked in the office, and fewer desks were installed than there were employees. Hence each morning in the office became a Caucus Race. "Change" is the buzz word of the age, whether it be necessary or no.

Taking the University sector as an example, one can reflect on a state of constant change except for perhaps in one or two very established Universities. One never knows when the race will be over – or perhaps if a new one has begun – as response to and anticipation of how government regulation, government decisions, the state of the economy and anxiety about, say immigration, affect the sector. At one time the British government was in favor of international students as a source of heightened income for universities, thus potentially reducing the government bill. Now the Borders' Agency is engaged in rigorously checking universities and their international students and bringing in rules making life far more difficult for both the students and the institutions. However, what happens in the contemporary world when the race is over? Well, like the decision of the Dodo, all have "won" and everyone has to have prizes, however idiosyncratic and trivialized they might be. Alice finds a box of comfits in her pocket (Carroll *Alice* 23). In a contemporary culture of assessment and award are we not raising expectations where that which was once prized now has the value of a sweetmeat? When the birds come to eat their comfits, they find that they are ill-designed: either the birds for the comfits or the comfits for the birds. Their reward is a great problem requiring the help of others in dislodging the sweet. Current policy in the UK for a considerable time has been to widen access to higher education, an applaudable aspiration, yet the policy of various governments has been to introduce student fees, which is a way of choking students with debt long after they have run their educational race and left university. Alice thought the whole matter of the race and prizes "very absurd," but she "did not dare to laugh" (*Alice* 23). The current fees situation in higher education in the UK is "absurd," in the most serious sense of the word as change, repercussions and a sense of instability characterize contemporary Western society.

Wonderland, like contemporary Western society, is in a state of flux, a place of instability. After the Caucus Race animals have left, Alice realizes that "everything seemed to have changed." The White Rabbit returns and orders Alice to fetch him a pair of gloves and a fan; however, he calls her Mary Ann. So even her identity has gone. One of the major tropes throughout *Alice's Adventures in Wonderland* is questioning Alice's identity, by herself and by other characters. Previously, when she was in the hallway trying to get to the key on the table, she admonished herself for crying with frustration, at which the narrator remarked that this: "curious child was very fond of pretending to be two people." Alice continued: "'But it's no use now . . . to pretend to be two people! Why, there's hardly enough of me left to make *one* respectable person!'" (*Alice* 12).

Alice's journey through Wonderland is a series of challenges to her sense of identity, from herself, when she asks "'Who in the world am I'" and the Caterpillar, who first asks her to "Explain" herself, her answer being that she is "not herself." He later retorts contemptuously: "'Who are *you*?'" Alice's strategy is to turn the question back on the Caterpillar, who then gives the puzzling response of "'Why?'" (*Alice* 36). Caterpillar's rebuttal of her question raises the pertinent question of why revealing one's identity to others is deemed to be an important factor. One internet search keying in "knowing who you are" returned twenty eight million responses in 0.53 seconds. The process of defining oneself is a matter of identifying difference and similarity. The Caterpillar does not understand Alice because she is confused by changes to her physicality, yet for the Caterpillar this is a matter of his being. The pigeon misidentifies Alice as a serpent through the slippage of logic in that as Alice eats eggs and so do serpents, then she must be a serpent. Alice is uncertain about her identity until she realizes at the Queen's croquet ground that the seemingly threatening figures are "nothing but a pack of cards." The final assertion of Alice's identity is in the courtroom scene, when she asserts herself against the Queen and declares: "'Who cares for you?' . . . (she had grown to her full size by this time.) 'You're nothing but a pack of cards!'" (*Alice* 97)

This declaration and realization is that which frees her and enables her to brush them all away like the leaves that have fallen on her as she lay on the riverbank. Alice's journey through Wonderland has been a quest for identity, a quest that typifies the years of adolescence and young adulthood and can be the source of insecurity and lack of mental well-being.

The actual direction of Alice's journey has not been important, which she realizes when she answers the Cheshire Cat's question regarding where she wants to go with " – so long as I get *somewhere*"(*Alice* 51). In the UK, from preschool to university, contemporary childhood is directed and channeled toward, as it were, getting "somewhere" in society. The State British education is a tightly controlled system of being tested – as is Alice – and having to pass the tests – as does Alice in her way by passing on in her journey. Children begin by being labelled pass or fail and may well continue so through life, with labels providing so-called aspects of their identity, whether it be achievement, gender, religious or spiritual affiliation. The problem is if you do not fit, for this leads to a lack of confidence and a questioning of identity. The best of education teaches one to deal with difficult and puzzling situations, thereby facilitating the development of a sense of confidence and identity. One can learn through literature. How Alice deals with the difficulties of her journey through Wonderland embeds a lesson in gaining confidence and in facing the questioning, as with the Caterpillar and in the final trial scene. Here Alice is physically getting larger and growing in confidence, for she realizes and states the truth that she is being tried by no more than a pack of cards. This has all been a complex game that ends when she takes control, as such is the game of life.

The worlds of Alice and Tom the chimney sweep, later-to-be Water Baby, are fantasies and playful texts. Yet my experience is that they teach ways of thinking, ways of negotiating unnegotiable realities. Lewis Carroll was applying his satirical wit to nineteenth-century systems and bureaucracy, whereas Kingsley was raising awareness of the plight of the poor and the chimney sweep children in his middle-class influential readership, as well as casting satirical blows at the arrogant and, to him, senseless attitudes of those in powerful positions. Interwoven in his playful "Fairy Tale for Land Babies" are Kingsley's post Darwinian ponderings and musings on creation. They are notably musings by an ordained member of the Church of England who was also a keen naturalist and corresponded with Charles Darwin for a decade. They were both engaged with the fabric and thinking of their age, taking their protagonists and their readers on journeys of discovery.

In conclusion, I would suggest that a return journey through childhood reading, embedded in and reinforced by intergenerational social experiences, exposes the ways in which thinking and attitudes are developed beyond the formalities of education. The text, narrative structure and techniques employed by authors are the keys to awareness and realization, unlocking divergent lateral thinking, which leads to problem solving itself and/or to creating the capacity in others. As Carroll, Kingsley and the ensuing generations of children's authors know, fantasy, play and creativity are most serious matters for the child reader, for the past re-shapes the future.

Works Cited

Carroll, Lewis. *Alice's Adventures in Wonderland*. W.W. Norton, 1992.

———. *Through the Looking-Glass*. W.W. Norton, 1992.

———. *The Hunting of the Snark: An Agony in Eight Fits*. Palgrave Macmillan, www.gutenberg.org/files/13/13-h/13-h.htm. Accessed 5 Apr. 2017.

Kingsley, Charles. *The Water-Babies*. Oxford UP, 2013.

"Life in the UK Practice Test 5." www.theuktest.com/life-in-the-uk-test/5. Accessed 5 Apr. 2017.

Mackey, Margaret. *One Child Reading: My Auto-Bibliography*. The U of Alberta P, 2016.

Silverman, Irwin W. "In Defense of the Play-Creativity Hypothesis." *Creativity Research Journal*, vol. 28, no. 2, pp. 136–43.

Contributors

Birgitte Beck Pristed is Associate Professor of Russian culture at Aarhus University, Denmark and author of *The New Russian Book: A Graphic Cultural History* (2017). Her current research focuses on Soviet children's books and history of paper.

Justyna Deszcz-Tryhubczak is Associate Professor of literature at the University of Wrocław. She has published among others on utopianism in children's literature and participatory approaches in children's literature studies. She is Director of The Center for Young People's Literature and Culture at the Institute of English Studies (University of Wrocław).

Jennifer Farrar (PhD) is a lecturer in children's literature and secondary English in the School of Education, University of Glasgow, UK. Her published work relates to her research interests in metafiction, children's literature, and critical literacy.

Ilaria Filograsso is Associate Professor of history of education and children's literature at the University of Chieti-Pescara, Italy. Her publications include *Bambini in trappola. Pedagogia nera e letteratura per l'infanzia* (2012), *Scrivere per liberare l'infanzia. Leila Berg tra impegno pedagogico, attivismo politico e letteratura per l'infanzia* (2019), and, with Marnie Campagnaro, *Children, Soldiers and Heroes: The Great War in Past and Present Italian Children's Literature* (2018).

Blanka Grzegorczyk teaches at the University of Cambridge and Manchester Metropolitan University. She is the author of *Discourses of Postcolonialism in Contemporary British Children's Literature* (2015) and *Terror and Counter-Terror in Contemporary British Children's Literature* (2020).

Sarah Hoem Iversen is Associate Professor in English at Western Norway University of Applied Sciences. She has published on historical children's dictionaries and nonfiction picturebooks including "Class,

Censorship, and the Construction of the Child Reader in Nineteenth-Century Children's Dictionaries" (2018), "Aesthetic Experience Through Students' Production of Digital Books" (2019), and "Organization and presentation of Knowledge in Picture Dictionaries" (2020).

Elżbieta Jamróz-Stolarska is Assistant Professor at the University of Wrocław. She has published on the children's book market, design, and illustration, including *Serie literackie dla dzieci i młodzieży w Polsce 1945–1989. Produkcja wydawnicza i ukształtowanie edytorskie* (2014). She also co-authored *Lilipucia rewolucja. Awangardowe wydawnictwa dla dzieci i młodzieży w Polsce w latach 2000–2015* (2018). She is a cofounder and a member of The Centre for Research on Children's and Young Adult Literature at the University of Wrocław.

Irena Barbara Kalla is Associate Professor at the University of Wrocław, Dutch Studies. She has published on Dutch and Flemish literature, including *Huisbeelden in de moderne Nederlandstalige poëzie* (2012) and *Minoes, Minnie, Minu en andere katse streken* (with Jan Van Coillie, 2017). She is Coordinator of The Centre for Research on Children's and Young Adult Literature at the University of Wrocław.

Taraneh Matloob Haghanikar is Assistant Professor in the Department of Curriculum and Instruction at the University of Northern Iowa. She has published on digital storytelling, multicultural children's literature, and the use of technology in teaching, including "Patterns in Multicultural Young Adults' Novels" (2017) and "Diversifying Our Curriculum: Values and Intercultural Experiences through Educational Technology" (2019).

Elizabeth L. Nelson is a funded PhD student at the University of Glasgow, UK, researching the intersection of traditional games, childhood, and participatory media. Her interests include playground lore and games, children's literature, and the digitalization of childlore practices.

Linda M. Pavonetti is Distinguished Professor and Chair of the department of Reading and Language Arts at Oakland University in Rochester, Michigan, USA. She has published *Children's Literature Remembered: Issues, Trends, and Favorite Books* (2004) and *Bridges to Understanding: Envisioning the World through Children's Books* (2011). She is currently serving on the 2021 Newbery Award Committee.

Sally Sims Stokes is Adjunct Professor of Library and Information Science at the Catholic University of America. Her publications include "Documenting the History of the White House Library Fireplace Tiles, 1944–1962" (*Art Documentation*, Journal of the Art Libraries Society of North America, 2017).

Elliott Schreiber is Associate Professor of German Studies at Vassar College, USA. He is the author of *The Topography of Modernity: Karl Philipp Moritz and the Space of Autonomy* (2012) and co-editor (with Edgar Landgraf) of *Play in the Age of Goethe: Theories, Narratives, and Practices of Play around 1800* (2020).

Yoo Kyung Sung is Associate Professor at the University of New Mexico, where she teaches children's literature and literacy courses. Her research focuses on critical content analysis of global and international children's literature. Her most recent (co-authored) article is "Schooling and Post-Immigration Experiences in Latinx Children's Literature" (2020).

Jan Van Coillie is Professor Emeritus of applied linguistics and children's literature at the KU Leuven, Belgium. He has published on children's poetry, (the history of) children's literature, and children's literature in translation, including *Minoes, Minnie, Minu en andere katse streken* (with I. B. Kalla, 2017) and *Children's Literature in Translation: Texts and Contexts* (with Jack McMartin, 2020).

Jean Webb is Professor of International Children's Literature at the University of Worcester. She has published widely on children's literature, including "Sickness and Literature for Children," in Maria Nikolajeva and Clémentine Beauvais (ed.) *The Edinburgh Companion to Children's Literature* (2017).

Zofia Zasacka is Assistant Professor and researcher at the National Library and the Educational Research Institute, Poland. She has published monographs and articles on youth reading habits and attitudes, including (with Krzysztof Bulkowski) "Reading engagement and school achievement of lower secondary school students" (2017).

Index

Note: Page numbers in *italic* indicate a figure and page numbers in **bold** indicate a table on the corresponding page. Page numbers followed by 'n' indicate a note.

Made in the USA
Las Vegas, NV
20 April 2026

45676007R00144